Martin H. Trauth

MATLAB® Recipes for Earth Sciences

Martin H. Trauth

MATLAB® Recipes
for Earth Sciences

Second Edition

With text contributions by
Robin Gebbers and Norbert Marwan
and illustrations by Elisabeth Sillmann

With 95 Figures and a CD-ROM

 Springer

Privatdozent Dr. rer. nat. habil.
M.H. Trauth
University of Potsdam
Department of Geosciences
Karl-Liebknecht-Str. 24
14476 Potsdam
Germany

E-Mail:
trauth@geo.uni-potsdam.de

Copyright disclaimer

MATLAB® is a trademark of The MathWorks, Inc. and is used with permission. The Math-Works does not warrant the accuracy of the text or exercises in this book. This book's use or discussion of MATLAB® software or related products does not constitute endorsement or sponsorship by The MathWorks of a particular pedagogical approach or particular use of the MATLAB® software.

For MATLAB® product information, please contact:

The MathWorks, Inc.
3 Apple Hill Drive
Natick, MA, 01760-2098 USA
Tel: 508-647-7000
Fax: 508-647-7001
E-mail: info@mathworks.com
Web: www.mathworks.com

Library of Congress Control Number: 2007928443

ISBN   978-3-540-72748-4   Springer Berlin Heidelberg New York
ISBN-10   3-540-27983-0 (first edition) Springer Berlin Heidelberg New York

Springer is a part of Springer Science+Business Media
Springer.com
© Springer-Verlag Berlin Heidelberg 2006, 2007

Cover design: deblik, Berlin
Typesetting: camera-ready by blätterwaldDesign, Elisabeth Sillmann, Landau
Production: Christine Adolph
Printing: Krips bv, Meppel
Binding: Stürtz AG, Würzburg

Printed on acid-free paper   32/2132/ca 5 4 3 2 1

Preface

The book *MATLAB Recipes for Earth Sciences* is designed to help undergraduate and PhD students, postdocs, and professionals to find quick solutions for common problems in data analysis in earth sciences. The book provides a minimum amount of theoretical background, but then tries to teach the application of all methods by examples. The software MATLAB is used since it provides numerous ready-to-use algorithms for most methods of data analysis, but also gives the opportunity to modify and expand the existing routines and even develop new software. The book contains MATLAB scripts to solve typical problems in earth sciences, such as simple statistics, time-series analysis, geostatistics and image processing. The book comes with a compact disk, which contains all MATLAB recipes and example data files. The MATLAB codes can be easily modified to be applied to the reader's data and projects.

The revised and updated Second Edition includes new subchapters on evolutionary Blackman-Tukey, Lomb-Scargle and Wavelet powerspectral analyses (Chapters 5.6–5.8), statistical analysis of point distributions and digital elevation models (Chapters 7.9 and 7.10), and a new chapter on the statistical analysis of directional data (Chapter 10). Whereas undergraduates participating in a course on data analysis might go through the entire book, the more experienced reader will use only one particular method to solve a specific problem. To facilitate the use of this book for the various readers, I outline the concept of the book and the contents of its chapters.

Chapter 1 – This chapter introduces some fundamental concepts of samples and populations. It also links the various types of data and questions to be answered from the data to the methods described in the following chapters.

Chapter 2 – A tutorial-style introduction to MATLAB designed for earth scientists. Readers already familiar with the software are advised to proceed directly to the following chapters.

Chapter 3 and 4 – Fundamentals in univariate and bivariate statistics. These two chapters contain basic concepts in statistics. The text also introduces advanced topics such as resampling schemes and cross validation. The reader already familiar with basic statistics might skip these two chapters.

Chapter 5 and 6 – Readers who wish to work with time series are recommended to read both chapters. Time-series analysis and signal processing are tightly linked. A solid knowledge of statistics is required to successfully work with these methods. However, the two chapters are independent of the previous chapters. The Second Edition of this book includes new subchapters on evolutionary Blackman-Tukey, Lomb-Scargle and Wavelet powerspectral analyses.

Chapter 7 and 8 – The second pair of chapters. I recommend to read both chapters since the methods of processing spatial data and images have many similarities. Moreover, spatial data and images are often combined in earth sciences, for instance while projecting satellite images upon digital elevation models. The Second Edition contains two new subchapters on the statistics of point distributions and on the analysis of digital elevation models.

Chapter 9 – Data sets in earth sciences often have many variables and data points. Multivariate methods are applied to a great variety of types of large data sets, including satellite images. The reader particularly interested in multivariate methods is advised to read Chapters 3 and 4 before proceeding to this chapter.

Chapter 10 – Methods to analyze circular and spherical data are widely used in earth sciences. Structural geologists measure and analyze the orientation of slickenlines (or striae) on a fault plane. The statistical analysis of circular data is also used in paleomagnetic applications. Microstructural investigations include the analysis of the grain shapes and quartz c-axis orientation in thin sections. This new chapter for the Second Edition is on the application of methods introduced in Chapter 3 to directional data.

The book has benefit from the comments of many colleagues and students, namely Robin Gebbers, Matthias Gerber, Mathis Hain, Martin Homann, Stefanie von Lonski, Norbert Marwan, Ira Ojala, Lydia Olaka, Oliver Rach, Jim Renwick, Jochen Rössler, Rolf Romer, Annette Witt and Max Zitzmann.

I very much appreciate the expertise and patience of Elisabeth Sillmann at blaetterwaldDesign.de who created the graphics and the complete page design of the book. I also acknowledge Courtney Esposito, Dee Savageau and Meg Vuillez of the Book Program at The MathWorks Inc., Claudia Olrogge and Annegret Schumann at The MathWorks Deutschland, Christian Witschel, Chris Bendall and their team at Springer, Martin Strathemann at Apple Deutschland, Michael Pöschl at HSD Berlin, Andreas Bohlen, Brunhilde Schulz and their team at UP Transfer GmbH. I thank the NASA/GSFC/METI/ERSDAC/JAROS and U.S./Japan ASTER Science Team and the director Mike Abrams for allowing me to include the ASTER images in the book.

Potsdam, April 2007

Martin Trauth

Contents

1 Data Analysis in Earth Sciences

1.1 Introduction

Earth scientists make observations and gather data about natural processes on Earth. They formulate and test hypotheses on the forces that have operated in a certain region to create its structure. They also make predictions about future changes of the planet. All these steps in exploring the system Earth include the acquisition and analysis of numerical data. An earth scientist needs a solid knowledge in statistical and numerical methods to analyze these data, as well as the ability to use suitable software packages on a computer.

This book introduces some of the most important methods of data analysis in earth sciences and illustrates the use of these methods by MATLAB examples. The examples can be used as recipes for the analysis of the reader's real data after learning their application on synthetic data. The introductory Chapter 1 deals with data acquisition (Chapter 1.2), the expected types of data (Chapter 1.3) and the suitable methods for analyzing data in earth sciences (Chapter 1.4). Therefore, we first explore the characteristics of a typical data set. Subsequently, we investigate the various ways of analyzing data with MATLAB.

1.2 Collecting Data

Data sets in earth sciences have a very limited sample size. They also contain a significant amount of uncertainties. Such data sets are typically used to describe rather large natural phenomena, such as a granite body, a large landslide and a widespread sedimentary unit. The methods described in this book help finding a way of predicting the characteristics of a larger *population* from the collected *samples* (Fig. 1.1). A proper sampling strategy is the first step to obtain a good data set. The development of a successful strategy for field sampling includes decisions on

- the *sample size* – This parameter includes the sample volume, the sample weight and the number of samples collected in the field. The rock weight or volume can be a critical factor if the samples are later analyzed in the laboratory. Most statistical methods also have a minimum required sample size. The sample size also restricts the number of subsamples that can be collected from the single sample. If the population is heterogeneous, then the sample needs to be large enough to represent the population's variability. On the other hand, a sample should be as small as possible to save time and effort to analyze it. It is recommended to collect a smaller pilot sample before defining a suitable sample size.

- the *spatial sampling scheme* – In most areas, samples are taken as the availability of outcrops permits. Sampling in quarries typically leads to

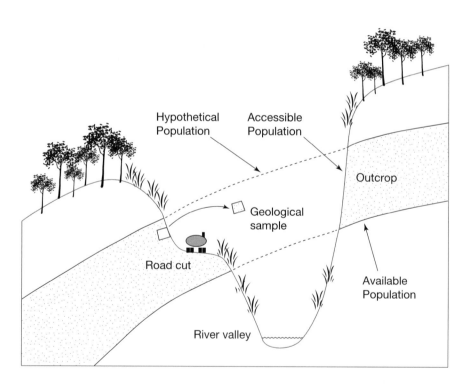

Fig. 1.1 Samples and population. Deep valley incision has eroded parts of a sandstone unit (*hypothetical population*). The remnants of the sandstone (*available population*) can only be sampled from outcrops, i.e., road cuts and quarries (*accessible population*). Note the difference between a statistical sample as a representative of a population and a geological sample as a piece of rock.

clustered data, whereas road cuts, shoreline cliffs or steep gorges cause traverse sampling schemes. If there are no financial limitations or the area allows hundred percent access to the rock body, a more uniform sampling pattern can be designed. A regular sampling scheme results in a gridded distribution of sample locations, whereas a uniform sampling strategy includes the random location of a sampling point within a grid square. You might expect that these sampling schemes represent the superior method to collect the samples. However, evenly-spaced sampling locations tend to miss small-scale variations in the area, such as thin mafic dykes in a granite body or the spatially-restricted occurrence of a fossil (Fig. 1.2).

The proper sampling strategy depends on the type of object to be analyzed, the aims of the investigation and the required level of confidence of the result. Having chosen a suitable sampling strategy, the quality of the set of samples can be influenced by a number of disturbances. The samples might not be representative of the larger population. Chemical or physical alteration, contamination by other material or dislocation by natural and anthropogenic processes may result in erroneous results and interpretations. Therefore, it is recommended to test the quality of the sample, the method of data analysis employed and the validity of the conclusions based on the analysis in all stages of the investigation.

1.3 Types of Data

Most data in geosciences consist of numerical measurements, although some information can also be represented by a list of names such as fossils and minerals (Fig. 1.3). The available methods for data analysis may require certain types of data in earth sciences. These are

- *nominal data* – Information in earth sciences is sometimes presented as a list of names, e.g., the various fossil species collected from a limestone bed or the minerals identified in a thin section. In some studies, these data are converted into a binary representation, i.e., *one* for present and *zero* for absent. Special statistical methods are available for the analysis of such data sets.

- *ordinal data* – These are numerical data representing observations that can be ranked, but the intervals along the scale are not constant. Mohs' hardness scale is one example for an ordinal scale. The hardness value

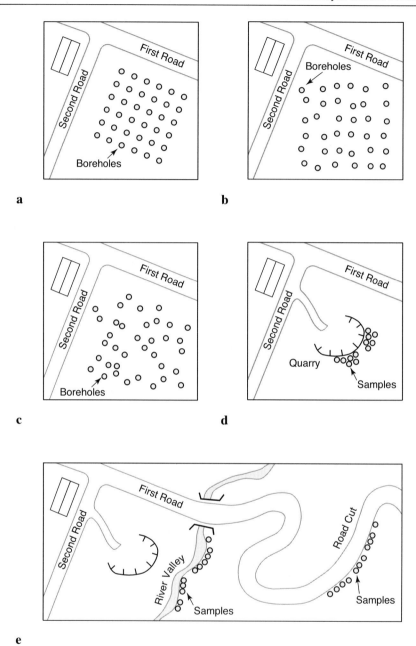

Fig. 1.2 Sampling schemes. **a** *Regular sampling* on an evenly-spaced rectangular grid, **b** *uniform sampling* by obtaining samples randomly-located within regular grid squares, **c** *random sampling* using uniform-distributed *xy* coordinates, **d** *clustered sampling* constrained by limited access in a quary, and **e** *traverse sampling* along road cuts and river valleys.

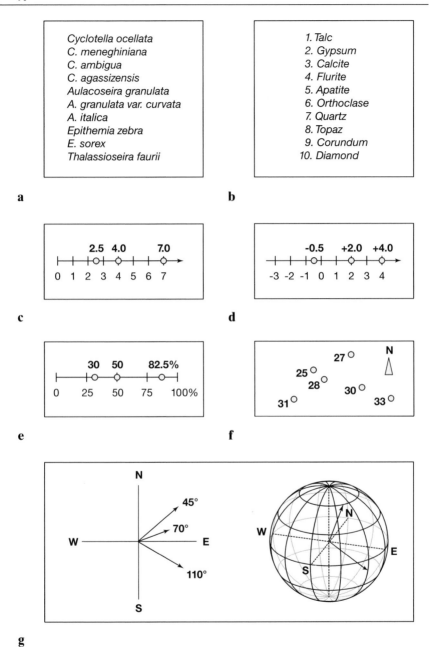

Fig. 1.3 Types of data in earth sciences. **a** *Nominal data,* **b** *ordinal data,* **c** *ratio data,* **d** *interval data,* **e** *closed data,* **f** *spatial data* and **g** *directional data.* All data types are described in the book.

indicates the materials resistance to scratching. Diamond has a hardness of 10, whereas this value for talc is 1. In terms of absolute hardness, diamond (hardness 10) is four times harder than corundum (hardness 9) and six times harder than topaz (hardness 8). The Modified Mercalli Scale to categorize the size of earthquakes is another example for an ordinal scale. It ranks earthquakes from intensity I (barely felt) to XII (total destruction).

- *ratio data* – These data are characterized by a constant length of successive intervals. Therefore, ratio data offer a great advantage in comparison to ordinal data. However, the zero point is the natural termination of the data scale. Examples of such data sets include length or weight data. This type of data allows either a discrete or continuous data sampling.

- *interval data* – These are ordered data that have a constant length of successive intervals. The data scale is not terminated by zero. Temperatures C and F represent an example of this data type although zero points exist for both scales. This types of data may be sampled continuously or in discrete intervals.

Besides these standard types of data, earth scientists frequently encounter special kinds of data, such as

- *closed data* – These data are expressed as proportions and added to a fixed total such as 100 percent. Compositional data represent the majority of closed data, such as element compositions of rock samples.

- *spatial data* – These are collected in a 2D or 3D study area. The spatial distribution of a certain fossil species, the spatial variation of the sandstone bed thickness and the 3D tracer concentration in groundwater are examples for this type of data. This is likely to be the most important data type in earth sciences.

- *directional data* – These data are expressed in angles. Examples include the strike and dip of a bedding, the orientation of elongated fossils or the flow direction of lava. This is a very common type of data in earth sciences.

Most of these data require special methods to be analyzed, that are outlined in the next chapter.

1.4 Methods of Data Analysis

Data analysis methods are used to describe the sample characteristics as precisely as possible. Having defined the sample characteristics we hypothesize about the general phenomenon of interest. The particular method that is used for describing the data depends on the data type and the project requirements.

- *Univariate methods* – Each variable is explored separately assuming the variables are independent of each other. The data are presented as a list of numbers representing a series of points on a scaled line. Univariate statistical methods include the collection of information about the variable, such as the minimum and maximum value, the average and the dispersion about the average. Examples are the sodium content of volcanic glass shards that were affected by chemical weathering or the size of snail shells in a sediment layer.

- *Bivariate methods* – Two variables are investigated together to detect relationships between these two parameters. For example, the correlation coefficient may be calculated to investigate whether there is a linear relationship between two variables. Alternatively, the bivariate regression analysis helps to find an equation that describes the relationship between the two variables. An example for a bivariate plot is the *Harker Diagram*, which is one of the oldest method to visualize geochemical data and plots oxides of elements against SiO_2 from igneous rocks.

- *Time-series analysis* – These methods investigate data sequences as a function of time. The time series is decomposed into a long-term trend, a systematic (periodic, cyclic, rhythmic) and an irregular (random, stochastic) component. A widely used technique is spectral analysis, to describe cyclic components of the time series. Examples for the application of these techniques are the investigation of cyclic climate variations in sedimentary rocks or the analysis of seismic data.

- *Signal processing* – This includes all techniques for manipulating a signal to minimize the effects of noise, to correct all kinds of unwanted distortions or to separate various components of interest. It includes the design, realization and application of filters to the data. These methods are widely used in combination with time-series analysis, e.g., to increase the signal-to-noise ratio in climate time series, digital images or geophysical data.

- *Spatial analysis* – The analysis of parameters in 2D or 3D space. Therefore, two or three of the required parameters are coordinate numbers. These methods include descriptive tools to investigate the spatial pattern of geographically distributed data. Other techniques involve spatial regression analysis to detect spatial trends. Finally, 2D and 3D interpolation techniques help to estimate surfaces representing the predicted continuous distribution of the variable throughout the area. Examples are drainage-system analysis, the identification of old landscape forms and lineament analysis in tectonically-active regions.

- *Image processing* – The processing and analysis of images has become increasingly important in earth sciences. These methods include manipulating images to increase the signal-to-noise ratio and to extract certain components of the image. Examples are the analysis of satellite images, the identification of objects in thin sections and counting annual layers in laminated sediments.

- *Multivariate analysis* – These methods involve the observation and analysis of more than one statistical variable at a time. Since the graphical representation of multidimensional data sets is difficult, most methods include dimension reduction. Multivariate methods are widely used on geochemical data, for instance in tephrochronology, where volcanic ash layers are correlated by geochemical fingerprinting of glass shards. Another important example is the comparison of species assemblages in ocean sediments to reconstruct paleoenvironments.

- *Analysis of directional data* – Methods to analyze circular and spherical data are widely used in earth sciences. Structural geologists measure and analyze the orientation of slickenlines (or striae) on a fault plane. Circular statistical methods are also common in paleomagnetic studies. Microstructural investigations include the analysis of grain shapes and quartz c-axis orientation in thin sections.

Some of these methods require the application of numerical methods, such as interpolation techniques and some methods of signal processing. The following text is mainly on statistical techniques, but also introduces several numerical methods used in earth sciences.

Recommended Reading

Borradaile G (2003) Statistics of Earth Science Data – Their Distribution in Time, Space and Orientation. Springer, Berlin Heidelberg New York

Carr JR (1995) Numerical Analysis for the Geological Sciences. Prentice Hall, Englewood Cliffs, New Jersey

Davis JC (2002) Statistics and Data Analysis in Geology, Third Edition. John Wiley and Sons, New York

Hanneberg WC (2004) Computational Geosciences with Mathematica. Springer, Berlin Heidelberg New York

Mardia KV (1972) Statistics of Directional Data. Academic Press, London

Middleton GV (1999) Data Analysis in the Earth Sciences Using MATLAB. Prentice Hall, New Jersey

Press WH, Teukolsky SA, Vetterling WT (1992) Numerical Recipes in Fortran 77. Cambridge University Press, Cambridge

Press WH, Teukolsky SA, Vetterling WT, Flannery BP (2002) Numerical Recipes in C++. Cambridge University Press, Cambridge

Swan ARH, Sandilands M (1995) Introduction to Geological Data Analysis. Blackwell Sciences, Oxford

Upton GJ, Fingleton B (1990) Spatial Data Analysis by Example, Categorial and Directional Data. John Wiley & Sons, New York

2 Introduction to MATLAB

2.1 MATLAB in Earth Sciences

MATLAB® is a software package developed by The MathWorks Inc. (http://www.mathworks.com) founded by Cleve Moler and Jack Little in 1984 and headquartered in Natick, Massachusetts. MATLAB was designed to perform mathematical calculations, to analyze and visualize data, and write new software programs. The advantage of this software is the combination of comprehensive math and graphics functions with a powerful high-level language. Since MATLAB contains a large library of ready-to-use routines for a wide range of applications, the user can solve technical computing problems much faster than with traditional programming languages, such as C++ and FORTRAN. The standard library of functions can be significantly expanded by add-on toolboxes, which are collections of functions for special purposes such as image processing, building map displays, performing geospatial data analysis or solving partial differential equations.

During the last few years, MATLAB has become an increasingly popular tool in earth sciences. It has been used for finite element modeling, the processing of seismic data and satellite images as well as the generation of digital elevation models from satellite images. The continuing popularity of the software is also apparent in the scientific reference literature. Many conference presentations and scientific publications have made reference to MATLAB. Universities and research institutions have also recognized the need for MATLAB training for staff and students. Many earth science departments across the world now offer MATLAB courses for undergraduates. Similarly, The MathWorks Inc. provides classroom kits for teachers at a reasonable price. It is also possible for students to purchase a low-cost edition of the software. This student version provides an inexpensive way for students to improve their MATLAB skills.

The following Chapters 2.2 to 2.7 contain a tutorial-style introduction to the software MATLAB, to the setup on the computer (Chapter 2.2), the syntax (2.3), data input and output (2.4 and 2.5), programming (2.6), and visualization (2.7). It is recommended to go through the entire chapter in order to obtain a solid knowledge in the software before proceeding to the following chapter. A more detailed introduction is provided by the MATLAB User's Guide (The MathWorks 2006). The book uses MATLAB Version 7.4 (Release 2007a), the Image Processing Toolbox Version 5.4, the Mapping Toolbox Version 2.5, the Signal Processing Toolbox Version 6.7, the Statistics Toolbox Version 6.0 and the Wavelet Toolbox Version 4.0.

2.2 Getting Started

The software package comes with extensive documentation, tutorials and examples. The first three chapters of the book *Getting Started with MATLAB* by The MathWorks, which is available printed, online and as PDF file is directed to the beginner. The chapters on programming, creating graphical user interfaces (GUI) and development environments are for the advanced users. Since *Getting Started with MATLAB* mediates all required knowledge to use the software, the following introduction concentrates on the most relevant software components and tools used in the following chapters.

After the installation of MATLAB on a hard disk or on a server, we launch the software either by clicking the shortcut icon on the desktop or by typing

```
matlab
```

at the operating system prompt. The software comes up with several window panels (Fig. 2.1). The default desktop layout includes the *Current Directory* panel that lists the files in the directory currently used. The *Workspace* panel lists the variables in the MATLAB workspace, which is empty after starting a new software session. The *Command Window* presents the interface between the software and the user, i.e., it accepts MATLAB commands typed after a prompt, >>. The *Command History* records all operations once typed in the Command Window and enables the user to recall these. The book mainly uses the Command Window and the built-in *Text Editor* that can be called by

```
edit
```

Before using MATLAB we have to (1) create a personal working directory where to store our MATLAB-related files, (2) add this directory to the MATLAB search path and (3) change into it to make this the current work-

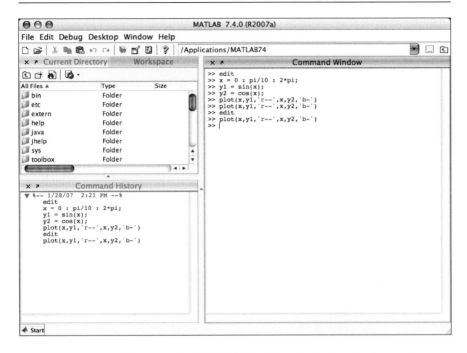

Fig. 2.1 Screenshot of the MATLAB default desktop layout including the *Current Directory* and *Workspace* panels (upper left), the *Command History* (lower left) and *Command Window* (right). This book only uses the Command Window and the built-in *Text Editor*, which can be called by typing `edit` after the prompt. All information provided by the other panels can also be accessed through the Command Window.

ing directory. The current working directory is the directory in which the software is installed, for instance, *c:/MATLAB74* on a personal computer running Microsoft Windows and */Applications/MATLAB74* on an Apple computer running Macintosh OS X. On the UNIX-based SUN Solaris operating system and on a LINUX system, the current working directory is the directory from which MATLAB has been launched. The command

```
pwd
```

prints the current working directory. Since you may have read-only permissions in this directory in a multi-user environment, you should change into your own home directory by typing

```
cd 'c:\Documents and Settings\username\My Documents'
```

after the prompt on a Windows system and

```
cd /users/username
```

or

```
cd /home/username
```

if you are *username* on a UNIX or LINUX system. You create a personal working directory by typing

```
mkdir mywork
```

The software uses a *search path* to find MATLAB-related files, which are organized in directories on the hard disk. The default search path includes only the MATLAB directory that has been created by the installer in the applications folder. To see which directories are in the search path or to add new directories, select *Set Path* from the *File* menu, and use the *Set Path* dialog box. Alternatively, the command

```
path
```

prints the complete list of directories in the search path. We add our personal working directory to this list by typing

```
path(path,'c:\Documents and Settings\user\My Documents\MyWork')
```

on a Windows machine assuming that you are *user*, you are working on *Hard Disk C* and your personal working directory is named *MyWork*. On a UNIX or LINUX computer the command

```
path(path,'/users/username/mywork')
```

is used instead. This command can be used whenever more working directories or toolboxes have to be added to the search path. Finally, you can change into the new directory by typing

```
cd mywork
```

making it the current working directory. The command

```
what
```

lists all MATLAB-related files in this directory. The modified search path is saved in a file *pathdef.m* in your home directory. In a future session, the software reads the contents of this file and makes MATLAB to use your custom path list.

2.3 The Syntax

The name MATLAB stands for *matrix laboratory*. The classic object han-
dled by MATLAB is a matrix, i.e., a rectangular two-dimensional array
of numbers. A simple 1-by-1 matrix is a scalar. Matrices with one column
or row are vectors, time series and other one-dimensional data fields. An
m-by-*n* matrix can be used for a digital elevation model or a grayscale image. RGB color images are usually stored as three-dimensional arrays, i.e.,
the colors red, green and blue are represented by an *m*-by-*n*-by-3 array.

Entering matrices in MATLAB is easy. To enter an arbitrary matrix, type

```
A = [2 4 3 7; 9 3 -1 2; 1 9 3 7; 6 6 3 -2]
```

after the prompt, which first defines a variable A, then lists the elements of
the matrix in square brackets. The rows of A are separated by semicolons,
whereas the elements of a row are separated by blanks, or, alternatively, by
commas. After pressing *return*, MATLAB displays the matrix

```
A =
    2    4    3    7
    9    3   -1    2
    1    9    3    7
    6    6    3   -2
```

Displaying the elements of A could be problematic in case of very large
matrices, such as digital elevation models consisting of thousands or mil-
lions of elements. You should end the line with a semicolon to suppress the
display of a matrix or the result of an operation in general.

```
A = [2 4 3 7; 9 3 -1 2; 1 9 3 7; 6 6 3 -2];
```

The matrix A is now stored in the workspace and we can do some basic
operations with it, such as computing the sum of elements,

```
sum(A)
```

which results in the display of

```
ans =
    18   22    8   14
```

Since we did not specify an output variable, such as A for the matrix entered
above, MATLAB uses a default variable ans, short for *answer*, to store the
results of the calculation. In general, we should define variables since the next
computation without a new variable name overwrites the contents of ans.

The above example illustrates another important point about MATLAB. Obviously the result of `sum(A)` are the four sums of the elements in the four columns of A. The software prefers working with the columns of matrices. If you wish to sum all elements of A and store the result in a scalar b, you simply type

```
b = sum(sum(A));
```

which first sums the columns of the matrix and then the elements of the resulting vector. Now we have two variables A and b stored in the workspace. We can easily check this by typing

```
whos
```

which is one the most frequently-used MATLAB commands. The software lists all variables in the workspace with information about their dimension, bytes and class.

```
Name      Size           Bytes  Class      Attributes
A         4x4              128  double
ans       1x4               32  double
b         1x1                8  double
```

Note that by default MATLAB is case sensitive, i.e., two different variables A and a can be defined. In this context, it is recommended to use capital letters for matrices and lower-case letters for vectors and scalars. You could now delete the contents of the variable ans by typing

```
clear ans
```

Next, we learn how specific matrix elements can be accessed or exchanged. Typing

```
A(3,2)
```

simply returns the matrix element located in the third row and second column. The matrix indexing therefore follows the rule *(row, column)*. We can use this to access single or several matrix elements. As an example, we type

```
A(3,2) = 30
```

to replace the element A(3,2) and to display the entire matrix.

```
A =
     2     4     3     7
     9     3    -1     2
     1    30     3     7
     6     6     3    -2
```

If you wish to replace several elements at one time, you can use the colon operator. Typing

```
A(3,1:4) = [1 3 3 5];
```

replaces all elements of the third row of the matrix A. The colon operator is used for several other things in MATLAB, for instance as an abbreviation for entering matrix elements such as

```
c = 0 : 10
```

which creates a row vector containing all integers from 0 to 10. The corresponding MATLAB response is

```
c =
    0  1  2  3  4  5  6  7  8  9  10
```

Note that this statement creates 11 elements, i.e., the integers from 1 to 10 and the zero. A common error while indexing matrices is the ignorance of the zero and therefore expecting 10 instead of 11 elements in our example. We can check this from the output of whos.

```
Name        Size            Bytes   Class      Attributes
A           4x4               128   double
ans         1x1                 8   double
b           1x1                 8   double
c           1x11               88   double
```

The above command creates only integers, i.e., the interval between the vector elements is one. However, an arbitrary interval can be defined, for example 0.5. This is later used to create evenly-spaced time axes for time series analysis.

```
c = 1 : 0.5 : 10;

c =
  Columns 1 through 6
    1.0000      1.5000      2.0000      2.5000      3.0000      3.5000
  Columns 7 through 12
    4.0000      4.5000      5.0000      5.5000      6.0000      6.5000
  Columns 13 through 18
    7.0000      7.5000      8.0000      8.5000      9.0000      9.5000
  Column 19
   10.0000
```

The display of the values of a variable can be interrupted by pressing *Ctrl-C* (*Control-C*) on the keyboard. This interruption affects only the output in the Command Window, whereas the actual command is processed before displaying the result.

MATLAB provides standard arithmetic operators for addition, +, and subtraction, -. The asterisk, *, denotes matrix multiplication involving inner products between rows and columns. For instance, we multiply the matrix A with a new matrix B.

```
B = [4 2 6 5; 7 8 5 6; 2 1 -8 -9; 3 1 2 3];
```

The matrix multiplication then is

```
C = A * B'
```

where ' is the complex conjugate transpose, i.e, turning rows into columns and columns into rows. This generates the output

```
C =
    69    103   -79    37
    46     94    11    34
    75    136   -76    39
    44     93    12    24
```

In linear algebra, matrices are used to keep track of the coefficients of linear transformations. The multiplication of two matrices represents the combination of two linear transformations to one single transformation. Matrix multiplication is not commutative, i.e., A*B' and B*A' yield different results in most cases. Accordingly, MATLAB provides matrix divisions, right, /, and left, \, representing different transformations. Finally, the software allows power of matrices, ^.

In earth sciences, however, matrices are often simply used as two-dimensional arrays of numerical data instead of an array representing a linear transformation. Arithmetic operations on such arrays are done element-by-element. Whereas this does not make any difference in addition and subtraction, the multiplicative operations are different. MATLAB uses a dot as part of the notation for these operations.

For instance, multiplying A and B element-by-element is performed by typing

```
C = A .* B
```

which generates the output

```
C =
     8      8    18    35
    63     24    -5    12
     2      3   -24   -45
    18      6     6    -6
```

2.4 Data Storage

This chapter is on how to store, import and export data with MATLAB. In earth sciences, data are collected in a great variety of formats, which often have to be converted before being analyzed with MATLAB. On the other hand, the software provides several import routines to read many binary data formats in earth sciences, such as the formats used to store digital elevation models and satellite data.

A computer generally stores data as *binary digits* or *bits*. A bit is analogous to a two-way switch with two states, on = 1 and off = 0. The bits are joined to larger groups, such as bytes consisting of 8 bits, to store more complex types of data. Such groups of bits are then used to encode data, e.g., numbers or characters. Unfortunately, different computer systems and software use different schemes for encoding data. For instance, the representation of text using the widely-used text processing software Microsoft Word is different from characters written in Word Perfect. Exchanging binary data therefore is difficult if the various users use different computer platforms and software. Binary data can be stored in relatively small files in case that both partners use similar systems of data exchange. The transfer rate of binary data is generally faster compared to the exchange of other file formats.

Various formats for exchanging data have been developed in the last decades. The classic example for the establishment of a data format that can be used on different computer platforms and software is the *American Standard Code for Information Interchange* (ASCII) that was first published in 1963 by the American Standards Association (ASA). ASCII as a 7-bit code consists of $2^7=128$ characters (codes 0 to 127). Whereas ASCII-1963 was lacking lower-case letters, in the update ASCII-1967, lower-case letters as well as various control characters such as *escape* and *line feed* and various symbols such as brackets and mathematical operators were also included. Since then, a number of variants appeared in order to facilitate the exchange of text written in non-English languages, such as the expanded ASCII containing 255 codes, e.g., the Latin-1 encoding.

2.5 Data Handling

The simplest way to exchange data between a certain piece of software and MATLAB is the ASCII format. Although the newer versions of MATLAB

provide various import routines for file types such as Microsoft Excel binaries, most data arrive as ASCII files. Consider a simple data set stored in a
table such as

```
SampleID   Percent C     Percent S
101        0.3657        0.0636
102        0.2208        0.1135
103        0.5353        0.5191
104        0.5009        0.5216
105        0.5415        -999
106        0.501         -999
```

The first row contains the variable names. The columns provide the data for
each sample. The absurd value -999 marks missing data in the data set. Two
things have to be changed to convert this table into MATLAB format. First,
MATLAB uses NaN as the arithmetic representation for *Not-a-Number* that
can be used to mark gaps. Second, you should comment the first line by typing a percent sign, %, at the beginning of the line.

```
%SampleID  Percent C     Percent S
101        0.3657        0.0636
102        0.2208        0.1135
103        0.5353        0.5191
104        0.5009        0.5216
105        0.5415        NaN
106        0.501         NaN
```

MATLAB ignores any text appearing after the percent sign and continues
processing on the next line. After editing this table in a text editor, such as
the *MATLAB Editor*, it is saved as ASCII text file *geochem.txt* in the current
working directory (Fig. 2.2). MATLAB now imports the data from this file
with the load command.

```
load geochem.txt
```

MATLAB loads the contents of file and assigns the matrix to a variable
named after the filename geochem. Typing

```
whos
```

yields

```
Name          Size            Bytes  Class      Attributes
geochem       6x3               144  double
```

The command save now allows to store workspace variables in a binary
format.

```
save geochem_new.mat
```

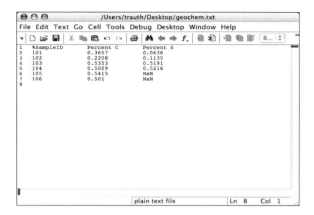

Fig. 2.2 Screenshot of MATLAB *Text Editor* showing the content of the file *geochem.txt*. The first line of the text is commented by a percent sign at the beginning of the line, followed by the actual data matrix.

MAT-files are double-precision binary files using *.mat* as extension. The advantage of these binary mat-files is that they are independent of the computer platforms running different floating-point formats. The command

```
save geochem_new.mat geochem
```

saves only the variable `geochem` instead of the entire workspace. The option `-ascii`, for example

```
save geochem_new.txt geochem -ascii
```

again saves the variable `geochem`, but in an ASCII file named *geochem_new. txt*. In contrast to the binary file *geochem_new.mat,* this ASCII file can be viewed and edited by using the MATLAB Editor or any other text editor.

2.6 Scripts and Functions

MATLAB is a powerful programming language. All files containing MATLAB code use *.m* as extension and are therefore called *M-files*. These files contain ASCII text and can be edited using a standard text editor. However, the built-in Editor color highlights various syntax elements such as comments (in green), keywords such as *if, for* and *end* (blue) and character strings (pink). This syntax highlighting eases MATLAB coding.

MATLAB uses two kinds of M-files, *scripts* and *functions*. Whereas scripts are a series of commands that operate on data in the workspace, functions are true algorithms with input and output variables. The advantages and disadvantages of both M-files will now be illustrated by an example. We start the Text Editor by typing

```
edit
```

This opens a new window named *untitled*. First, we generate a simple MATLAB script. We type a series of commands calculating the average of the elements of a data vector x.

```
[m,n] = size(x);
if m == 1
    m = n;
end
sum(x)/m
```

The first line returns the dimension of the variable x using the command size. In our example, x should be either a column vector with dimension (m,1) or a row vector with dimension (1,n). The if statement evaluates a logical expression and executes a group of commands when this expression is true. The end keyword terminates the last group of commands. In the example, the if loop picks either m or n depending on if m==1 is false or true. The last line computes the average by dividing the sum of elements by m or n. We do not use a semicolon here to enable the output of the result. We save our new M-file as *average.m* and type

```
x = [3 6 2 -3 8];
```

in the Command Window to define an example vector x. Then, we type

```
average
```

without the extension .*m* to run our script. We obtain the average of the elements of the vector x as output.

```
ans =
    3.2000
```

After typing

```
whos
```

we see that the workspace now contains

```
Name          Size              Bytes  Class      Attributes
ans           1x1                   8  double
```

```
m                    1x1                    8   double
n                    1x1                    8   double
x                    1x5                   40   double
```

The listed variables are the example vector x and the output of the size function, m and n. The result of the operation is stored in the variable ans. Since the default variable ans might be overwritten during one of the following operations, we wish to define a different variable. Typing

```
a = average
```

however, causes the error message

```
??? Attempt to execute SCRIPT average as a function.
```

Obviously, we cannot assign a variable to the output of a script. Moreover, all variables defined and used in the script appear in the workspace, in our example, the variables m and n. Scripts contain sequences of commands applied to variables in the workspace. MATLAB functions instead allow to define inputs and outputs. They do not automatically import variables from the workspace. To convert the above script into a function, we have to introduce the following modifications (Fig. 2.3):

```
function y = average(x)
%AVERAGE    Average value.
%    AVERAGE(X) is the average of the elements in the vector X.

% By Martin Trauth, Feb 18, 2005.

[m,n] = size(x);
if m == 1
    m = n;
end
y = sum(x)/m;
```

The first line now contains the keyword function, the function name average and the input x and output y. The next two lines contain comments as indicated by the percent sign. After one empty line, we see another comment line containing the author and version of the M-file. The remaining file contains the actual operations. The last line now defines the value of the output variable y. This line is now terminated by a semicolon to suppress the display of the result in the Command Window. We first type

```
help average
```

which displays the first block of contiguous comment lines. The first executable statement or blank line – as in our example – effectively ends the help

Fig. 2.3 Screenshot of the MATLAB *Text Editor* showing the function `average`. The function starts with a line containing the keyword `function`, the name of the function `average` and the input variable `x` and the output variable `y`. The following lines contain the output for `help average`, the copyright and version information as well as the actual MATLAB code for computing the average using this function.

section and therefore the output of *help*. Now we are independent of the variable names used in our function. We clear the workspace and define a new data vector.

```
clear

data = [3 6 2 -3 8];
```

We run our function by the statement

```
result = average(data);
```

This clearly illustrates the advantages of functions compared to scripts. Typing

```
whos
```

results in

```
Name           Size            Bytes  Class      Attributes
data           1x5                40  double
result         1x1                 8  double
```

indicates that all variables used in the function do not appear in the workspace. Only the input and output as defined by the user are stored in the workspace. The M-files can therefore be applied to data like real functions, whereas scripts contain sequences of commands are applied to the variables in workspace.

2.7 Basic Visualization Tools

MATLAB provides numerous routines for displaying your data as graphs. This chapter introduces the most important graphics functions. The graphs will be modified, printed and exported to be edited with graphics software other than MATLAB. The simplest function producing a graph of a variable y versus another variable x is plot. First, we define two vectors x and y, where y is the sine of x. The vector x contains values between 0 and 2π with $\pi/10$ increments, whereas y is the element-by-element sine of x.

```
x = 0 : pi/10 : 2*pi;
y = sin(x);
```

These two commands result in two vectors with 21 elements each, i.e., two 1-by-21 arrays. Since the two vectors x and y have the same length, we can use plot to produce a linear 2D graph y against x.

```
plot(x,y)
```

This command opens a *Figure Window* named *Figure 1* with a gray background, an *x*-axis ranging from 0 to 7, a *y*-axis ranging from −1 to +1 and a blue line. You may wish to plot two different curves in one single plot, for example, the sine and the cosine of x in different colors. The command

```
x = 0 : pi/10 : 2*pi;
y1 = sin(x);
y2 = cos(x);

plot(x,y1,'r--',x,y2,'b-')
```

creates a dashed red line displaying the sine of x and a solid blue line representing the cosine of this vector (Fig. 2.4). If you create another plot, the window *Figure 1* is cleared and a new graph is displayed. The command figure, however, can be used to create a new figure object in a new window.

```
plot(x,y1,'r--')
figure
plot(x,y2,'b-')
```

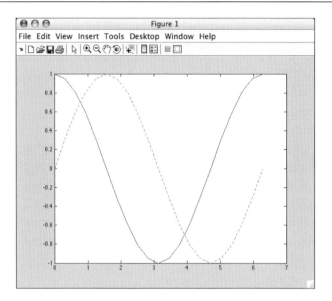

Fig. 2.4 Screenshot of the MATLAB *Figure Window* showing two curves in different line types. The Figure Window allows to edit all elements of the graph after choosing *Edit Plot* from the *Tools* menu. Double clicking on the graphics elements opens an options window for modifying the appearance of the graphs. The graphics is exported using *Save as* from the *File* menue. The command *Generate M-File* from the *File* menu creates MATLAB code from an edited graph.

Instead of plotting both lines in one graph simultaneously, you can also plot the sine wave, hold the graph and then plot the second curve. The command `hold` is particularly important while using different plot functions for displaying your data. For instance, if you wish to display the second graph as a bar plot.

```
plot(x,y1,'r--')
hold on
bar(x,y2)
hold off
```

This command plots `y1` versus `x` as dashed line, whereas `y2` versus `x` is shown as group of blue vertical bars. Alternatively, you can plot both graphs in the same Figure Window, but in different plots using the `subplot`. The syntax `subplot(m,n,p)` divides the Figure Window into an *m*-by-*n* matrix of display regions and makes the `p`-th display region active.

```
subplot(2,1,1), plot(x,y1,'r--')
subplot(2,1,2), bar(x,y2)
```

The Figure Window is divided into two rows and one column in our example. The 2D linear plot is displayed in the upper half, whereas the bar plot appears in the lower half of the Figure Window. In the following, it is recommended to close the Figure Windows before proceeding to the next example. Subsequent plots would replace the graph in the lower display region only, or more general, the last generated graph in a Figure Window.

An important modification to graphs is the scaling of the axis. By default, MATLAB uses axis limits close to the minima and maxima of the data. Using the command `axis`, however, allows to change the settings for scaling. The syntax for this command is simply `axis([xmin xmax ymin ymax])`. The command

```
plot(x,y1,'r--')
axis([0 pi -1 1])
```

sets the limits of the *x*-axis to 0 and π, whereas the limits of the *y*-axis are set to the default values -1 and $+1$. Important options of `axis` are

```
plot(x,y1,'r--')
axis square
```

making the current axes region square and

```
plot(x,y1,'r--')
axis equal
```

setting the aspect ratio in a way that the data units are equal in both directions of the plot. The function `grid` adds a grid to the current plot, whereas the functions `title`, `xlabel` and `ylabel` allow to define a title and labels the *x*- and *y*-axis.

```
plot(x,y1,'r--')
title('My first plot')
xlabel('x-axis')
ylabel('y-axis')
grid
```

These are a few examples how MATLAB functions can be used in the Command Window to edit the plot. However, the software also supports various ways to edit all objects in a graph interactively using a computer mouse. First, the *Edit Mode* of the Figure Window has to be activated by clicking on the arrow icon. The Figure Window also contains some other options, such as *Rotate 3D*, *Zoom* or *Insert Legend*. The various objects in a graph, however, are selected by double-clicking on the specific component, which opens the *Property Editor*. The Property Editor allows to make changes to many properties of the graph such as axes, lines, patches and text objects. After having made all necessary changes to the graph, the corresponding commands can even be exported by selecting *Generate M-File* from the *File* menu of the Figure Window.

Although the software now provides enormous editing facilities for graphs, the more reasonable way to modify a graph for presentations or publications is to export the figure, import it into a software such as CorelDraw or Adobe Illustrator. MATLAB graphs are exported by selecting the command *Save as* from the *File* menu or by using the command `print`. This function exports the graph either as raster image, e.g., JPEG or vector file, e.g., as EPS or PDF format into the working directory (see Chapter 8 for more details on graphic file formats). In practice, the user should check the various combinations of export file format and the graphics software used for final editing the graphs.

Recommended Reading

Davis TA, Sigmon K (2005) The MATLAB Primer, Seventh Edition. Chapman & Hall/ CRC, London

Etter DM, Kuncicky DC, Moore H (2004) Introduction to MATLAB 7. Prentice Hall, New Jersey

Gilat A (2007) MATLAB: An Introduction with Applications. John Wiley & Sons, New York

Hanselman DC, Littlefield BL (2004) Mastering MATLAB 7. Prentice Hall, New Jersey

Palm WJ (2004) Introduction to MATLAB 7 for Engineers. McGraw-Hill, New York

The Mathworks (2006) MATLAB – The Language of Technical Computing – Getting Started with MATLAB Version 7. The MathWorks, Natick, MA

3 Univariate Statistics

3.1 Introduction

The statistical properties of a single parameter are investigated by means of univariate analysis. Such variable could be the organic carbon content of a sedimentary unit, the thickness of a sandstone layer, the age of sanidine crystals in a volcanic ash or the volume of landslides. The number and size of *samples* we collect from a larger *population* are often limited by financial and logistical constraints. The methods of univariate statistics help conclude from the samples for the larger phenomenon, i.e., the population.

Firstly, we describe the sample characteristics by statistical parameters and compute an *empirical distribution* (*descriptive statistics*) (Chapters 3.2 and 3.3). A brief introduction to the most important measures of central tendency and dispersion is followed by MATLAB examples. Next, we select a *theoretical distribution*, which shows similar characteristics as the empirical distribution (Chapters 3.4 and 3.5). A suite of theoretical distributions is then introduced and their potential applications outlined, before we use MATLAB tools to explore these distributions. Finally, we try to conclude from the sample for the larger phenomenon of interest (*hypothesis testing*) (Chapters 3.6 to 3.8). The corresponding chapters introduce the three most important statistical tests for applications in earth sciences, the t-test to compare the means of two data sets, the F-test comparing variances and the χ^2-test to compare distributions.

3.2 Empirical Distributions

Assume that we have collected a number of measurements of a specific object. The collection of data can be written as a vector x

$$x = (x_1, x_2, \ldots, x_N)$$

containing N observations x_i. The vector x may contain a large number of data points. It may be difficult to understand its properties as such. This is why descriptive statistics are often used to summarize the characteristics of the data. Similarly, the statistical properties of the data set may be used to define an empirical distribution which then can be compared against a theoretical one.

The most straight-forward way of investigating the sample characteristics is to display the data in a graphical form. Plotting all the data points along one single axis does not reveal a great deal of information about the data set. However, the density of the points along the scale does provide some information about the characteristics of the data. A widely-used graphical display of univariate data is the *histogram* (Fig. 3.1). A histogram is a bar plot of a frequency distribution that is organized in intervals or *classes*. Such histogram plot provides valuable information on the characteristics of the data, such as the *central tendency*, the *dispersion* and the *general shape* of the distribution. However, quantitative measures provide a more accurate way of describing the data set than the graphical form. In purely quantitative terms, the *mean* and the *median* define the central tendency of the data set, while data dispersion is expressed in terms of the *range* and the *standard deviation*.

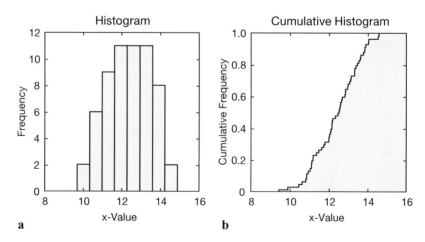

Fig. 3.1 Graphical representation of an empirical frequency distribution. **a** In a *histogram*, the frequencies are organized in classes and plotted as a bar plot. **b** The *cumulative histogram* of a frequency distribution displays the counts of all classes lower and equal than a certain value. The cumulative histogram is normalized to a total number of observations of one.

Measures of Central Tendency

Parameters of central tendency or location represent the most important measures for characterizing an empirical distribution (Fig. 3.2). These values help locate the data on a linear scale. They represent a typical or best value that describes the data. The most popular indicator of central tendency is the *arithmetic mean*, which is the sum of all data points divided by the number of observations:

$$\bar{x} = \frac{1}{N}\sum_{i=1}^{N} x_i$$

The arithmetic mean can also be called the mean or the average of an univariate data set. The sample mean is often used as an estimate of the population mean μ for the underlying theoretical distribution. The arithmetic mean is sensitive to outliers, i.e., extreme values that may be very different from the majority of the data. Therefore, the *median* is often used as an alternative measure of central tendency. The median is the x-value which is in the middle of the data, i.e., 50% of the observations are larger than the median and 50% are smaller. The median of a data set sorted in ascending order is defined as

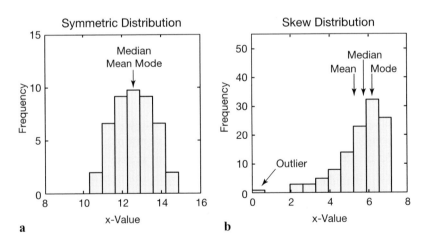

Fig. 3.2 Measures of *central tendency*. **a** In an unimodal symmetric distribution, the mean, the median and the mode are identical. **b** In a skew distribution, the median is between the mean and the mode. The mean is highly sensitive to outliers, whereas the median and the mode are not much influenced by extremely high and low values.

$$\tilde{x} = x_{(N+1)/2}$$

if N is odd and

$$\tilde{x} = \left(x_{(N/2)} + x_{(N/2)+1} \right) / 2$$

if N is even. Although outliers also affect the median, their absolute values do not influence it. *Quantiles* are a more general way of dividing the data sample into groups containing equal numbers of observations. For example, *quartiles* divide the data into four groups, *quintiles* divide the observations in five groups and *percentiles* define one hundred groups.

The third important measure for central tendency is the *mode*. The mode is the most frequent x value or – if the data are grouped in classes – the center of the class with the largest number of observations. The data have no mode if there aren't any values that appear more frequently than any of the other values. Frequency distributions with one mode are called *unimodal*, but there may also be two modes (*bimodal*), three modes (*trimodal*) or four or more modes (*multimodal*).

The measures mean, median and mode are used when several quantities add together to produce a total, whereas the *geometric mean* is often used if these quantities are multiplied. Let us assume that the population of an organism increases by 10% in the first year, 25% in the second year, then 60% in the last year. The average increase rate is not the arithmetic mean, since the number of individuals is multiplied by (not added to) 1.10 in the first year, by 1.375 in the second year and 2.20 in the last year. The average growth of the population is calculated by the geometric mean:

$$\bar{x}_G = \left(x_1 \cdot x_2 \cdot \ldots \cdot x_N \right)^{1/N}$$

The average growth of these values is 1.4929 suggesting a ~49% growth of the population. The arithmetic mean would result in an erroneous value of 1.5583 or ~56% growth. The geometric mean is also an useful measure of central tendency for skewed or log-normally distributed data. In other words, the logarithms of the observations follow a gaussian distribution. The geometric mean, however, is not calculated for data sets containing negative values. Finally, the *harmonic mean*

$$\bar{x}_H = N / \left(\frac{1}{x_1} + \frac{1}{x_2} + \ldots + \frac{1}{x_N} \right)$$

is used to take the mean of asymmetric or log-normally distributed data, similar to the geometric mean, but they are both not robust to outliers. The harmonic mean is a better average when the numbers are defined in relation to some unit. The common example is averaging velocity. The harmonic mean is also used to calculate the mean of samples sizes.

Measures of Dispersion

Another important property of a distribution is the dispersion. Some of the parameters that can be used to quantify dispersion are illustrated in Figure 3.3. The simplest way to describe the dispersion of a data set is the *range*, which is the difference between the highest and lowest value in the data set given by

$$\Delta x = x_{max} - x_{min}$$

Since the range is defined by the two extreme data points, it is very susceptible to outliers. Hence, it is not a reliable measure of dispersion in most cases. Using the interquartile range of the data, i.e., the middle 50% of the data attempts to overcome this. A most useful measure for dispersion is the *standard deviation*.

$$s = \sqrt{\frac{1}{N-1}\sum_{i=1}^{N}(x_i - \bar{x})^2}$$

The standard deviation is the average deviation of each data point from the mean. The standard deviation of an empirical distribution is often used as an estimate for the population standard deviation σ. The formula of the population standard deviation uses N instead of $N-1$ in the denominator. The sample standard deviation s is computed with $N-1$ instead of N since it uses the sample mean instead of the unknown population mean. The sample mean, however, is computed from the data x_i, which reduces the degrees of freedom by one. The *degrees of freedom* are the number of values in a distribution that are free to be varied. Dividing the average deviation of the data from the mean by N would therefore underestimate the population standard deviation σ.

The *variance* is the third important measure of dispersion. The variance is simply the square of the standard deviation.

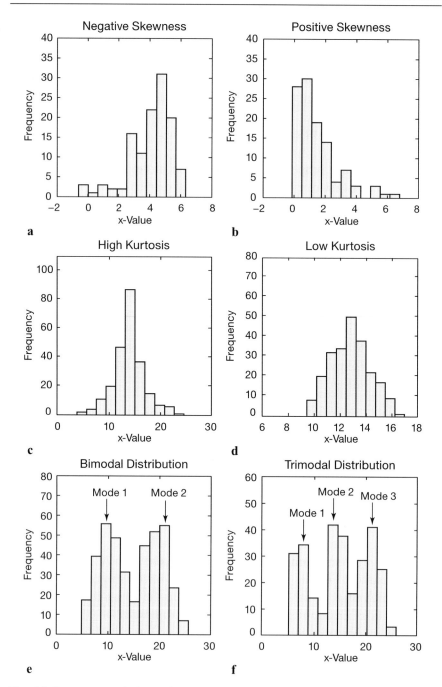

Fig. 3.3 *Dispersion* and *shape* of a distribution. **a-b** Unimodal distributions showing a negative or positive skew. **c-d** Distributions showing a high or low kurtosis. **e-f** Bimodal and trimodal distribution showing two or three modes.

$$s^2 = \frac{1}{N-1}\sum_{i=1}^{N}(x_i - \bar{x})^2$$

Although the variance has the disadvantage of not sharing the dimension of the original data, it is extensively used in may applications instead of the standard deviation.

Furthermore, both *skewness* and *kurtosis* can be used to describe the shape of a frequency distribution. Skewness is a measure of asymmetry of the tails of a distribution. The most popular way to compute the asymmetry of a distribution is Pearson's mode skewness:

skewness = (mean-mode) / standard deviation

A negative skew indicates that the distribution is spread out more to the left of the mean value, assuming increasing values on the axis to the right. The sample mean is smaller than the mode. Distributions with positive skewness have large tails that extend to the right. The skewness of the symmetric normal distribution is zero. Although Pearson's measure is a useful one, the following formula by Fisher for calculating the skewness is often used instead, including the corresponding MATLAB function.

$$skewness = \sum_{i=1}^{N}\frac{(x_i - \bar{x})^3}{s^3}$$

The second important measure for the shape of a distribution is the *kurtosis*. Again, numerous formulas to compute the kurtosis are available. MATLAB uses the following formula:

$$kurtosis = \sum_{i=1}^{N}\frac{(x_i - \bar{x})^4}{s^4}$$

The kurtosis is a measure of whether the data are peaked or flat relative to a normal distribution. A high kurtosis indicates that the distribution has a distinct peak near the mean, whereas a distribution characterized by a low kurtosis shows a flat top near the mean and heavy tails. Higher peakedness of a distribution is resulting from rare extreme deviations, whereas a low kurtosis is caused by frequent moderate deviations. A normal distribution has a kurtosis of three. Therefore, some definitions for kurtosis subtract three from the above term in order to set the kurtosis of the normal distribution to zero.

After having defined the most important parameters to describe an empirical distribution, the measures of central tendency and dispersion are illustrated by examples. The text and binary files used in the following chapters are on the CD that comes with this book. It is recommended to save the files in the personal working directory.

3.3 Example of Empirical Distributions

Let us describe the data contained in the file *organicmatter_one.txt*. This file contains the organic matter content (in weight percentage, wt%) of lake sediments. In order to load the data type

```
corg = load('organicmatter_one.txt');
```

The data file contains 60 measurements that can be displayed by

```
plot(corg,zeros(1,length(corg)),'o')
```

This graph shows some of the characteristics of the data. The organic carbon content of the samples range between 9 and 15 wt%. Most data cluster between 12 and 13 wt%. Values below 10 and above 14 are rare. While this kind of representation of the data has its advantages, univariate data are generally displayed as histograms.

```
hist(corg)
```

By default, the function hist divides the range of the data into ten equal intervals or classes, counts the observation within each interval and displays the frequency distribution as bar plot. The midpoints of the default intervals v and the number of observations n per interval can be accessed using

```
[n,v] = hist(corg);
```

The number of classes should be not lower than six and not higher than fifteen for practical purposes. In practice, the square root of the number of observations, rounded to the nearest integer, is often used as the number of classes. In our example, we use eight classes instead of the default ten classes.

```
hist(corg,8)
```

We can even define the midpoint values of the histogram classes. Here, it is recommended to choose interval endpoints that avoid data points falling between two intervals. The maximum and minimum values contained in the data vector are

```
max(corg)

ans =
    14.5615

min(corg)

ans =
    9.4168
```

The range of the data values, i.e., the difference between maximum and minimum values is

```
range(corg)

ans =
    5.1447
```

The range of the data is the information that we need in order to define the classes. Since we have decided to use eight classes, we split the range of the data into eight equally-sized bins. The approximate width of the intervals is

```
5.1447/8

ans =
    0.6431
```

We round this number up and define

```
v = 10 : 0.65 : 14.55;
```

as midpoints of the histogram intervals. The commands for displaying the histogram and calculating the frequency distribution are

```
hist(corg,v);

n = hist(corg,v);
```

The most important parameters describing the distribution are the averages and the dispersion about the average. The most popular measure for average is the arithmetic mean of our data.

```
mean(corg)

ans =
    12.3448
```

Since this measure is very susceptible to outliers, we use the median as an alternative measure of central tendency,

```
median(corg)

ans =
    12.4712
```

which is not much different in this example. However, we will later see that
this difference can be significant for distributions that are not symmetric.
A more general parameter to define fractions of the data less or equal to a
certain value is the quantile. Some of the quantiles have special names, such
as the three quartiles dividing the distribution into four equal parts, 0–25%,
25–50%, 50–75% and 75–100% of the total number of observations.

```
prctile(corg,[25 50 75])

ans =
    11.4054    12.4712    13.2965
```

The third parameter in this context is the mode, which is the midpoint of the
interval with the highest frequency. MATLAB does not provide a function
to compute the mode. We use the function find to located the class that has
the largest number of observations.

```
v(find(n == max(n)))

ans =
    11.9500    12.6000    13.2500
```

This statement simply identifies the largest element in n. The index of this
element is then used to display the midpoint of the corresponding class v.
If there are several n's with similar values, this statement returns several
solutions suggesting that the distribution has several modes. The median,
quartiles, minimum and maximum of a data set can be summarized and
displayed in a *box and whisker plot*.

```
boxplot(corg)
```

The boxes have lines at the lower quartile, median, and upper quartile values. The whiskers are lines extending from each end of the boxes to show
the extent of the rest of the data.

The most popular measures for dispersion are range, standard deviation
and variance. We have already used the range to define the midpoints of the
classes. The variance is the average-squared deviation of each number from
the mean of a data set.

```
var(corg)

ans =
    1.3595
```

The standard deviation is the square root of the variance.

```
std(corg)

ans =
    1.1660
```

Note that by default the functions `var` and `std` calculate the sample variance and standard deviation representing an unbiased estimate of the dispersion of the population. While using `skewness` to describe the shape of the distribution, we observe a slightly negative skew.

```
skewness(corg)

ans =
    -0.2529
```

Finally, the peakedness of the distribution is described by the kurtosis. The result from the function `kurtosis`,

```
kurtosis(corg)

ans =
    2.4670
```

suggests that our distribution is slightly flatter than a gaussian distribution since its kurtosis is lower than three. Most of these functions have corresponding versions for data sets containing gaps, such as `nanmean` and `nanstd`, which treat `NaN`'s as missing values. To illustrate the use of these functions we introduce a gap to our data set and compute the mean using `mean` and `nanmean` for comparison.

```
corg(25,1) = NaN;

mean(corg)

ans =
    NaN

nanmean(corg)

ans =
    12.3371
```

In this example the function `mean` follows the rule that all operations with

NaN's result in NaN's, whereas the function nanmean simply skips the missing value and computes the mean of the remaining data. As a second example, we now explore a data set characterized by a significant skew. The data represent 120 microprobe analyses on glass shards hand-picked from a volcanic ash. The volcanic glass has been affected by chemical weathering in an initial stage. Therefore, the glass shards show glass hydration and sodium depletion in some sectors. We study the distribution of sodium contents (in wt%) in the 120 measurements using the same principle as above.

```
sodium = load('sodiumcontent.txt');
```

As a first step, it is always recommended to visualize the data as a histogram. The square root of 120 suggests 11 classes, therefore we display the data by typing

```
hist(sodium,11)

[n,v] = hist(sodium,11);
```

Since the distribution has a negative skew, the mean, the median and the mode are significantly different.

```
mean(sodium)

ans =
    5.6628

median(sodium)

ans =
    5.9741

v(find(n == max(n)))

ans =
    6.5407
```

The mean of the data is lower than the median, which is in turn lower than the mode. We observe a strong negative skew as expected from our data.

```
skewness(sodium)

ans =
    -1.1086
```

Now we introduce a significant outlier to the data and explore its effect on the statistics of the sodium contents. We use a different data set, which is better suited for this example than the previous data set. The new data set contains higher sodium values of around 17 wt% and is stored in the file *sodiumcontent_two.txt*.

```
sodium = load('sodiumcontent_two.txt');
```

This data set contains only 50 measurements to better illustrate the effect of an outlier. We can use the script used in the previous example to display the data in a histogram and compute the number of observations n with respect to the classes v. The mean of the data is 16.6379, the media is 16.9739 and the mode is 17.2109. Now we introduce one single value of 1.5 wt% in addition to the 50 measurements contained in the original data set.

```
sodium(51,1) = 1.5;
```

The histogram of this data set illustrates the distortion of the frequency distribution by this single outlier. The corresponding histogram shows several empty classes. The influence of this outlier on the sample statistics is substantial. Whereas the median of 16.9722 is relatively unaffected, the mode of 17.0558 is slightly different since the classes have changed. The most significant changes are observed in the mean (16.3411), which is very sensitive to outliers.

3.4 Theoretical Distributions

Now we have described the empirical frequency distribution of our sample. A histogram is a convenient way to picture the frequency distribution of the variable x. If we sample the variable sufficiently often and the output ranges are narrow, we obtain a very smooth version of the histogram. An infinite number of measurements $N \rightarrow \infty$ and an infinite small class width produce the random variable's *probability density function* (PDF). The probability distribution density $f(x)$ defines the probability that the variate has the value equal to x. The integral of $f(x)$ is normalized to unity, i.e., the total number of observations is one. The *cumulative distribution function* (CDF) is the sum of a discrete PDF or the integral of a continuous PDF. The cumulative distribution function $F(x)$ is the probability that the variable takes a value less than or equal x.

As a next step, we have to find a suitable theoretical distribution that fits the empirical distributions described in the previous chapters. In this section, the most important theoretical distributions are introduced and their application is described.

Uniform Distribution

A *uniform* or *rectangular distribution* is a distribution that has a constant probability (Fig. 3.4). The corresponding probability density function is

$$f(x) = 1/N = const.$$

where the random variable x has any of N possible values. The cumulative distribution function is

$$F(x) = x \cdot 1/N$$

The probability density function is normalized to unity

$$\int_{-\infty}^{+\infty} f(x)\, dx = 1$$

i.e., the sum of probabilities is one. Therefore, the maximum value of the cumulative distribution function is one.

$$F(x)_{max} = 1$$

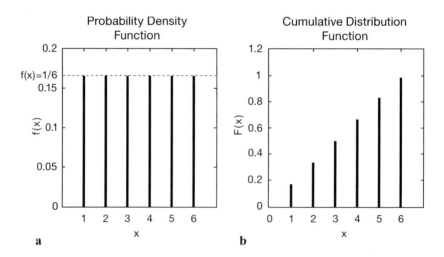

Fig. 3.4 a Probability density function $f(x)$ and **b** cumulative distribution function $F(x)$ of a uniform distribution with $N = 6$. The 6 discrete values of the variable x have the same probability of $1/6$.

An example is a rolling die with $N=6$ faces. A discrete variable such as the faces of a die can only take a countable number of values x. The probability of each face is 1/6. The probability density function of this distribution is

$$f(x) = 1/6$$

The corresponding cumulative distribution function is

$$F(x) = x \cdot 1/6$$

where x takes only discrete values, $x=1, 2, \ldots, 6$.

Binomial or Bernoulli Distribution

A *binomial* or *Bernoulli distribution*, named after the Swiss scientist Jakob Bernoulli (1654–1705), gives the discrete probability of x successes out of N trials, with probability p of success in any given trial (Fig. 3.5). The probability density function of a binomial distribution is

$$f(x) = \binom{N}{x} p^x (1-p)^{N-x}$$

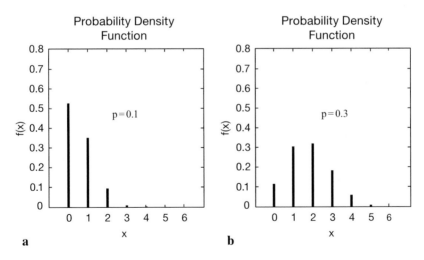

Fig. 3.5 Probability density function $f(x)$ of a binomial distribution, which gives the probability p of x successes out of $N=6$ trials, with probability **a** $p=0.1$ and **b** $p=0.3$ of success in any given trial.

The cumulative distribution function is

$$F(x) = \sum_{i=1}^{x} \binom{N}{i} p^i (1-p)^{N-i}$$

where

$$\binom{n}{r} = \frac{n!}{r!(n-r)!}$$

The binomial distribution has two parameters N and p. An example for the application of this distribution is the outcome of oil drilling. Let us assume that the probability of a drilling success is 0.1 or 10%. The probability of $x=3$ successful wells out of a total number of $N=10$ wells is

$$f(3) = \binom{10}{3} 0.1^3 (1-0.1)^{10-3} = 0.057 \approx 6\%$$

Therefore, the probability of exact 3 successful wells out of 10 trials is 6%.

Poisson Distribution

When the number of trials is $N \rightarrow \infty$ and the success probability is $p \rightarrow 0$, the binomial distribution approaches the *Poisson distribution* with one single parameter $\lambda = Np$ (Fig. 3.6) (Poisson 1837). This works well for $N > 100$ and $p < 0.05$ or 5%. Therefore, we use the Poisson distribution for processes characterized by extremely low occurrence, e.g., earthquakes, volcano eruptions, storms and floods. The probability density function is

$$f(x) = \frac{e^{-\lambda} \lambda^x}{x!}$$

and the cumulative distribution function is

$$F(x) = \sum_{i=0}^{x} \frac{e^{-\lambda} \lambda^i}{i!}$$

The single parameter λ describes both the mean and the variance of this distribution.

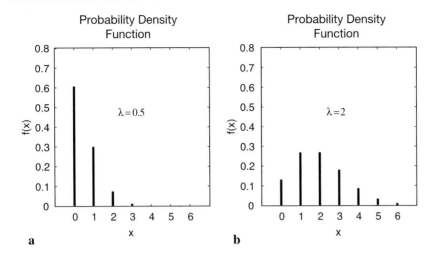

Fig. 3.6 Probability density function $f(x)$ of a Poisson distribution with different values for λ. **a** $\lambda = 0.5$ and **b** $\lambda = 2$.

Normal or Gaussian Distribution

When $p = 0.5$ (symmetric, no skew) and $N \rightarrow \infty$, the binomial distribution approaches the *normal* or *gaussian distribution* with the parameters mean μ and standard deviation σ (Fig. 3.7). The probability density function of a normal distribution in the continuous case is

$$f(x) = \frac{1}{\sigma\sqrt{2\pi}} \exp\left(-\frac{1}{2}\left(\frac{x-\mu}{\sigma}\right)^2\right)$$

and the cumulative distribution function is

$$F(x) = \frac{1}{\sigma\sqrt{2\pi}} \int_{-\infty}^{x} \exp\left(-\frac{1}{2}\left(\frac{y-\mu}{\sigma}\right)^2\right) dy$$

The normal distribution is used when the mean is the most frequent and most likely value. The probability of deviations is equal towards both directions and decrease with increasing distance from the mean.

The *standard normal distribution* is a special member of the normal family that has a mean of *zero* and a standard deviation of *one*. We transform the equation of the normal distribution by substitute $z = (x-\mu)/\sigma$. The probability density function of this distribution is

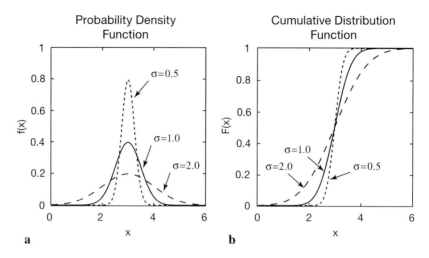

Fig. 3.7 a Probability density function $f(x)$ and **b** cumulative distribution function $F(x)$ of a gaussian or normal distribution with mean $\mu=3$ and different values for standard deviation σ.

$$f(x) = \frac{1}{\sqrt{2\pi}} \exp\left(-\frac{z^2}{2}\right)$$

This definition of the normal distribution is often called z *distribution*.

Logarithmic Normal or Log-Normal Distribution

The *logarithmic normal distribution* is used when the data have a lower limit, e.g., mean-annual precipitation or the frequency of earthquakes (Fig. 3.8). In such cases, distributions are usually characterized by significant skewness, which is best described by a logarithmic normal distribution. The probability density function of this distribution is

$$f(x) = \frac{1}{\sigma\sqrt{2\pi}x} \exp\left(-\frac{1}{2}\left(\frac{\ln x - \mu}{\sigma}\right)^2\right)$$

and the cumulative distribution function is

$$F(x) = \frac{1}{\sigma\sqrt{2\pi}} \int_{-\infty}^{x} \frac{1}{y} \exp\left(-\frac{1}{2}\left(\frac{\ln y - \mu}{\sigma}\right)^2\right) dy$$

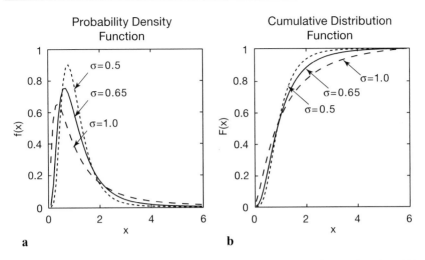

Fig. 3.8 a Probability density function $f(x)$ and **b** cumulative distribution function $F(x)$ of a logarithmic normal distribution with mean $\mu = 0$ and with different values for σ.

where $x > 0$. The distribution can be described by the two parameters mean μ and variance σ^2. The formulas for the mean and the variance, however, are different from the ones used for normal distributions. In practice, the values of x are logarithmized, the mean and the variance are computed using the formulas for the normal distribution and the empirical distribution is compared with a normal distribution.

Student's t Distribution

The *Student's t distribution* was first introduced by William Gosset (1876–1937) who needed a distribution for small samples (Fig. 3.9). W. Gosset was an Irish Guinness Brewery employee and was not allowed to publish research results. For that reason he published his t distribution under the pseudonym *Student* (Student, 1908). The probability density function is

$$f(x) = \frac{\Gamma\left(\dfrac{\Phi+1}{2}\right)}{\Gamma\left(\dfrac{\Phi}{2}\right)} \frac{1}{\sqrt{\Phi\pi}} \frac{1}{\left(1+\dfrac{x^2}{\Phi}\right)^{\frac{\Phi+1}{2}}}$$

where Γ is the Gamma function

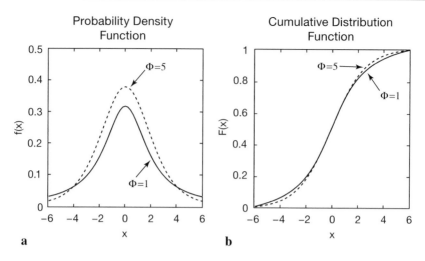

Fig. 3.9 a Probability density function $f(x)$ and **b** cumulative distribution function $F(x)$ of a Student's t distribution with different values for Φ.

$$\Gamma(x) = \lim_{n \to \infty} \frac{n! n^{x-1}}{x(x+1)(x+2)...(x+n-1)}$$

which can be written as

$$\Gamma(x) = \int_0^\infty e^{-y} y^{x-1} dy$$

if $x>0$. The single parameter Φ of the t distribution is the degrees of free-dom. In the analysis of univariate data, this parameter is $\Phi=n-1$, where n is the sample size. As $\Phi \to \infty$, the t distribution converges to the standard normal distribution. Since the t distribution approaches the normal distri-bution for $\Phi>30$, it is not often used for distribution fitting. However, the t distribution is used for hypothesis testing, namely the t-test (Chapter 3.6).

Fisher's F Distribution

The *F distribution* was named after the statistician Sir Ronald Fisher (1890–1962). It is used for hypothesis testing, namely for the F-test (Chapter 3.7). The F distribution has a relatively complex probability density function (Fig. 3.10):

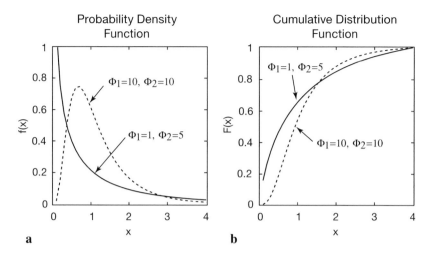

Fig. 3.10 a Probability density function $f(x)$ and **b** cumulative distribution function $F(x)$ of a Fisher's F distribution with different values for Φ_1 and Φ_2.

$$f(x) = \frac{\Gamma\left(\dfrac{\Phi_1 + \Phi_2}{2}\right)\left(\dfrac{\Phi_1}{\Phi_2}\right)^{\frac{\Phi_1}{\Phi_2}}}{\Gamma(\Phi_1/2)\Gamma(\Phi_1/2)} x^{\frac{\Phi_1-2}{2}}\left(1 + \frac{\Phi_1}{\Phi_2}x\right)^{\frac{\Phi_1+\Phi_2}{2}}$$

where $x > 0$ and Γ is again the Gamma function. The two parameters Φ_1 and Φ_2 are the degrees of freedom.

χ^2 or Chi-Squared Distribution

The χ^2 distribution was introduced by Friedrich Helmert (1876) and Karl Pearson (1900). It is not used for fitting a distribution, but has important applications in statistical hypothesis testing, namely the χ^2-test (Chapter 3.8). The probability density function of the χ^2 distribution is

$$f(x) = \frac{1}{2^{\Phi/2}\,\Gamma(\Phi/2)} x^{\frac{\Phi-2}{2}} e^{-\frac{x}{2}}$$

where $x > 0$, otherwise $f(x) = 0$, and Γ is again the Gamma function. Again, Φ is the degrees of freedom (Fig. 3.11).

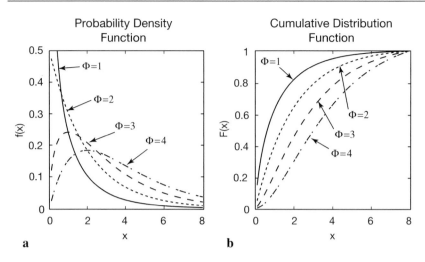

Fig. 3.11 a Probability density function $f(x)$ and **b** cumulative distribution function $F(x)$ of a χ^2 distribution with different values for Φ.

3.5 Example of Theoretical Distributions

The function `randtool` is a tool to simulate discrete data with a statistics similar to our data. This function creates a histogram of *random numbers* from the distributions in the Statistics Toolbox. The random numbers that have been generated by using this tool can be exported into the workspace. We start the *graphical user interface* (GUI) of the function by typing

```
randtool
```

after the prompt. We can now create a data set similar to the one in the file *organicmatter_one.txt*. The 60 measurements have a mean of 12.3448 wt% and a standard deviation of 1.1660 wt%. The GUI uses *Mu* for μ (the mean of a population) and *Sigma* for σ (the standard deviation). After choosing *Normal* for a gaussian distribution and 60 for the number of samples, we get a histogram similar to the one of the first example. This synthetic distribution based on 60 samples represents a rough estimate of the true normal distribution. If we increase the sample size, the histogram looks much more like a true gaussian distribution.

Instead of simulating discrete distributions, we can use the probability density function (PDF) or cumulative distribution function (CDF) to compute a theoretical distribution. The MATLAB Help gives an overview of the available theoretical distributions. As an example, we use the functions `normpdf(x,mu,sigma)` and `normcdf(x,mu,sigma)` to compute the PDF and CDF of a gaussian distribution with `Mu=12.3448` and `Sigma=1.1660`, evaluated at the values in `x` to compare the result with our sample data set.

```
x = 9 : 0.1 : 15;
pdf = normpdf(x,12.3448,1.1660);
cdf = normcdf(x,12.3448,1.1660);
plot(x,pdf,x,cdf)
```

MATLAB also provides a GUI-based function for generating PDF's and CDF's with specific statistics, which is called `disttool`.

```
disttool
```

We choose `pdf` as function type and `Mu=12.3448` and `Sigma=1.1660`. The function `disttool` uses the non-GUI functions for calculating probability density functions and cumulative distribution functions, such as `normpdf` and `normcdf`.

3.6 The t-Test

The Student's t-test by William Gossett (1876–1937) compares the means of two distributions. Let us assume that two independent sets of n_a and n_b measurements that have been carried out on the same object. For instance, several samples were taken from two different outcrops. The t-test can be used to test the hypothesis that both samples come from the same population, e.g., the same lithologic unit (*null hypothesis*) or from two different populations (*alternative hypothesis*). Both, the sample and population distribution have to be gaussian. The variances of the two sets of measurements should be similar. Then, the proper test statistic for the difference of two means is

$$\hat{t} = \frac{\left|\bar{a} - \bar{b}\right|}{\sqrt{\dfrac{n_a + n_b}{n_a n_b} \cdot \dfrac{(n_a - 1) \cdot s_a^{\,2} + (n_b - 1) \cdot s_b^{\,2}}{n_a + n_b - 2}}}$$

where n_a and n_b are the sample sizes, s_a^2 and s_b^2 are the variances of the two samples a and b. The alternative hypothesis can be rejected if the measured *t*-value is lower than the critical *t*-value, which depends on the degrees of freedom $\Phi = n_a + n_b - 2$ and the significance level α. If this is the case, we cannot reject the null hypothesis without another cause. The significance level α of a test is the maximum probability of accidentally rejecting a true null hypothesis. Note that we cannot prove the null hypothesis, in other words *not guilty* is not the same as *innocent* (Fig. 3.12).

The t-test can be performed by the function `ttest2`. We load an example data set of two independent series of measurements. The first example shows the performance of the t-test on two distributions with the means 25.5 and 25.3, whereas the standard deviations are 1.3 and 1.5.

```
clear

load('organicmatter_two.mat');
```

The binary file *organicmatter_two.mat* contains two data sets `corg1` and `corg2`. First, we plot both histograms in one single graph

```
[n1,x1] = hist(corg1);
[n2,x2] = hist(corg2);

h1 = bar(x1,n1);
hold on
h2 = bar(x2,n2);

set(h1,'FaceColor','none','EdgeColor','r')
set(h2,'FaceColor','none','EdgeColor','b')
```

Here we use the command `set` to change graphic objects of the bar plots `h1` and `h2`, such as the face and edge colors of the bars. Now we apply the function `ttest2(x,y,alpha)` to the two independent samples `corg1` and `corg2` at an `alpha=0.05` or 5% significance level. The command

```
[h,significance,ci] = ttest2(corg1,corg2,0.05)
```

yields

```
h =
     0

significance =
    0.0745

ci =
   -0.0433     0.9053
```

The result `h=0` means that you cannot reject the null hypothesis without another cause at a 5% significance level. The significance of 0.0745 means that by chance you would have observed more extreme values of *t* than the one in the example in 745 of 10,000 similar experiments. A 95% confidence interval on the mean is [−0.0433 0.9053], which includes the theoretical (and hypothesized) difference of 0.2.

The second synthetic example shows the performance of the t-test on very different distributions in the means. The means are 24.3 and 25.5, whereas the standard deviations are again 1.3 and 1.5.

```
clear

load('organicmatter_three.mat');
```

This file again contains two data sets `corg1` and `corg2`. The t-test at a 5% significance level

```
[h,significance,ci] = ttest2(corg1,corg2,0.05)
```

yields

```
h =
     1

significance =
    6.1138e-06

ci =
    0.7011    1.7086
```

The result `h=1` suggests that you can reject the null hypothesis. The significance is extremely low and very close to zero. The 95% confidence interval on the mean is [0.7011 1.7086], which again includes the theoretical (and hypothesized) difference of 1.2.

3.7 The F-Test

The F-test by Snedecor and Cochran (1989) compares the variances s_a^2 and s_b^2 of two distributions, where $s_a^2 > s_b^2$. An example is the comparison of the natural heterogeneity of two samples based on replicated measurements. The sample sizes n_a and n_b should be above 30. Then, the proper test statistic to compare variances is

$$\hat{F} = \frac{s_a^{\,2}}{s_b^{\,2}}$$

The two variances are not significantly different, i.e., we reject the alternative hypothesis, if the measured F-value is lower than the critical F-value, which depends on the degrees of freedom $\Phi_a = n_a - 1$ and $\Phi_b = n_b - 1$, respectively, and the significance level α.

Although MATLAB does not provide a ready-to-use F-test, this hypothesis test can easily be implemented. We first apply this test to two distributions with very similar standard deviations of 1.3 and 1.2.

```
load('organicmatter_four.mat');
```

The quantity F is the quotient between the larger and the smaller variance. First, we compute the standard deviations, where

```
s1 = std(corg1)

s2 = std(corg2)
```

yields

```
s1 =
    1.2550

s2 =
    1.2097
```

The F-distribution has two parameters, df1 and df2, which are the numbers of observations of both distributions reduced by one, where

```
df1 = length(corg1) - 1

df2 = length(corg2) - 1
```

yields

```
df1 =
    59

df2 =
    59
```

Next we sort the standard deviations by their absolute value,

```
if s1 > s2
  slarger  = s1
  ssmaller = s2
else
  slarger  = s2
  ssmaller = s1
end
```

and get

```
slarger =
    1.2550
```

```
ssmaller =
    1.2097
```

Now we compare the calculated F with the critical F. This can be accomplished using the function `finv` on a 95% significance level. The function `finv` returns the inverse of the F distribution function with `df1` and `df2` degrees of freedom, at the value of 0.95. Typing

```
Freal = slarger^2 / ssmaller^2

Ftable = finv(0.95,df1,df2)
```

yields

```
Freal =
    1.0762

Ftable =
    1.5400
```

The F calculated from the data is smaller than the critical F. Therefore, we cannot reject the null hypothesis without another cause. We conclude that the variances are identical on a 95% significance level.

We now apply this test to two distributions with very different standard deviations, 2.0 and 1.2.

```
load('organicmatter_five.mat');
```

We compare the calculated F with the critical F at a 95% significance level. The critical F can be computed using the function `finv`. We again type

```
s1 = std(corg1);

s2 = std(corg2);

df1 = length(corg1) - 1;

df2 = length(corg2) - 1;

if s1 > s2
  slarger  = s1;
  ssmaller = s2;
else
  slarger  = s2;
  ssmaller = s1;
end

Freal = slarger^2 / ssmaller^2

Ftable = finv(0.95,df1,df2)
```

and get

```
Freal =
    3.4967

Ftable =
    1.5400
```

The F calculated from the data is now larger than the critical F. Therefore, we can reject the null hypothesis. The variances are different on a 95% significance level.

3.8 The χ^2-Test

The χ^2-test introduced by Karl Pearson (1900) involves the comparison of distributions, permitting a test that two distributions were derived from the same population. This test is independent of the distribution that is being used. Therefore, it can be applied to test the hypothesis that the observations were drawn from a specific theoretical distribution. Let us assume that we have a data set that consists of 100 chemical measurements from a sandstone unit. We could use the χ^2-test to test the hypothesis that these measurements can be described by a gaussian distribution with a typical central value and a random dispersion around. The n data are grouped in K classes, where n should be above 30. The frequencies within the classes O_k should not be lower than four and never be zero. Then, the proper statistic is

$$\hat{\chi}^2 = \sum_{k=1}^{K} \frac{\left(O_k - E_k\right)^2}{E_k}$$

where E_k are the frequencies expected from the theoretical distribution. The alternative hypothesis is that the two distributions are different. This can be rejected if the measured χ^2 is lower than the critical χ^2, which depends on the degrees of freedom $\Phi = K - Z$, where K is the number of classes and Z is the number of parameters describing the theoretical distribution plus the number of variables (for instance, $Z = 2 + 1$ for the mean and the variance for a gaussian distribution of a data set of one variable, $Z = 1 + 1$ for a Poisson distribution of one variable) (Fig. 3.12).

As an example, we test the hypothesis that our organic carbon measurements contained in *organicmatter_one.txt* follow a gaussian distribution. We first load the data into the workspace and compute the frequency distribution n_exp of the data.

```
corg = load('organicmatter_one.txt');

v = 10 : 0.65 : 14.55;
n_exp = hist(corg,v);
```

We use the function `normpdf` to create the synthetic frequency distribution `n_syn` with a mean of 12.3448 and a standard deviation of 1.1660.

```
n_syn = normpdf(v,12.3448,1.1660);
```

The data need to be scaled so that they are similar to the original data set.

```
n_syn = n_syn ./ sum(n_syn);
n_syn = sum(n_exp) * n_syn;
```

The first line normalizes `n_syn` to a total of one. The second command scales `n_syn` to the sum of `n_exp`. We can display both histograms for comparison.

```
subplot(1,2,1), bar(v,n_syn,'r')
subplot(1,2,2), bar(v,n_exp,'b')
```

Visual inspection of these plots reveals that they are similar. However, it is advisable to use a more quantitative approach. The χ^2-test explores the

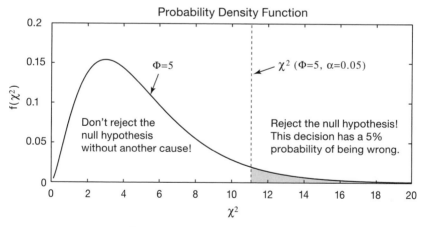

Fig. 3.12 Principles of a χ^2-test. The alternative hypothesis that the two distributions are different can be rejected if the measured χ^2 is lower than the critical χ^2. χ^2 depends on $\Phi = K - Z$, where K is the number of classes and Z is the number of parameters describing the theoretical distribution plus the number of variables. In the example, the critical χ^2 ($\Phi = 5$, $\alpha = 0.05$) is 11.0705. If the measured $\chi^2 = 2.1685$ is below the critical χ^2, we cannot reject the null hypothesis. In our example, we can conclude that the sample distribution is not significantly different from a gaussian distribution.

squared differences between the observed and expected frequencies. The quantity χ^2 is the sum of the squared differences divided by the expected frequencies.

```
chi2 = sum((n_exp - n_syn).^2 ./ n_syn)

chi2 =
    2.1685
```

The critical χ^2 can be calculated using chi2inv. The χ^2-test requires the degrees of freedom Φ. In our example, we test the hypothesis that the data are gaussian distributed, i.e., we estimate two parameters μ and σ. The number of degrees of freedom is $\Phi = 8 - (2+1) = 5$. We test our hypothesis on a $p = 95\%$ significance level. The function chi2inv computes the inverse of the χ^2 CDF with parameters specified by Φ for the corresponding probabilities in p.

```
chi2inv(0.95,5)

ans =
    11.0705
```

The critical χ^2 of 11.0705 is well above the measured χ^2 of 2.1685. Therefore, we cannot reject the null hypothesis. Hence, we conclude that our data follow a gaussian distribution.

Recommended Reading

Bernoulli J (1713) Ars Conjectandi. Reprinted by Ostwalds Klassiker Nr. 107–108. Leipzig 1899

Fisher RA (1935) Design of Experiments. Oliver and Boyd, Edinburgh

Helmert FR (1876) Über die Wahrscheinlichkeit der Potenzsummen der Beobachtungsfehler und über einige damit im Zusammenhang stehende Fragen. Zeitschrift für Mathematik und Physik 21:192–218

Pearson ES (1990) Student – A Statistical Biography of William Sealy Gosset. In: Plackett RL, with the assistance of Barnard GA, Oxford University Press, Oxford

Pearson K (1900) On the criterion that a given system of deviations from the probable in the case of a correlated system of variables is such that it can be reasonably supposed to have arisen from random sampling. Philos. Mag. 5, 50:157–175

Poisson SD (1837) Recherches sur la Probabilité des Jugements en Matière Criminelle et en Matière Civile, Précédées des Regles du Calcul des Probabilités, Bachelier, Imprimeur-Libraire pour les Mathematiques, Paris

Sachs L, Hedderich J (2006) Angewandte Statistik – Anwendung statistischer Methoden, Elfte, überarbeitete und aktualisierte Auflage. Springer, Berlin Heidelberg New York

Snedecor GW, Cochran WG (1989) Statistical Methods, Eighth Edition. Blackwell

Publishers, Oxford

Spiegel MR, Schiller JJ, Srinivasan RA (2000) Probability and Statistics, 2nd Edition. Schaum's Outline Series, McGraw-Hill, New York

Student (1908) On the Probable Error of the Mean. Biometrika 6:1–25

Taylor JR (1997) An Introduction to Error Analysis – The Study of Uncertainties in Physical Measurements, Second Edition. University Science Books, Sausalito, California

The Mathworks (2006) Statistics Toolbox User's Guide – For the Use with MATLAB®. The MathWorks, Natick, MA

4 Bivariate Statistics

4.1 Introduction

Bivariate analysis aims to understand the relationship between two variables x and y. Examples are the length and the width of a fossil, the sodium and potassium content of volcanic glass or the organic matter content along a sediment core. When the two variables are measured on the same object, x is usually identified as the *independent variable*, whereas y is the *dependent variable*. If both variables were generated in an experiment, the variable manipulated by the experimenter is described as the independent variable. In some cases, both variables are not manipulated and therefore independent. The methods of bivariate statistics help describe the strength of the relationship between the two variables, either by a single parameter such as Pearson's correlation coefficient for linear relationships or by an equation obtained by regression analysis (Fig. 4.1). The equation describing the relationship between x and y can be used to predict the y-response from arbitrary x's within the range of original data values used for regression. This is of particular importance if one of the two parameters is difficult to measure. Here, the relationship between the two variables is first determined by regression analysis on a small training set of data. Then, the regression equation is used to calculate this parameter from the first variable.

This chapter first introduces Pearson's correlation coefficient (Chapter 4.2), then explains the widely-used methods of linear and curvilinear regression analysis (Chapter 4.3, 4.9 and 4.10). Moreover, a selection of methods is explained that are used to assess the uncertainties in regression analysis (Chapters 4.4 to 4.8). All methods are illustrated by means of synthetic examples since they provide excellent means for assessing the final outcome.

4.2 Pearson's Correlation Coefficient

Correlation coefficients are often used at the exploration stage of bivariate

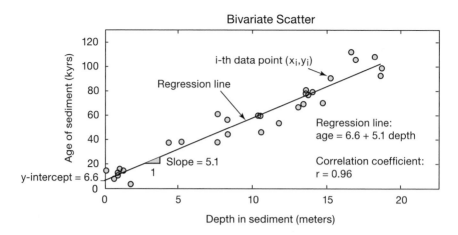

Fig. 4.1 Display of a bivariate data set. The thirty data points represent the *age* of a sediment (in kiloyears before present) in a certain *depth* (in meters) below the sediment-water interface. The joint distribution of the two variables suggests a linear relationship between *age* and *depth*, i.e., the increase of the sediment age with depth is constant. Pearson's correlation coefficient (explained in the text) of $r = 0.96$ supports the strong linear dependency of the two variables. Linear regression yields the equation *age* = 6.6 + 5.1 *depth*. This equation indicates an increase of the sediment age of 5.1 kyrs per meter sediment depth (the slope of the regression line). The inverse of the slope is the sedimentation rate of ca. 0.2 meters/kyrs. Furthermore, the equation defines the age of the sediment surface of 6.6 kyrs (the intercept of the regression line with the *y*-axis). The deviation of the surface age from zero can be attributed either to the statistical uncertainty of regression or any natural process such as erosion or bioturbation. Whereas the assessment of the statistical uncertainty will be discussed in this chapter, the second needs a careful evaluation of the various processes at the sediment-water interface.

statistics. They are only a very rough estimate of a rectilinear trend in the bivariate data set. Unfortunately, the literature is full of examples where the importance of correlation coefficients is overestimated and outliers in the data set lead to an extremely biased estimator of the population correlation coefficient.

The most popular correlation coefficient is *Pearson's linear product-moment correlation coefficient* ρ (Fig. 4.2). We estimate the population's correlation coefficient ρ from the sample data, i.e., we compute the sample correlation coefficient r, which is defined as

$$r_{xy} = \frac{\sum_{i=1}^{n}(x_i - \bar{x})(y_i - \bar{y})}{(n-1)s_x s_y}$$

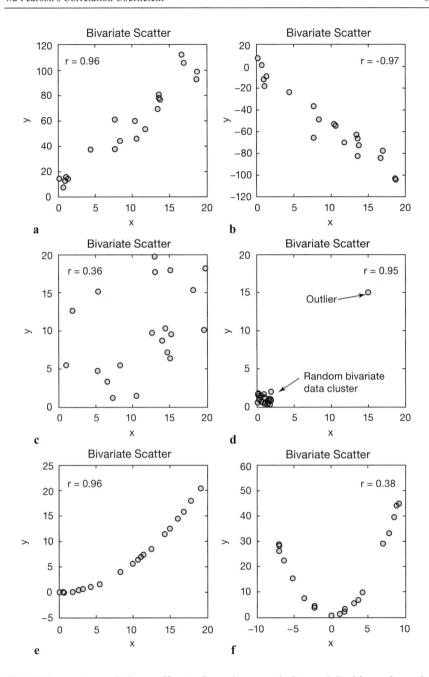

Fig. 4.2 Pearson's correlation coefficent r for various sample data. **a–b** Positive and negative linear correlation, **c** random scatter without a linear correlation, **d** an outlier causing a misleading value of r, **e** curvilinear relationship causing a high r since the curve is close to a straight line, **f** curvilinear relationship clearly not described by r.

where n is the number of xy pairs of data points, s_x and s_y are the univariate standard deviations. The numerator of Pearson's correlation coefficient is known as the *corrected sum of products* of the bivariate data set. Dividing the numerator by $(n-1)$ yields the *covariance*

$$cov_{xy} = \frac{1}{(n-1)} \sum_{i=1}^{n} (x_i - \bar{x})(y_i - \bar{y})$$

which is the summed products of deviations of the data from the sample means, divided by $(n-1)$. The covariance is a widely-used measure in bivariate statistics, although it has the disadvantage of depending on the dimension of the data. We will use the covariance in time-series analysis, which is a special case of bivariate statistics with time as one of the two variables (Chapter 5). Dividing the covariance by the univariate standard deviations removes this effect and leads to Pearson's correlation coefficient.

Pearson's correlation coefficient is very sensitive to various disturbances in the bivariate data set. The following example illustrates the use of the correlation coefficients and highlights the potential pitfalls when using this measure of linear trends. It also describes the resampling methods that can be used to explore the confidence of the estimate for ρ. The synthetic data consist of two variables, the age of a sediment in kiloyears before present and the depth below the sediment-water interface in meters. The use of synthetic data sets has the advantage that we fully understand the linear model behind the data.

The data are represented as two columns contained in file *agedepth.txt*. These data have been generated using a series of thirty random levels (in *meters*) below the sediment surface. The linear relationship *age* = 5.6 *meters* + 1.2 was used to compute noisefree values for the variable *age*. This is the equation of a straight line with a slope of 5.6 and an intercept with the *y*-axis of 1.2. Finally, some gaussian noise of amplitude 10 was added to the *age* data. We load the data from the file *agedepth.txt*.

```
agedepth = load('agedepth_1.txt');
```

We define two new variables, `meters` and `age`, and generate a scatter plot of the data.

```
meters = agedepth(:,1);
age = agedepth(:,2);

plot(meters,age,'o')
```

We observe a strong linear trend suggesting some dependency between the variables, meters and age. This trend can be described by Pearson's correlation coefficient r, where $r=1$ represents a perfect positive correlation, i.e., age increases with meters, $r=0$ suggests no correlation, and $r=-1$ indicates a perfect negative correlation. We use the function corrcoef to compute Pearson's correlation coefficient.

```
corrcoef(meters,age)
```

which causes the output

```
ans =
      1.0000      0.9342
      0.9342      1.0000
```

The function corrcoef calculates a matrix of correlation coefficients for all possible combinations of the two variables. The combinations (meters, age) and (age, meters) result in $r=0.9342$, whereas (age, age) and (meters, meters) yield $r=1.000$.

The value of $r=0.9342$ suggests that the two variables age and meters depend on each other. However, Pearson's correlation coefficient is highly sensitive to outliers. This can be illustrated by the following example. Let us generate a normally-distributed cluster of thirty (x,y) data with zero mean and standard deviation one. To obtain identical data values, we reset the random number generator by using the integer 5 as seed.

```
randn('seed',5);
x = randn(30,1); y = randn(30,1);

plot(x,y,'o'), axis([-1 20 -1 20]);
```

As expected, the correlation coefficient of these random data is very low.

```
corrcoef(x,y)

ans =
      1.0000      0.1021
      0.1021      1.0000
```

Now we introduce one single outlier to the data set, an exceptionally high (x,y) value, which is located precisely on the one-by-one line. The correlation coefficient for the bivariate data set including the outlier $(x,y) = (5,5)$ is much higher than before.

```
x(31,1) = 5; y(31,1) = 5;

plot(x,y,'o'), axis([-1 20 -1 20]);

corrcoef(x,y)
```

```
ans =
    1.0000      0.4641
    0.4641      1.0000
```

After increasing the absolute (x,y) values of this outlier, the correlation coefficient increases dramatically.

```
x(31,1) = 10; y(31,1) = 10;

plot(x,y,'o'), axis([-1 20 -1 20]);

corrcoef(x,y)

ans =
    1.0000      0.7636
    0.7636      1.0000
```

and reaches a value close to $r=1$ if the outlier has a value of $(x,y) = (20,20)$.

```
x(31,1) = 20; y(31,1) = 20;

plot(x,y,'o'), axis([-1 20 -1 20]);

corrcoef(x,y)

ans =
    1.0000      0.9275
    0.9275      1.0000
```

Still, the bivariate data set does not provide much evidence for a strong dependence. However, the combination of the random bivariate (x,y) data with one single outlier results in a dramatic increase of the correlation coefficient. Whereas outliers are easy to identify in a bivariate scatter, erroneous values might be overlooked in large multivariate data sets.

Various methods exist to calculate the significance of Pearson's correlation coefficient. The function corrcoef provides the possibility for evaluating the quality of the result. Furthermore, *resampling schemes* or *surrogates* such as the *bootstrap* or *jackknife* method provide an alternative way of assessing the statistical significance of the results. These methods repeatedly resample the original data set with N data points either by choosing $N-1$ subsamples N times (the jackknife) or picking an arbitrary set of subsamples with N data points with replacements (the bootstrap). The statistics of these subsamples provide a better information on the characteristics of the population than statistical parameters (mean, standard deviation, correlation coefficients) computed from the full data set. The function bootstrp allows resampling of our bivariate data set including the outlier $(x,y) = (20,20)$.

```
rhos1000 = bootstrp(1000,'corrcoef',x,y);
```

This command first resamples the data a thousand times, calculates the correlation coefficient for each new subsample and stores the result in the variable `rhos1000`. Since `corrcoef` delivers a 2×2 matrix as mentioned above, `rhos1000` has the dimension 1000×4, i.e., 1000 values for each element of the 2×2 matrix. Plotting the histogram of the 1000 values of the second element, i.e., the correlation coefficient of (x,y) illustrates the dispersion of this parameter with respect to the presence or absence of the outlier. Since the distribution of `rhos1000` contains many empty classes, we use a large number of bins.

```
hist(rhos1000(:,2),30)
```

The histogram shows a cluster of correlation coefficients at around $r = 0.2$ that follow the normal distribution and a strong peak close to $r = 1$ (Fig. 4.3). The interpretation of this histogram is relatively straightforward. When the subsample contains the outlier, the correlation coefficient is close to one. Samples without the outlier yield a very low (close to zero) correlation coefficient suggesting no strong dependence between the two variables x and y.

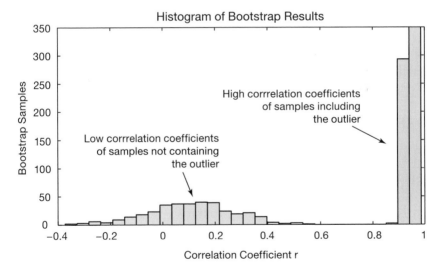

Fig. 4.3 Bootstrap result for Pearson's correlation coefficient r from 1000 subsamples. The histogram shows a roughly normally-distributed cluster of correlation coefficients at around $r = 0.2$ suggesting that these subsamples do not contain the outlier. The strong peak close to $r = 1$, however, suggests that such an outlier with high values of the two variables x and y is present in the corresponding subsamples.

Bootstrapping therefore represents a powerful and simple tool for accepting or rejecting our first estimate of the correlation coefficient. The application of the above procedure applied to the synthetic sediment data yields a clear unimodal gaussian distribution of the correlation coefficients.

```
corrcoef(meters,age)

ans =
     1.0000     0.9342
     0.9342     1.0000

rhos1000 = bootstrp(1000,'corrcoef',meters,age);

hist(rhos1000(:,2),30)
```

Most `rhos1000` fall within the interval between 0.88 and 0.98. Since the resampled correlation coefficients obviously are gaussian distributed, we can use the mean as a good estimate for the true correlation coefficient.

```
mean(rhos1000(:,2))

ans =
     0.9315
```

This value is not much different to our first result of $r = 0.9342$. However, now we can be certain about the validity of this result. However, in our example, the bootstrap estimate of the correlations from the age-depth data is quite skewed, as there is a hard upper limit of one. Nevertheless, the bootstrap method is a valuable tool for obtaining valuable information on the reliability of Pearson's correlation coefficient of bivariate data sets.

4.3 Classical Linear Regression Analysis and Prediction

Linear regression provides another way of describing the dependence between the two variables x and y. Whereas Pearson's correlation coefficient provides only a rough measure of a linear trend, linear models obtained by regression analysis allow to predict arbitrary y values for any given value of x within the data range. Statistical testing of the significance of the linear model provides some insights into the quality of prediction.

Classical regression assumes that y responds to x, and the entire dispersion in the data set is in the y-value (Fig. 4.4). Then, x is the independent, regressor or predictor variable. The values of x are defined by the experimenter and are often regarded as to be free of errors. An example is the location x of a sample in a sediment core. The dependent variable y contains

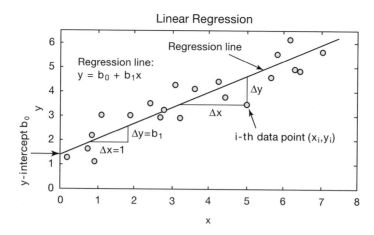

Fig. 4.4 Linear regression. Whereas classical regression minimizes the Δy deviations, reduced major axis regression minimizes the triangular area $0.5(\Delta x\, \Delta y)$ between the points and the regression line, where Δx and Δy are the distances between the predicted and the true x and y values. The intercept of the line with the y-axis is b_0, whereas the slope is b_1. These two parameters define the equation of the regression line.

errors as its magnitude cannot be determined accurately. Linear regression minimizes the Δy deviations between the xy data points and the value predicted by the best-fit line using a least-squares criterion. The basis equation for a general linear model is

$$y = b_0 + b_1 x$$

where b_0 and b_1 are the regression coefficients. The value of b_0 is the intercept with the y-axis and b_1 is the slope of the line. The squared sum of the Δy deviations to be minimized is

$$\sum_{i=1}^{n}\left(\Delta y_i\right)^2 = \sum_{i=1}^{n}\left(y_i - (b_0 + b_1 x_i)\right)^2$$

Partial differentiation of the right-hand term and equation to zero yields a simple equation for the first regression coefficient b_1:

$$b_1 = \frac{\sum_{i=1}^{n}\left(x_i - \bar{x}\right)\left(y_i - \bar{y}\right)}{\sum_{i=1}^{n}\left(x_i - \bar{x}\right)^2}$$

The regression line passes through the data centroid defined by the sample-means. We can therefore compute the other regression coefficient b_0,

$$b_0 = \bar{y} - b_1 \bar{x}$$

using the univariate sample means and the slope b_1 computed earlier.

Let us again load the synthetic age-depth data from the file *agedepth.txt*. We define two new variables, `meters` and `age`, and generate a scatter plot of the data.

```
agedepth = load('agedepth_1.txt');

meters = agedepth(:,1);
age = agedepth(:,2);
```

A significant linear trend in the bivariate scatter plot and a correlation co-efficient of more than $r = 0.9$ suggests a strong linear dependence between `meters` and `age`. In geologic terms, this suggests that the sedimentation rate is constant through time. We now try to fit a linear model to the data that helps us predict the age of the sediment at levels without age data. The function `polyfit` computes the coefficients of a polynomial $p(x)$ of a certain degree that fits the data y in a least-squared sense. In our example, we fit a polynomial of degree 1 (linear) to the data.

```
p = polyfit(meters,age,1)

p =
    5.6393      0.9986
```

Since we are working with synthetic data, we know the values for slope and intercept with the y-axis. While the estimated slope agrees well with the true value (5.6 vs. 5.6393), the intercept with the y-axis is significantly different (1.2 vs. 0.9986). Both the data and the fitted line can be plotted on the same graph.

```
plot(meters,age,'o'), hold

plot(meters,p(1)*meters+p(2),'r')
```

Instead of using the equation for the regression line, we can also use the function `polyval` to calculate the y-values.

```
plot(meters,age,'o'), hold

plot(meters,polyval(p,meters),'r')
```

Both, the functions `polyfit` and `polyval` are incorporated in the GUI function `polytool`.

```
polytool(meters,age)
```

The coefficients `p(x)` and the equation obtained by linear regression can now be used to predict *y*-values for any given *x*-value. However, we can only do this for the depth interval for which the linear model was fitted, i.e., between 0 and 20 meters. As an example, the age of the sediment at the depth of 17 meters depth is given by

```
polyval(p,17)

ans =
   96.8667
```

This result suggests that the sediment at 17 meters depth has an age of ca. 97 kyrs. The goodness-of-fit of the linear model can be determined by calculating error bounds. These are obtained by using an additional output parameter for `polyfit` and as an input parameter for `polyval`.

```
[p,s] = polyfit(meters,age,1);
[p_age,delta] = polyval(p,meters,s);
```

This code uses an interval of $\pm 2s$, which corresponds to a 95% confidence interval. `polyfit` returns the polynomial coefficients p, and a structure s that `polyval` uses to calculate the error bounds. *Structures* are MATLAB arrays with named data containers called *fields*. The fields of a structure can contain any type of data, such as text strings representing names. Another might contain a scalar or a matrix. In our example, the structure s contains fields for the statistics of the residuals that we use to compute the error bounds. `delta` is an estimate of the standard deviation of the error in predicting a future observation at x by $p(x)$. We plot the results.

```
plot(meters,age,'+',meters,p_age,'g-',...
    meters,p_age+2*delta,'r--',meters,p_age-2*delta,'r--')
xlabel('meters'), ylabel('age')
```

Since the `plot` statement does not fit on one line, we use an *ellipsis* (three periods), . . ., followed by *return* or *enter* to indicate that the statement continues on the next line. The plot now shows the data points, the regression line as well as the error bounds of the regression (Fig. 4.5). This graph already provides some valuable information on the quality of the result. However, in many cases a better knowledge on the validity of the model is required and therefore more sophisticated methods for confidence testing of the results are introduced in the following chapters.

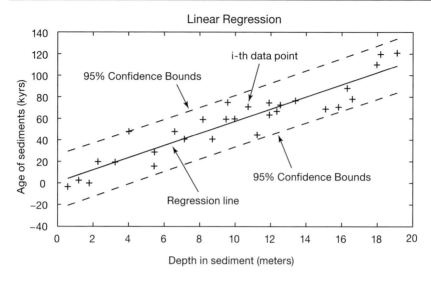

Fig. 4.5 The result of linear regression. The plot shows the original data points (plus signs), the regression line (solid line) as well as the error bounds (dashed lines) of the regression. Note that the error bounds are actually curved though they seem to be almost straight lines in the example.

4.4 Analyzing the Residuals

When you compare how far the predicted values are from the actual or observed values, you are performing an analysis of the residuals. The statistics of the residuals provides valuable information on the quality of a model fitted to the data. For instance, a significant trend in the residuals suggests that the model not fully describes the data. In such a case, a more complex model, such as a polynomial of a higher degree should be fitted to the data. Residuals ideally are purely random, i.e., gaussian distributed with zero mean. Therefore, we test the hypothesis that our residuals are gaussian distributed by visual inspection of the histogram and by employing a χ^2-test introduced in Chapter 3.

```
res = age - polyval(p,meters);
```

Plotting the residuals does not show obvious patterned behavior. Thus, no more complex model than a straight line should be fitted to the data.

```
plot(meters,res,'o')
```

An alternative way to plot the residuals is a stem plot using `stem`.

```
subplot(2,1,1)
plot(meters,age,'o'), hold
plot(meters,p(1)*meters+p(2),'r')

subplot(2,1,2)
stem(meters,res);
```

Let us explore the distribution of the residuals. We choose six classes and calculate the corresponding frequencies.

```
[n_exp,x] = hist(res,6)

n_exp =
     5     4     8     7     4     2

x =
   -16.0907   -8.7634   -1.4360   5.8913   13.2186   20.5460
```

By basing the bin centers in the locations defined by the function hist, a more practical set of classes can be defined.

```
v = -13 : 7 : 23;

n_exp = hist(res,v);
```

Subsequently, the mean and standard deviation of the residuals are computed. These are then used for generating a theoretical frequency distribution that can be compared with the distribution of the residuals. The mean is close to zero, whereas the standard deviation is 11.5612. The function normpdf is used for creating the frequency distribution n_syn similar to our example. The theoretical distribution is scaled according to our original sample data and displayed.

```
n_syn = normpdf(v,0,11.5612);

n_syn = n_syn ./ sum(n_syn);
n_syn = sum(n_exp) * n_syn;
```

The first line normalizes n_syn to a total of one. The second command scales n_syn to the sum of n_exp. We plot both distributions for comparison.

```
subplot(1,2,1), bar(v,n_syn,'r')
subplot(1,2,2), bar(v,n_exp,'b')
```

Visual inspection of the bar plots reveals similarities between the data sets. Hence, the χ^2-test can be used to test the hypothesis that the residuals follow a gaussian distribution.

```
chi2 = sum((n_exp - n_syn) .^2 ./ n_syn)
```

```
chi2 =
    2.3465
```

The critical χ^2 can be calculated by using chi2inv. The χ^2 test requires the degrees of freedom Φ, which is the number of classes reduced by one and the number of parameters estimated. In our example, we test for a gaussian distribution with two parameters, the mean and the standard deviation. Therefore, the degrees of freedom is $\Phi=6-(1+2)=3$. We test at a 95% significance level.

```
chi2inv(0.95,3)

ans =
    7.8147
```

The critical χ^2 of 7.8147 is well above the measured χ^2 of 2.3465. It is not possible to reject the null hypothesis. Hence, we conclude that our residuals follow a gaussian distribution and the bivariate data set is well described by the linear model.

4.5 Bootstrap Estimates of the Regression Coefficients

We use the *bootstrap* method to obtain a better estimate of the regression coefficients. Again, we use the function bootstrp with 1000 samples (Fig. 4.6).

```
p_bootstrp = bootstrp(1000,'polyfit',meters,age,1);
```

The statistics of the first coefficient, i.e., the slope of the regression line is

```
hist(p_bootstrp(:,1),15)

mean(p_bootstrp(:,1))

ans =
    5.6023

std(p_bootstrp(:,1))

ans =
    0.4421
```

Your results might be slightly different because of the different state of the built-in random number generator used by bootstrp. The small standard deviation indicates that we have an accurate estimate. In contrast, the statistics of the second parameter shows a significant dispersion.

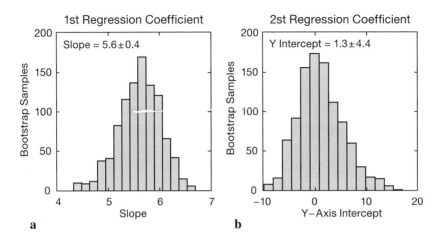

Fig. 4.6 Histogram of the **a** first (slope of the line) and **b** second (y-axis intercept of the regression line) regression coefficient as estimated from bootstrap resampling. Whereas the first coefficient is very-well constrained, the second coefficient shows a large scatter.

```
hist(p_bootstrp(:,2),15)
mean(p_bootstrp(:,2))

ans =
    1.3366

std(p_bootstrp(:,2))

ans =
    4.4079
```

The true values as used to simulate our data set are 5.6 for the slope and 1.2 for the intercept with the y-axis, whereas the coefficients calculated using the function `polyfit` were 5.6393 and 0.9986, respectively. We see that indeed the intercept with the y-axis has a large uncertainty, whereas the slope is well defined.

4.6 Jackknife Estimates of the Regression Coefficients

The *jackknife* method is a resampling technique that is similar to the bootstrap. From a sample with n data points, n subsets with $n-1$ data points are taken. The parameters of interest are calculated from each subset, e.g., the regression coefficients. The mean and dispersion of the coefficients are computed. The disadvantage of this method is the limited number of n samples. The jackknife estimate of the regression coefficients is therefore less precise in comparison to the bootstrap results.

MATLAB does not provide a jackknife routine. However, the corresponding code is easy to generate:

```
for i = 1 : 30
    % Define two temporary variables j_meters and j_age
    j_meters = meters;
    j_age = age;
    % Eliminate the i-th data point
    j_meters(i) = [];
    j_age(i) = [];
    % Compute regression line from the n-1 data points
    p(i,:) = polyfit(j_meters,j_age,1);
end
```

The jackknife for $n-1=29$ data points can be obtained by a simple `for` loop. Within each iteration, the i-th element is deleted and the regression coefficients are calculated for the remaining samples. The mean of the i samples gives an improved estimate of the coefficients. Similar to the bootstrap result, the slope of the regression line (first coefficient) is well defined, whereas the intercept with the y-axis (second coefficient) has a large uncertainty,

```
mean(p(:,1))

ans =
    5.6382
```

compared to $5.6023 +/- 0.4421$ and

```
mean(p(:,2))

ans =
    1.0100
```

compared to $1.3366 +/- 4.4079$ as calculated by the bootstrap method. The true values are 5.6 and 1.2. The histogram of the jackknife results from 30 subsamples

```
hist(p(:,1));
figure
hist(p(:,2));
```

does not display the distribution of the coefficients as clearly as the bootstrap estimates (Fig. 4.7). We have seen that resampling using the jackknife or bootstrap methods provides a simple and valuable tool to test the quality of regression models. The next chapter introduces an alternative approach for quality estimation, which is by far more often used than resampling.

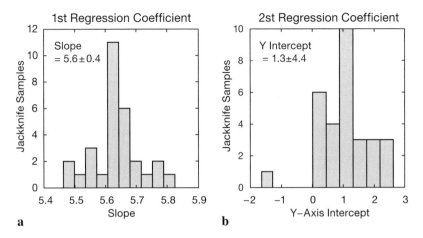

Fig. 4.7 Histogram of the **a** first (slope of the line) and **b** second (*y*-axis intercept of the regression line) regression coefficient as estimated from jackknife resampling. Note that the parameters are not as clearly defined as from bootstrapping.

4.7 Cross Validation

A third method to test the goodness-of-fit of the regression is *cross valida-tion*. The regression line is computed by using $n-1$ data points. The n-th data point is predicted and the discrepancy between the prediction and the actual value is computed. Subsequently, the mean of the discrepancies be-tween the actual and predicted values is determined.

In this example, the cross validation for n data points is computed. The corresponding 30 regression lines display some dispersion in slope and *y*-axis intercept.

```
for i = 1 : 30
    % Define temporary variables j_meters and j_age
    j_meters = meters;
    j_age = age;
    % Eliminate the i-th data point
    j_meters(i) = [];
    j_age(i) = [];
    % Compute regression line from the n-1 data points
    p(i,:) = polyfit(j_meters,j_age,1);
    % Plot the i-th regression line and hold plot for next loop
    plot(meters,polyval(p(i,:),meters),'r'), hold on
    % Store the regression result and errors in p_age and p_error
    p_age(i) = polyval(p(i,:),meters(i));
    p_error(i) = p_age(i) - age(i);
end
```

The prediction error is – in the best case – gaussian distributed with zero mean.

```
mean(p_error)

ans =
     0.0122
```

The standard deviation is an unbiased mean deviation of the true data points from the predicted straight line.

```
std(p_error)

ans =
    12.4289
```

Cross validation gives valuable information of the goodness-of-fit of the regression result. This method can be used also for quality control in other fields, such as spatial and temporal prediction.

4.8 Reduced Major Axis Regression

In some cases, both variables are not manipulated and can therefore be considered to be independent. Here, several methods are available to compute a best-fit line that minimizes the distance from both x and y. As an example, the method of *reduced major axis* (RMA) minimizes the triangular area $0.5 (\Delta x \Delta y)$ between the points and the regression line, where Δx and Δy are the distances between predicted and true x and y values (Fig. 4.4). This optimization appears to be complex. However, it can be shown that the first regression coefficient b_1 (the slope) is simply the ratio of the standard deviations of x and y.

$$b_1 = s_y / s_x$$

Similar to classic regression, the regression line passes through the data centroid defined by the sample mean. We can therefore compute the second regression coefficient b_0 (the y-intercept),

$$b_0 = \bar{y} - b_1 \bar{x}$$

using the univariate sample means and the slope b_1 computed earlier. Let us load the age-depth data from the file *agedepth.txt* and define two variables, `meters` and `age`. It is ssumed that both of the variables contain errors and the scatter of the data can be explained by dispersion of `meters` and `age`.

```
clear
agedepth = load('agedepth_1.txt');

meters = agedepth(:,1);
age = agedepth(:,2);
```

The above formula is used for computing the slope of the regression line b_1.

```
p(1,1) = std(age)/ std(meters)

p =
   6.0367
```

The second coefficient b_0, i.e., the y-axis intercept can therefore be computed by

```
p(1,2) = mean(age) - p(1,1) * mean(meters)

p =
   6.0367    -2.9570
```

The regression line can be plotted by

```
plot(meters,age,'o'), hold
plot(meters,polyval(p,meters),'r')
```

This linear fit slightly differs from the line obtained from classic regression. Note that the regression line from RMA is *not* the bisector of the angle between the x-y and y-x classical linear regression analysis, i.e., using either x or y as independent variable while computing the regression lines.

4.9 Curvilinear Regression

It has become apparent from our previous analysis that a linear regression model provides a good way of describing the scaling properties of the data. However, we may wish to check whether the data could be equally-well described by a polynomial fit of a higher degree.

$$y = b_0 + b_1 x + b_2 x^2$$

To clear the workspace and reload the original data, type

```
agedepth = load('agedepth_1.txt');

meters = agedepth(:,1);
age = agedepth(:,2);
```

Subsequently, a polynomial of degree 2 can be fitted by using the function `polyfit`.

```
p = polyfit(meters,age,2)

p =
   -0.0132    5.8955    0.1265
```

The first coefficient is close to zero, i.e., has not much influence on prediction. The second and third coefficients are similar to the coefficients obtained by linear regression. Plotting the data yields a curve that resembles a straight line.

```
plot(meters,age,'o'), hold
plot(meters,polyval(p,meters),'r')
```

Let us compute and plot the error bounds obtained by passing an optional second output parameter from `polyfit` as an input parameter to `polyval`.

```
[p,s] = polyfit(meters,age,2);
[p_age,delta] = polyval(p,meters,s);
```

This code uses an interval of $\pm 2s$, corresponding to a 95% confidence interval. `polyfit` returns the polynomial coefficients p, but also a structure s for use with `polyval` to obtain error bounds for the predictions. The structure s contains fields for the norm of the residuals that we use to compute the error bounds. `delta` is an estimate of the standard deviation of the prediction error of a future observation at x by p(x). We plot the results.

```
plot(meters,age,'+',meters,p_age,'g-',...
   meters,p_age+2*delta,'r', meters,p_age-2*delta,'r')
grid on
```

We now use another synthetic data set that we generate using a quadratic relationship between meters and age.

```
meters = 20 * rand(30,1);
age =   1.6 * meters.^2 - 1.1 * meters + 1.2;
age = age + 40.* randn(length(meters),1);

plot(meters,age,'o')

agedepth = [meters age];
```

```
agedepth = sortrows(agedepth,1);

save agedepth_2.txt agedepth -ascii
```

The synthetic bivariate data set can be loaded from the file *agedepth_2.txt*.

```
agedepth = load(agedepth_2.txt');

meters = agedepth(:,1);
age = agedepth(:,2);

plot(meters,age,'o')
```

Fitting a polynomial of degree 2 yields a convincing regression result compared to the linear model.

```
p = polyfit(meters,age,2)

p =
    1.7199    -5.6948    33.3508
```

As shown above, the true values for the three coefficients are $+1.6$, -1.1 and $+1.2$. There are some discrepancies between the true values and the coefficients estimated using `polyfit`. The regression curve and the error bounds can be plotted by typing (Fig. 4.8)

```
plot(meters,age,'o'), hold
plot(meters,polyval(p,meters),'r')

[p,s] = polyfit(meters,age,2);
[p_age,delta] = polyval(p,meters,s);

plot(meters,age,'+',meters,p_age,'g',meters,...
    p_age+2*delta,'r--',meters,p_age-2*delta,'r--')
grid on
xlabel('meters'), ylabel('age')
```

The plot shows that the quadratic model for this data is a good one. The quality of the result could again be tested by exploring the residuals, employing resampling schemes or cross validation. The combination of regression analysis with one of these methods represent a powerful tool in bivariate data analysis, whereas Pearson's correlation coefficient should be used only as a first test for linear relationships.

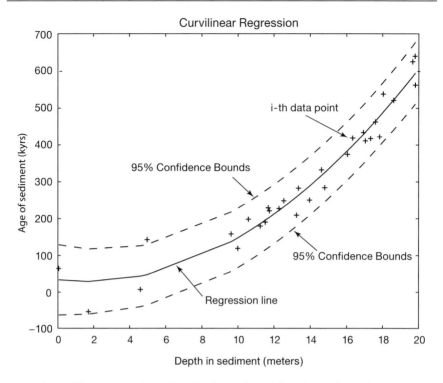

Fig. 4.8 Curvilinear regression. The plot shows the original data points (plus signs), the regression line for a polynomial of degree 2 (solid line) as well as the error bounds (dashed lines) of the regression.

Recommended Reading

Alberède F (2002) Introduction to Geochemical Modeling. Cambridge University Press, Cambridge

Davis JC (2002) Statistics and Data Analysis in Geology, Third Edition. John Wiley and Sons, New York

Draper NR, Smith, H (1998) Applied Regression Analysis. Wiley Series in Probability and Statistics, John Wiley and Sons, New York

Efron B (1982) The Jackknife, the Bootstrap, and Other Resampling Plans. Society of Industrial and Applied Mathematics CBMS-NSF Monographs 38

Fisher RA (1922) The Goodness of Fit of Regression Formulae, and the Distribution of Regression Coefficients. Journal of the Royal Statistical Society 85:597–612

MacTavish JN, Malone PG, Wells TL (1968) RMAR; a Reduced Major Axis Regression Program Designed for Paleontologic Data. Journal of Paleontology 42/4:1076–1078

Pearson K (1894–98) Mathematical Contributions to the Theory of Evolution, Part I to IV. Philosophical Transactions of the Royal Society 185–191

The Mathworks (2006) Statistics Toolbox User's Guide – For the Use with MATLAB®. The MathWorks, Natick, MA

5 Time-Series Analysis

5.1 Introduction

Time-series analysis aims to understand the temporal behavior of one of several variables $y(t)$. Examples are the investigation of long-term records of mountain uplift, sea-level fluctuations, orbitally-induced insolation variations and their influence on the ice-age cycles, millenium-scale variations of the atmosphere-ocean system, the effect of the El Niño/Southern Oscillation on tropical rainfall and sedimentation (Fig. 5.1) and tidal influences on nobel gas emissions of bore holes. The temporal structure of a sequence of events can be random, clustered, cyclic or chaotic. Time-series analysis provides various tools to detect these temporal structures. The understanding of the underlying process that produced the observed data allows us to predict future values of the variable. We use the Signal Processing and Wavelet Toolbox, which contain all necessary routines for time-series analysis.

The first section is on signals in general and contains a technical description of how to generate synthetic signals for time-series analysis (Chapter 5.2). Then, spectral analysis to detect cyclicities in a single time series (autospectral analysis) and to determine the relationship between two time series as a function of frequency (crossspectral analysis) is demonstrated in Chapters 5.3 and 5.4. Since most time series in earth sciences are not evenly-spaced in time, various interpolation techniques and subsequent spectral analysis are introduced in Chapter 5.5. Evolutionary powerspectra to map changes in the cyclicities through time are shown in Chapter 5.6. An alternative technique to analyze unevenly-spaced data is in Chapter 5.7. In the subsequent Chapter 5.8, the very popular wavelets are introduced having the capability to map temporal variations in the spectra, similar to the method shown in Chapter 5.6.. The chapter closes with an overview of nonlinear techniques, in particular the method of recurrence plots (Chapter 5.9).

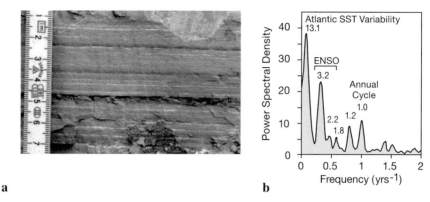

a   b

Fig. 5.1 a Photograph of ca. 30 kyr-old varved sediments from a landslide-dammed lake in the Northwest Argentine Andes. The mixed clastic-biogenic varves consist of reddish-brown and green to buff-colored clays sourced from Cretaceous redbeds (red-brown) and Precambrian to early Paleozoic greenshists (green-buff colored). The clastic varves are topped by thin white diatomite layers documenting the bloom of silica algae after the austral-summer rainy season. The distribution of the two source rocks and the interannual precipitation pattern in the area suggests that the reddish-brown layers reflect cyclic recurrence of enhanced precipitation, erosion and sediment input in the landslide-dammed lake. **b** The powerspectrum of a red-color intensity transect across 70 varves is dominated by significant peaks at frequencies of ca. 0.076, 0.313, 0.455 and 1.0 yrs^{-1} corresponding to periods of 13.1, 3.2, 2.2, and around 1.0 years. This cyclicities suggest a strong influence of the tropical Atlantic sea-surface temperature (SST) variability (characterized by 10 to 15 year cycles), the El Niño/Southern Oscillation (ENSO) (cycles between two and seven years) and the annual cycle at 30 kyrs ago, similar to today (Trauth et al. 2003).

5.2 Generating Signals

A time series is an ordered sequence of values of a variable $y(t)$ at certain times t_k.

$$y(t_k) = y(t_1), y(t_2), \ldots, y(t_N)$$

If the time-indexed distance between any two successive observation t_k and t_{k+1} is constant, the time series is equally spaced and the sampling interval is

$$\Delta t = t_{k+1} - t_k$$

The sampling frequency f_s is the inverse of the sampling interval Δt. In most cases, we try to sample at constant time intervals or sampling frequencies. However, in some cases equally-spaced data are not available. As

an example, assume deep-sea sediments sampled at five-centimeter intervals along a sediment core. Radiometric age determination of certain levels
of the sediment core revealed significant fluctuations in the sedimentation
rates. The samples evenly spaced along the sediment core are therefore not
equally spaced on the time axis. Here, the quantity

$$\Delta t = T / N$$

where T is the full length of the time series and N is the number of data points,
represents only an average sampling interval. In general, a time series $y(t_k)$
can be represented as a linear sum of a long-term component or trend $y_{tr}(t_k)$,
a periodic component $y_p(t_k)$ and a random noise $y_n(t_k)$.

$$y(t_k) = y_{tr}(t_k) + y_p(t_k) + y_n(t_k)$$

The long-term component is a linear or higher-degree trend that can be
extracted by fitting a polynomial of a certain degree and subtracting the
values of this polynomial from the data (see Chapter 4). Noise removal will
be described in Chapter 6. The periodic – or cyclic in a mathematically less
rigorous sense – component can be approximated by a linear combination
of cosine (or sine) waves that have different amplitudes A_i, frequencies f_i
and phase angles ψ_i.

$$y_p(t_k) = \sum_i A_i \cdot \cos(2\pi f_i t_k - \psi_i)$$

The phase angle ψ helps to detect temporal shifts between signals of the
same frequency. Two signals y_1 and y_2 of the same period are out of phase
if the difference between ψ_1 and ψ_2 is not zero (Fig. 5.2).

The frequency f of a periodic signal is the inverse of the period τ. The
Nyquist frequency f_{Nyq} is half the sampling frequency f_s and provides a maximum frequency the data can produce. As an example, audio compact disks
(CDs) are sampled at frequencies of 44,100 Hz (Hertz, which is 1/second).
The corresponding Nyquist frequency is 22,050 Hz, which is the highest
frequency a CD player can theoretically produce. The limited performance
of anti-alias filters used by CD players again reduces the frequency band
and causes a cutoff frequency at around 20,050 Hz, which is the true upper
frequency limit of a CD player.

We now generate synthetic signals to illustrate the use of time-series
analysis tools. While using synthetic data we know in advance which fea-

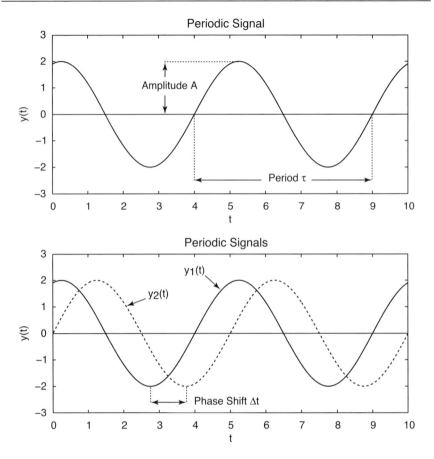

Fig. 5.2 Two periodic signals y_1 and y_2 as a function of time t defined by the amplitudes A_1 and A_2, the period $\tau_1 = \tau_2$, which is the inverse of the frequency $f_1 = f_2$. Two signals y_1 and y_2 of the same period are out of phase if the difference between ψ_1 and ψ_2 is not zero.

tures the time series contains, such as periodic or stochastic components, and we can introduce artifacts such as a linear trend or gaps. This knowledge is particularly important if you are new to time series analysis. The user encounters plenty of possible effects of parameter settings, potential artifacts and errors in the application of spectral analysis tools. Therefore, we start with simple data before we apply the methods to more complex time series.

The next example illustrates how to generate a basic synthetic data series that is characteristic to earth sciences data. First, we create a time axis t running from 0.01 to 100 in 0.01 intervals. Next, we generate a strictly periodic signal y(t), a sine wave with a period 5 and an amplitude 2 by typing

```
t = 0.01 : 0.01 : 100;
y = 2*sin(2*pi*t/5);

plot(t,y)
```

The period of $\tau=5$ corresponds to a frequency of $f=1/5=0.2$. Natural data series, however, are more complex than a simple periodic signal. The next-complicated signal is generated by superposition of several periodic components with different periods. As an example, we compute such a signal by adding three sine waves with the periods $\tau_1=50$ ($f_1=0.02$), $\tau_2=15$ ($f_2\approx0.07$) and $\tau_3=5$ ($f_3=0.2$). The corresponding amplitudes are $A_1=2$, $A_2=1$ and $A_3=0.5$. The new time axis t runs from 1 to 1000 with 1.0 intervals.

```
t = 1 : 1000;
y = 2*sin(2*pi*t/50) + sin(2*pi*t/15) + 0.5*sin(2*pi*t/5);

plot(t,y), axis([0 200 -4 4])
```

Only one fifth of the original data series is displayed by restricting the x-axis limits to the interval [0 200]. It is, however, recommended to generate long data series as in the example in order to avoid edge effects while applying spectral-analysis tools for the first time.

In contrast to our synthetic time series, real data also contain various disturbances, such as random noise and first or higher-order trends. Firstly, a random-number generator can be used to compute gaussian noise with zero mean and standard deviation one. The seed of the algorithm needs to be set to zero. Subsequently, one thousand random numbers are generated using the function randn.

```
randn('seed',0)
n = randn(1,1000);
```

We add this noise to the original data, i.e., we generate a signal containing additive noise (Fig. 5.3). Displaying the data illustrates the effect of noise on a periodic signal. In reality, no record that is free of noise. Hence, it is important to familiarize oneself with the influence of noise on powerspectra.

```
yn = y + n;

plot(t,y,'b-',t,yn,'r-'), axis([0 200 -4 4])
```

The methods of signal processing methods are often applied to remove most of the noise although many filtering methods make arbitrary assumptions

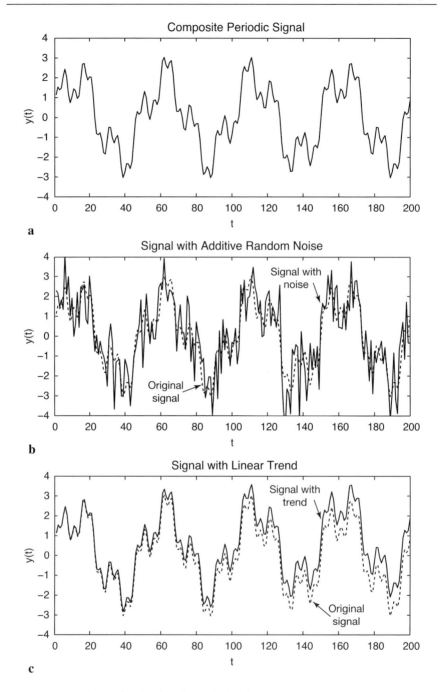

a

b

c

Fig. 5.3 a Synthetic signal with the periodicities $\tau_1=50$, $\tau_2=15$ and $\tau_3=5$, different amplitudes, **b** overlain by gaussian noise and **c** a linear trend.

on the signal-to-noise ratio. Moreover, filtering introduces artifacts and statistical dependencies to the data. These may have a profound influence on the resulting powerspectra.

Finally, we introduce a linear long-term trend to the data by adding a straight line with a slope 0.005 and an intercept of zero with the y-axis (Fig. 5.3). Such trends are common features in earth sciences. As an example, consider the glacial-interglacial cycles observed in marine oxygen-isotope records overlain by a long-term cooling trend during the last six million years.

```
yt = y + 0.005 * t;

plot(t,y,'b-',t,yt,'r-'), axis([0 200 -4 4])
```

In reality, more complex trends exist, such as higher-order trends or trends characterized by changing slopes. In practice, it is recommended to eliminate such a trend by fitting polynomials to the data and to subtract the corresponding values. This synthetic time series now contains many characteristics of a typical data set in the earth sciences. It can be used to illustrate the use of spectral-analysis tools that are introduced in the next chapter.

5.3 Blackman-Tukey Autospectral Analysis

Autospectral analysis aims to describe the distribution of variance contained in one single signal $x(t)$ over frequency or wavelength. A simple way to describe the variance in a signal over a time lag k is the autocovariance. An unbiased estimator of the autocovariance cov_{xx} of the signal $x(t)$ with N data points sampled at constant time intervals Δt is

$$cov_{xx}(k) = \frac{1}{N-k-1} \sum_{t=1}^{N-k} (x_i - \overline{x})(x_{i+k} - \overline{x})$$

The autocovariance series clearly depends on the amplitude of $x(t)$. Normalizing the covariance by the variance σ^2 of $x(t)$ yields the autocorrelation sequence. Autocorrelation involves correlating a series of data with itself, depending on a time lag k.

$$corr_{xx}(k) = \frac{cov_{xx}(k)}{cov_{xx}(0)} = \frac{cov_{xx}(k)}{\sigma_x^2}$$

The most popular method to compute powerspectra in earth sciences is the method introduced by Blackman and Tukey (1958). The *Blackman-Tukey method* uses the complex Fourier transform $X(f)$ of the autocorrelation sequence $corr_{xx}(k)$,

$$X_{xx}(f) = \sum_{k=0}^{M} corr_{xx}(k)\, e^{i2\pi fk/f_s}$$

where M is the maximum lag and f_s the sampling frequency. The Blackman-Tukey *powerspectral density PSD* is estimated by

$$PSD_{xx}(f) = |X_{xx}(f)|$$

The actual computation of *PSD* can be performed only at a finite number of frequency points by employing a *Fast Fourier Transformation* (FFT). The FFT is a method to compute a discrete Fourier Transform with reduced execution time. Most FFT algorithms divide the transform into two pieces of size $N/2$ at each step. It is therefore limited to blocks of a power of two. In practice, the *PSD* is computed by using a number of frequencies close to the number of data points in the original signal $x(t)$.

The discrete Fourier transform is an approximation of the continuous Fourier transform. The Fourier transform expects an infinite signal. However, real data are limited at both ends, i.e., the signal amplitude is zero beyond the limits of the time series. In the time domain, a finite signal corresponds to an infinite signal multiplied by a rectangular window that is one within the limits of the signal and zero elsewhere. In the frequency domain, the multiplication of the time series with this window equals to a convolution of the powerspectrum of the signal with the spectrum of the rectangular window. The spectrum of the window, however, equals a *sin (x)/x* function, which has a main lobe and several side lobes at both sides of the main peak. Therefore, all maxima in a powerspectrum *leak*, i.e., they lose power about the minor peaks (Fig. 5.4).

A popular way to overcome the problem of *spectral leakage* is windowing. The sequence of data is simply multiplied by a window with smooth ends. Several window shapes are available, e.g., *Bartlett* (triangular), *Hamming* (cosinusoidal) and *Hanning* (slightly different cosinusoidal). The use of these windows slightly modifies the equation of the Fourier transform of the autocorrelation sequence:

$$X_{xx}(f) = \sum_{k=0}^{M} corr_{xx}(k)w(k)\, e^{i2\pi fk/f_s}$$

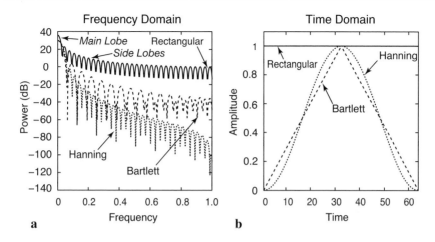

Fig. 5.4 Spectral leakage. **a** The relative amplitude of the side lobes compared to the main lobe is reduced by multiplying the corresponding time series with **b** a window with smooth ends. A number of different windows with advantages and disadvantages are available instead of using the default rectangular window, including *Bartlett* (triangular) and *Hanning* (cosinusoidal) windows. Graph generated using the function wvtool.

where M is the maximum lag considered and window length, and $w(k)$ is the windowing function. The Blackman-Tukey method therefore performs autospectral analysis in three steps, calculation of the autocorrelation sequence $corr_{xx}(k)$, windowing and finally computation of the discrete fourier transform. MATLAB allows to perform this powerspectral analysis with a number of modifications of the above method. A useful modification is the method by Welch (1967) (Fig. 5.5). The Welch method includes dividing the time series into overlapping segments, computing the powerspectrum for each segment and averaging the powerspectra. The advantage of averaging spectra is obvious, it simply improves the signal-to-noise ratio of a spectrum. The disadvantage is a loss of resolution of the spectrum.

The Welch spectral analysis that is included in the Signal Processing Toolbox can be applied to the synthetic data sets. The function periodog ram(y,window,nfft,fs) computes the powerspectral density of y(t). We use the default rectangular window by choosing an empty vector [] for window. The powerspectrum is computed using a FFT of length nfft of 1024. We then compute the magnitude of the complex output Pxx of peri-odogram by using the function abs. Finally, the sampling frequency fs of one is supplied to the function in order to obtain a correct frequency scaling of the f-axis.

```
[Pxx,f] = periodogram(y,[],1024,1);
magnitude = abs(Pxx);

plot(f,magnitude), grid
xlabel('Frequency')
ylabel('Power')
title('Autospectrum')
```

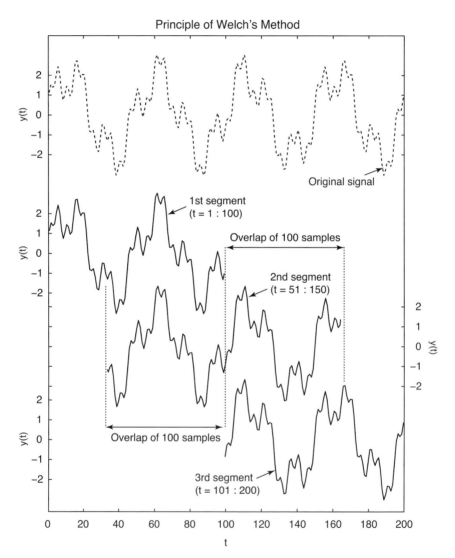

Fig. 5.5 Principle of Welch powerspectral analysis. The time series is divided into overlapping segments, then the powerspectrum for each segment is computed and all spectra are averaged to improve the signal-to-noise ratio of the powerspectrum.

The graphical output shows that there are three significant peaks at the position of the original frequencies of the three sine waves. The same procedure can be applied to the noisy data:

```
[Pxx,f] = periodogram(yn,[],1024,1);
magnitude = abs(Pxx);

plot(f,magnitude), grid
xlabel('Frequency')
ylabel('Power')
title('Autospectrum')
```

Let us increase the noise level. The gaussian noise has now a standard deviation of five and zero mean.

```
randn('seed',0);
n = 5 * randn(size(y));
yn = y + n;

[Pxx,f] = periodogram(yn,[],1024,1);
magnitude = abs(Pxx);

plot(f,magnitude), grid
xlabel('Frequency')
ylabel('Power')
title('Autospectrum')
```

This spectrum resembles a real data spectrum in the earth sciences. The spectral peaks now sit on a significant noise floor. The peak of the highest frequency even disappears in the noise. It cannot be distinguished from maxima which are attributed to noise. Both spectra can be compared on the same plot (Fig. 5.6):

```
[Pxx,f] = periodogram(y,[],1024,1);
magnitude = abs(Pxx);

plot(f,magnitude,'b')
hold

[Pxx,f] = periodogram(yn,[],1024,1);
magnitude = abs(Pxx);

plot(f,magnitude,'r'), grid
xlabel('Frequency')
ylabel('Power')
title('Autospectrum')
```

Next, we explore the influence of a linear trend on a spectrum. Long-term trends are common features in earth science data. We will see that this trend is misinterpreted as a very long period by the FFT. The spectrum therefore contains a large peak with a frequency close to zero (Fig. 5.7).

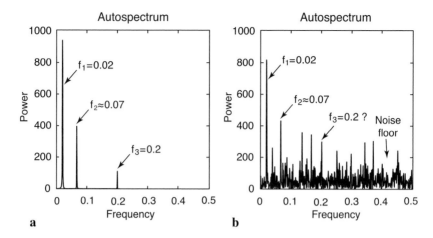

Fig. 5.6 Comparison of the Welch powerspectra of the **a** noise-free and **b** noisy synthetic signal with the periods τ_1=50 (f_1=0.02), τ_2=15 ($f_2 \approx 0.07$) and τ_3=5 (f_3=0.2). In particular, the peak with the highest frequency disappears in the noise floor and cannot be distinguished from peaks attributed to the gaussian noise.

```
yt = y + 0.005 * t;

[Pxx,f] = periodogram(y,[],1024,1);
magnitude = abs(Pxx);

[Pxxt,f] = periodogram(yt,[],1024,1);
magnitudet = abs(Pxxt);

subplot(1,2,1), plot(f,abs(Pxx))
xlabel('Frequency')
ylabel('Power')

subplot(1,2,2), plot(f,abs(Pxxt))
xlabel('Frequency')
ylabel('Power')
```

To eliminate the long-term trend, we use the function detrend.

```
ydt = detrend(yt);

subplot(2,1,1)
plot(t,y,'b-',t,yt,'r-'), axis([0 200 -4 4])

subplot(2,1,2)
plot(t,y,'b-',t,ydt,'r-'), axis([0 200 -4 4])
```

The corresponding spectrum does not show the low-frequency peak anymore. Some data contain a high-order trend that can be removed by fitting a higher-order polynomial to the data and by subtracting the corresponding $Y(t)$ values.

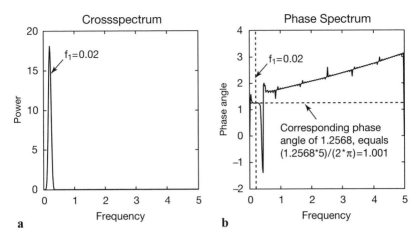

Fig. 5.8 Crossspectrum of two sine waves with identical periodicities $\tau=5$ (equivalent to $f=0.2$) and amplitudes two. The sine waves show a relative phase shift of $t=1$. In the argument of the second sine wave this corresponds to $2\pi/5$, which is one fifth of the full wavelength of $\tau=5$. **a** The magnitude shows the expected peak at $f=0.2$. **b** The corresponding phase difference in radians at this frequency is 1.2568, which equals $(1.2568*5)/(2*\pi) = 1.0001$, which is the phase shift of one we introduced at the beginning.

in our example, therefore the default rectangular window is used to obtain eight sections of y1 and y2. The parameter noverlap defines the number of samples of overlap from section to section, zero in our example. The sampling frequency fs is 10 in the example. Coherence does not make much sense if we have noise-free data with only one frequency. This results in a correlation coefficient that equals one everywhere. Since the coherence is plotted on a log scale (in *decibel*, dB), the corresponding graph shows a log coherence of zero for all frequencies.

```
[Cxy,f] = mscohere(y1,y2,[],0,512,10);

plot(f,Cxy)
xlabel('Frequency')
ylabel('Magnitude Squared Coherence')
title('Coherence')
```

The function mscohere(y1,y2,window,noverlap,nfft,fs) specifies the number of FFT points nfft=512, the default rectangular window, which overlaps by ten data points. The complex part of Pxy is required for computing the phase shift using the function angle between the two signals.

```
phase = angle(Pxy);

plot(f,phase), grid
xlabel('Frequency')
ylabel('Phase Angle')
title('Phase spectrum')
```

The phase shift at a frequency of f=0.2 (period τ=5) can be interpolated from the phase spectrum

```
interp1(f,phase,0.2)
```

which produces the output

```
ans =
  -1.2567
```

The phase spectrum is normalized to one full period τ=2π, therefore a phase shift of -1.2567 equals $(-1.2567*5)/(2*\pi) = -1.0001$, which is the phase shift of one that we introduced at the beginning.

We now use two sine waves with different periodicities to illustrate the crossspectral analysis. Both signals have a periodicity of 5, but with a phase shift of 1, then they both have one other, but different period.

```
clear

t = 0.1 : 0.1 : 1000;
y1 = sin(2*pi*t/15) + 0.5*sin(2*pi*t/5);
y2 = 2*sin(2*pi*t/50) + 0.5*sin(2*pi*t/5+2*pi/5);

plot(t,y1,'b-',t,y2,'r-')
```

Now we compute the crossspectrum, which clearly shows the common period of τ=5 or frequency of f=0.2.

```
[Pxy,f] = cpsd(y1,y2,[],0,512,10);
magnitude = abs(Pxy);

plot(f,magnitude);
xlabel('Frequency')
ylabel('Power')
title('Crossspectrum')
```

The coherence shows a large value of approximately one at f=0.2.

```
[Cxy,f] = mscohere(y1,y2,[],0,512,10);

plot(f,Cxy)
xlabel('Frequency')
ylabel('Magnitude Squared Coherence')
title('Coherence')
```

The complex part is required for calculating the phase shift between the two sine waves.

```
[Pxy,f] = cpsd(y1,y2,[],0,512,10);
phase=angle(Pxy);

plot(f,phase)
```

The phase shift at a frequency of $f=0.2$ (period $\tau=5$) is

```
interp1(f,phase,0.2)
```

which produces the output of

```
ans =
   -1.2604
```

The phase spectrum is normalized to one full period $\tau=2\pi$, therefore a phase shift of -1.2604 equals $(-1.2604*5)/(2*\pi) = -1.0001$, which is again the phase shift of one that we introduced at the beginning.

5.5 Interpolating and Analyzing Unevenly-Spaced Data

Now we use our experience in analyzing evenly-spaced data to run a spectral analysis on unevenly-spaced data. Such data are very common in earth sciences. For example, in the field of paleoceanography, deep-sea cores are typically sampled at constant depth intervals. The transformation of evenly-spaced length-parameter data to time-parameter data in an environment with changing length-time ratios results in unevenly-spaced time series. Numerous methods exist for interpolating unevenly-spaced sequences of data or time series. The aim of these *interpolation techniques* for $x(t)$ data is to estimate the x-values for an equally-spaced t vector from the actual irregular-spaced $x(t)$ measurements. *Linear interpolation* predicts the x-values by effectively drawing out a straight line between two neighboring measurements and by calculating the appropriate point along that line. However, the method also has its limitations. It assumes linear transitions in the data, which introduces a number of artifacts, including the loss of high-frequency components of the signal and limiting the data range to that of the original measurements.

Cubic-spline interpolation is another method for interpolating data that are unevenly spaced. Cubic splines are piecewise continuous curves, passing through at least four data points for each step. The method has the advantage that it preserves the high-frequency information contained in the data. However, steep gradients in the data sequence could cause spurious amplitudes in the interpolated time series, which typically occur at neighboring extreme minima and maxima. Since all these and other interpolation techniques might introduce some artifacts into the data, it is always advisable to (1) preserve the number of data points before and after interpolation, (2) report the method employed for estimating the evenly-spaced data sequence and (3) explore the effect of interpolation on the variance of the data.

After this brief introduction to interpolation techniques, we apply the most popular linear and cubic-spline interpolation techniques to unevenly-spaced data. Having interpolated the data, we use the spectral tools that have already been applied to evenly-spaced data (Chapters 5.3 and 5.4). First, we load the two time series:

```
series1 = load('series1.txt');
series2 = load('series2.txt');
```

Both synthetic data sets contain a two-column matrix with 339 rows. The first column contains ages in kiloyears that are not evenly spaced. The second column contains oxygen-isotope values measured on foraminifera. The data sets contain 100, 40 and 20 kyr cyclicities and they are overlain by gaussian noise. In the 100 kyr frequency band, the second data series is shifted by 5 kyrs with respect to the first data series. To plot the data we type

```
plot(series1(:,1),series1(:,2))
figure
plot(series2(:,1),series2(:,2))
```

The statistics of the spacing of the first data series can be computed by

```
intv1 = diff(series1(:,1));

plot(intv1)
```

The plot shows that the spacing varies around a mean interval of 3 kyrs with a standard deviation of ca. 1 kyrs. The minimum and maximum value of the time axis

```
min(series1(:,1))

max(series1(:,1))
```

of $t_{min}=0$ and $t_{max}=997$ kyrs gives some information about the temporal range of the data. The second data series

```
intv2 = diff(series2(:,1));

plot(intv2)

min(series2(:,1))

max(series2(:,1))
```

has a similar range from 0 to 997 kyrs. We see that both series have a mean spacing of 3 kyrs and range from 0 to ca. 1000 kyrs. We now interpolate the data to an evenly-spaced time axis. While doing this, we follow the rule that number of data points should not be increased. The new time axis runs from 0 to 996 kyrs with 3 kyr intervals.

```
t = 0 : 3 : 996;
```

We now interpolate the two time series to this axis with linear and spline-interpolation methods using the function interp1.

```
series1L = interp1(series1(:,1),series1(:,2),t,'linear');
series1S = interp1(series1(:,1),series1(:,2),t,'spline');

series2L = interp1(series2(:,1),series2(:,2),t,'linear');
series2S = interp1(series2(:,1),series2(:,2),t,'spline');
```

The results are compared by plotting the first series before and after interpolation.

```
plot(series1(:,1),series1(:,2),'ko')
hold
plot(t,series1L,'b-',t,series1S,'r-')
```

We already observe some significant artifacts at ca. 370 kyrs. Whereas the linearly-interpolated points are always within the range of the original data, the spline interpolation method produces values that are unrealistically high or low (Fig. 5.9). The results can be compared by plotting the second data series.

```
plot(series2(:,1),series2(:,2),'ko')
hold
plot(t,series2L,'b-',t,series2S,'r-')
```

In this series, only a few artifacts can be observed. We can apply the function used above to calculate the powerspectral density. We compute the FFT for 256 data points, the sampling frequency is $1/3$ kyrs^{-1}.

```
[Pxx,f] = periodogram(series1L,[],256,1/3);
magnitude = abs(Pxx);
```

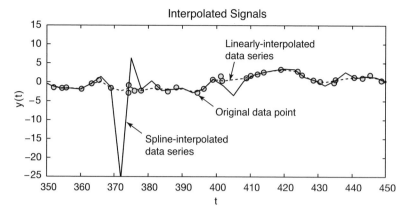

Fig. 5.9 Interpolation artifacts. Whereas the linearly interpolated points are always within the range of the original data, the spline interpolation method causes unrealistic high and low values.

```
plot(f,magnitude)
xlabel('Frequency')
ylabel('Power')
title('Autospectrum')
```

Significant peaks occur at frequencies of 0.01, 0.025 and 0.05 approximately, corresponding to the 100, 40 and 20 kyr cycles. Analysis of the second time series

```
[Pxx,f] = periodogram(series2L,[],256,1/3);
magnitude = abs(Pxx);

plot(f,magnitude)
xlabel('Frequency')
ylabel('Power')
title('Autospectrum')
```

also yields significant peaks at frequencies of 0.01, 0.025 and 0.05 (Fig. 5.10). Now we compute the crossspectrum of both data series.

```
[Pxy,f] = cpsd(series1L,series2L,[],128,256,1/3);
magnitude = abs(Pxy);

plot(f,magnitude)
xlabel('Frequency')
ylabel('Power')
title('Crossspectrum')
```

The coherence is quite convincing.

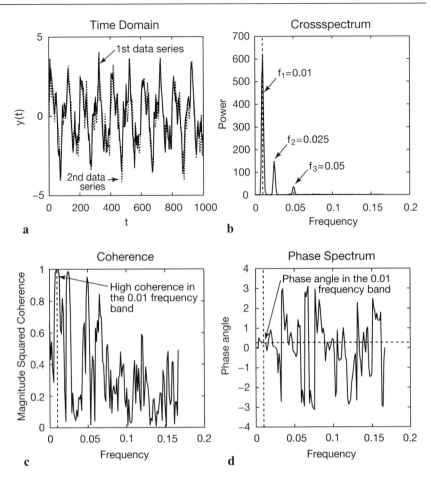

Fig. 5.10 Result from crossspectral analysis of the two linearly-interpolated signals. **a** Signals in the time domain, **b** crossspectrum of both signals, **c** coherence of the signals in the frequency domain and **d** phase spectrum in radians.

```
[Cxy,f] = mscohere(series1L,series2L,[],128,256,1/3);

plot(f,Cxy)
xlabel('Frequency')
ylabel('Magnitude Squared Coherence')
title('Coherence')
```

We observe a fairly high coherence in the frequency bands of the 0.01, 0.025 and 0.05. The complex part of P_{xy} is required for calculating the phase difference per frequency.

```
phase = angle(Pxy);

plot(f,phase)
xlabel('Frequency')
ylabel('Phase Angle')
title('Phase spectrum')
```

The phase shift at a frequency of $f=0.01$ is calculated by

```
interp1(f,phase,0.01)
```

which produces the output of

```
ans =
  -0.2796
```

The phase spectrum is normalized to a full period $\tau=2\pi$. Hence, a phase shift of -0.2796 equals $(-0.2796*100 \text{ kyr})/(2*\pi)=-4.45$ kyr. This corresponds roughly to the phase shift of 5 kyr introduced to the second data series with respect to the first series.

As a more comfortable tool for spectral analysis, the Signal Processing Toolbox also contains a GUI function named `sptool`, which stands for *Signal Processing Tool*.

5.6 Evolutionary Blackman-Tukey Powerspectrum

The amplitude of spectral peaks usually changes through time. This is particularly true for paleoclimate time series. Paleoclimate records usually show trends in the mean and variance, but also in the relative contributions of rhythmic components such as the Milankovitch cycles in marine oxygen-isotope records. Evolutionary powerspectra have the capability to map such changes in the frequency domain. The *evolutionary* or *windowed Blackman-Tukey powerspectrum* is a modification of the method introduced in Chapter 5.3, which computes the spectrum of overlapping segments of the time series. These overlapping segments are relatively short compared to the windowed segments used by the Welch method (Chapter 5.3), which is used to increase the signal-to-noise ratio of powerspectra. Therefore, the windowed Blackman-Tukey method uses the short-time Fourier transform (STFT) instead of the Fast Fourier Transformation (FFT). The output of windowed Blackman-Tukey powerspectrum is the short-term, time-localized frequency content of the signal. There are various methods to display the results. For instance, time and frequency are plotted on the x- and y-axis, or *vice versa*, where the color of the plot is proportional to the height of the spectral peaks.

As an example, we generate a synthetic data set that is similar to the ones used in Chapter 5.5. The data series contains three main periodicities of 100, 40 and 20 kyrs and additive gaussian noise. The amplitudes, however, change through time. Therefore, this example can be used to illustrate the advantage of the windowed Blackman-Tukey method. First, we create a time vector t.

```
clear
t = 0 : 3 : 1000;
```

In a first step, we introduce some gaussian noise to the time vector t to make the data unevenly spaced.

```
randn('seed',0);
t = t + randn(size(t));
```

In a second step, we compute the signal with the three periodicities and varying amplitudes. The 40 kyr cycle appears after ca. 450 kyrs, whereas the 100 and 20 kyr cycles are present through the time series.

```
x1 = 0.5*sin(2*pi*t/100) + ...
     1.0*sin(2*pi*t/40)  + ...
     0.5*sin(2*pi*t/20);
x2 = 0.5*sin(2*pi*t/100) + ...
     0.5*sin(2*pi*t/20);

x = x1; x(1,150:end) = x2(1,150:end);
```

We add gaussian noise to the signal.

```
x = x + 0.5*randn(size(x));
```

Finally, we save the synthetic data series to the file *series3.txt* on the hard disk and clear the workspace.

```
series3(:,1) = t;
series3(:,2) = x;
series3(1,1) = 0;
series3(end,1) = 1000;
series3 = sortrows(series3,1);
save series3.txt series3 -ascii
clear
```

The above series of commands illustrates how to generate synthetic time series that show the same characteristics as oxygen-isotope data from calcareous algae (foraminifera) in deep-sea sediments. This synthetic data set is suitable to demonstrate the application of methods for spectral analysis. The following sequence of commands assumes that real data are contained in a file named *series3.txt*. We load and display the data (Fig. 5.11).

```
series3 = load('series3.txt');
plot(series3(:,1),series3(:,2))
xlabel('Time (kyr)')
ylabel('d18O (permille)')
title('Signal with Varying Cyclicities')
```

Both, the standard and the windowed Blackman-Tukey method require evenly-spaced data. Therefore, we interpolate the data to an evenly-spaced time vector t as demonstrated in Chapter 5.5.

```
t = 0 : 3 : 1000;
y = interp1(series3(:,1),series3(:,2),t,'linear');
```

First, we compute a non-evolutionary powerspectrum for the full length

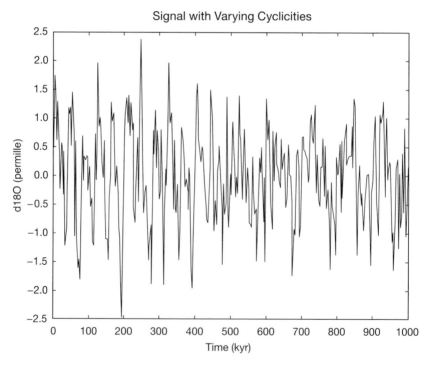

Fig. 5.11 Synthetic data set containing three main periodicities of 100, 40, and 20 kyrs and additive gaussian noise. Whereas the 100 and 20 kyr cycles are present throughout the time series, the 40 kyr cycle appears at around 450 kyr before present.

of the time series (Fig. 5.12). This exercise helps us to compare the differences between the results of the standard and windowed Blackman-Tukey powerspectral analysis.

```
[Pxx,f] = periodogram(y,[],1024,1/3);
plot(f,abs(Pxx))
xlabel('Frequency')
ylabel('Power')
title('Blackman-Tukey Powerspectrum')
```

The Blackman-Tukey autospectrum shows significant peaks at 100, 40 and 20 kyr cyclicities and some noise. The powerspectrum, however, does not provide any information about fluctuations of the amplitudes of these peaks. The non-evolutionary Blackman-Tukey powerspectrum simply represents an average of the spectral information contained in the data.

We use the function `spectrogram` to map the changes of the powerspectrum through time. By default, the time series is divided into eight segments

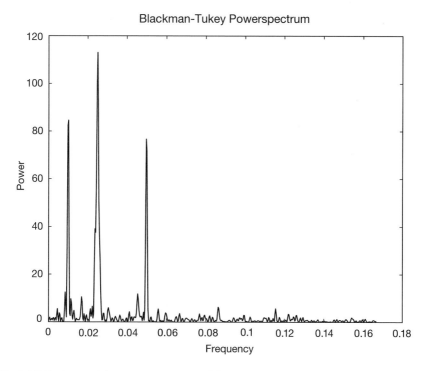

Fig. 5.12 Blackman-Tukey powerspectrum of the full time series showing significant peaks at 100, 40 and 20 kyrs. The plot, however, does not provide any information on the temporal behaviour of the cyclicities.

with a 50% overlap. Each segment is windowed with a Hamming window to suppress spectral leakage (Chapter 5.3). The function `spectrogram` uses similar input parameters as `periodogram` used in Chapter 5.3. We compute the evolutionary Blackman-Tukey powerspectrum for a window of 64 data points and 50 data points overlap. The STFT is computed for `nfft=256`. Since the spacing of the interpolated time vector is 3 kyrs, the sampling frequency is 1/3 kyr^{-1}.

```
spectrogram(y,64,50,256,1/3)
title('Blackman-Tukey Evolutionary Powerspectrum')
xlabel('Frequency (1/kyr)')
ylabel('Time (kyr)')
```

The output of `spectrogram` is a color plot (Fig. 5.13) that displays vertical stripes in red representing significant maxima at frequencies of 0.01 and

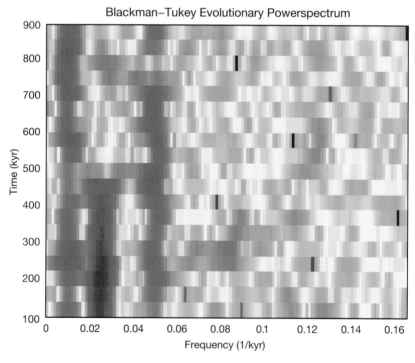

Fig. 5.13 Evolutionary Blackman-Tukey powerspectrum using `spectrogram` that computes the short-time Fourier transform STFT of overlapping segments of the time series. We use a Hamming window of 64 data points and 50 data points overlap. The STFT is computed for a `nfft=256`. Since the spacing of the interpolated time vector is 3 kyrs the sampling frequency is 1/3 kyr^{-1}. The plot shows the onset of the 40 kyr cycle at around 450 kyrs before present.

0.05 kyr^{-1}, or 100 and 20 kyr cyclicities. The 40 kyr cycle (corresponding to a frequency of 0.025 kyr^{-1}), however, only occurs after ca. 450 kyr, as documented by the vertical red stripe in the lower half of the graph.

For better visibility of the significant cycles, the coloration of the graph can be modified using the colormap editor.

```
colormapeditor
```

The colormap editor displays the colormap of the figure as a strip of rectangular cells. Nodes separate regions of uniform slope in the RGB colormap. The nodes can be shifted by using the mouse that introduces distortions to the colormap and therefore a modified coloration of the spectrogram. For example, shifting the yellow node towards the right increases the contrast between vertical peak areas at 100, 40 and 20 kyrs compared to the background.

5.7 Lomb-Scargle Powerspectrum

The Blackman-Tukey method requires evenly-spaced data. In earth sciences, however, time series are often unevenly spaced. Interpolating the unevenly-spaced data to a grid of evenly-spaced times is one way to overcome this problem (Chapter 5.5). However, interpolation introduces numerous artifacts to the data, both in the time and the frequency domain. For this reason, an alternative method of time-series analysis has become increasingly popular in earth sciences, the *Lomb-Scargle algorithm* (e.g., Scargle 1981, 1982, 1989, 1990, Press et al. 1992, Schulz et al. 1998).

In contrast to the Blackman-Tukey method, the Lomb-Scargle algorithm evaluates the data of the time series only at times t_i that are actually measured. Suppose a series $y(t)$ of N data points. Then, the Lomb-Scargle normalized periodogram P_x as a function of angular frequency $\omega = 2\pi f > 0$ is given by

$$P_x(\omega) = \frac{1}{2\sigma^2} \left\{ \frac{\left[\sum_j (y_j - \bar{y}) \cos \omega(t_j - \tau) \right]^2}{\sum_j \cos^2 \omega(t_j - \tau)} + \frac{\left[\sum_j (y_j - \bar{y}) \sin \omega(t_j - \tau) \right]^2}{\sum_j \sin^2 \omega(t_j - \tau)} \right\}$$

where

$$\bar{y} = \frac{1}{N}\sum_{i=1}^{N} y_i$$

$$s^2 = \frac{1}{N-1}\sum_{i=1}^{N}(y_i - \bar{y})^2$$

are the arithmetic mean and the variance of the data (Chapter 3.2). The constant τ is a kind of offset that makes $P_x(\omega)$ independent of shifting the t_i's by any constant. Scargle (1982) showed that this particular choice of the offset τ has the consequence that the solution for $P_x(\omega)$ is identical to a least-squares fit of sine and cosine functions to the data series $y(t)$:

$$y(t) = A\cos\omega t + B\sin\omega t$$

The least-squares fit of harmonic functions to data series in conjunction with spectral analysis was already investigated by Lomb (1976) and therefore, the method is called normalized Lomb-Scargle Fourier transform. The term *normalized* refers to the factor σ in the dominator of the equation for the periodogram.

Scargle (1982) has shown that the Lomb-Scargle periodogram has an exponential probability distribution with unit mean. The probability that $P_x(\omega)$ will be between some positive quantity z and $z+dz$ is $\exp(-z)dz$. If we scan M independent frequencies, the probability of none of them give larger values than z is $(1-\exp(-z))^M$. Therefore, we can compute the false-alarm probability of the null hypothesis, e.g., the probability that a given peak in the periodogram is not significant, by

$$P(>z) \equiv 1 - (1 - e^{-z})^M$$

Press et al. (1992) suggest to use the Nyquist criterion (Chapter 5.2) to determine the number of independent frequencies M assuming that the data were evenly spaced. In this case, the best value for the number of independent frequencies is $M = 2N$, where N is the length of the time series.

More detailed discussions of the Lomb-Scargle method are given in Scargle (1989) and Press et al. (1992). An excellent summary of the method and a TURBO PASCAL program to compute the normalized Lomb-Scargle powerspectrum of paleoclimatic data has been published by Schulz and Stattegger (1998). A comfortable MATLAB algorithm `lombscargle` to compute the

Lomb-Scargle periodogram has been published by Brett Shoelson (The MathWorks Inc.) and can be downloaded from File Exchange at

```
http://www.mathworks.com/matlabcentral/fileexchange/
```

The following MATLAB code bases on the original FORTRAN code published by Scargle (1989). Significance testing uses the methods proposed by Press et al. (1992) explained above.

At first, we load the synthetic data that were generated to illustrate the use of the windowed Blackman-Tukey method in Chapter 5.6. The data contain periodicities of 100, 40 and 20 kyrs and additive gaussian noise. The data are unevenly spaced about the time axis. We define two new vectors t and y that contain the original time vector and the synthetic oxygen-isotope data sampled at times t.

```
clear
series3 = load('series3.txt');
t = series3(:,1);
y = series3(:,2);
```

We generate a frequency axis f. The Lomb-Scargle method is not able to deal with the zero-frequency piece, i.e., infinite periods. Therefore, we start at a frequency value that is equivalent to the spacing of the frequency vector. opac is the oversampling parameter that influences the resolution of the frequency axis about the N(frequencies)=N(datapoints) case. We also need the highest frequency fhi that can be analyzed by the Lomb-Scargle algorithm. A common way to choose fhi is to take the Nyquist frequency fnyq that would be obtained if the N data points were evenly spaced over the same time interval. The following code uses the input parameter hifac, which is defined as hifac=fhi/fnyq according to Press et al. (1992),

```
int = mean(diff(t));
ofac = 4; hifac = 1;
f = ((2*int)^(-1))/(length(y)*ofac): ...
    ((2*int)^(-1))/(length(y)*ofac): ...
    hifac*(2*int)^(-1);
```

where int is the mean sampling interval. We normalize the data by subtracting the mean.

```
y = y - mean(y);
```

We now compute the normalized Lomb-Scargle periodogram px as a function of the angular frequency wrun using the translation of the first equation in Chapter 5.7 into MATLAB code.

```
for k = 1:length(f)
    wrun = 2*pi*f(k);
    px(k) = 1/(2*var(y)) * ...
        ((sum(y.*cos(wrun*t - ...
        atan2(sum(sin(2*wrun*t)),sum(cos(2*wrun*t)))/2))).^2) ...
        /(sum((cos(wrun*t - ...
        atan2(sum(sin(2*wrun*t)),sum(cos(2*wrun*t)))/2)).^2)) + ...
        ((sum(y.*sin(wrun*t - ...
        atan2(sum(sin(2*wrun*t)),sum(cos(2*wrun*t)))/2))).^2) ...
        /(sum((sin(wrun*t - ...
        atan2(sum(sin(2*wrun*t)),sum(cos(2*wrun*t)))/2)).^2));
end
```

Now, the significance level of any peak in the powerspectrum `px` can be computed. The variable `prob` indicates the false-alarm probability of the null hypothesis. Therefore, a low `prob` indicates a highly significant peak in the powerspectrum.

```
prob = 1-(1-exp(-px)).^length(y);
```

We plot the powerspectrum and the probabilities (Fig. 5.14).

```
plot(f,px)
xlabel('Frequency')
ylabel('Power')
title('Lomb-Scargle Powerspectrum')

figure
plot(f,prob)
xlabel('Frequency')
ylabel('Probability')
title('Probabilities')
```

The two plots suggest that all three peaks are highly significant since the errors are extremely low at the cyclicities of 100, 40 and 20 kyrs.

An alternative way to display the significance levels was suggested by Press et al. (1992). Here, the equation for the false-alarm probability of the null hypothesis is inverted to compute the corresponding power of the significance levels. As an example, we choose a significance level of 95%. However, this number can also be replaced by a vector of several significance levels such as `signif=[0.90 0.95 0.99]`. We type

```
m = floor(0.5*ofac*hifac*length(y));
effm = 2*m/ofac;
signif = 0.95;
levels = log((1-signif.^(1/effm)).^(-1));
```

where `m` is the true number of independent frequencies and `effm` is the effective number of frequencies using the oversampling factor `ofac`. The

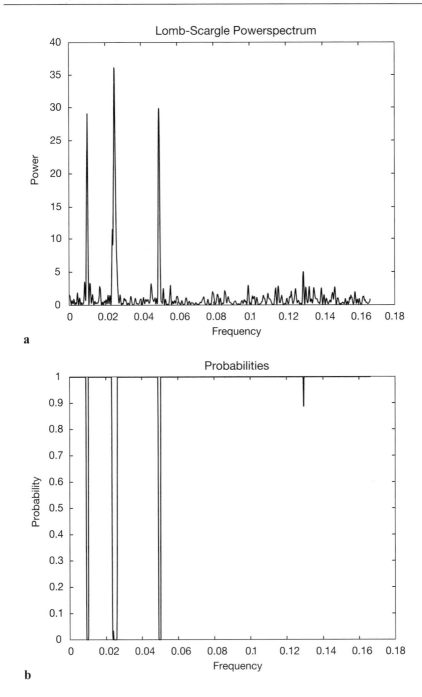

Fig. 5.14 a Lomb-Scargle powerspectrum and **b** the false-alarm probability of the null hypothesis. The plot suggests that the 100, 40 and 20 kyr cycles are highly significant.

second plot displays the spectral peaks and the corresponding probabilities.

```
plot(f,px)
hold on
for k = 1:length(signif)
    line(f,levels(:,k)*ones(size(f)),'LineStyle','--')
end
xlabel('Frequency')
ylabel('Power')
title('Lomb-Scargle Powerspectrum')
hold off
```

All three spectral peaks at frequencies of 0.01, 0.025 and 0.05 kyr^{-1} exceed the 95% significant level suggesting that they represent significant cyclicities. Therefore, we obtain similar results as for the Blackman-Tukey method. However, the Lomb-Scargle method does not require any interpolation of un-evenly-spaced data. Furthermore, it allows for quantitative significance testing.

5.8 Wavelet Powerspectrum

Chapter 5.6 has illustrated a modification of the Blackman-Tukey meth-od to map nonstationarities in the powerspectrum. In principle, a similar modification could be applied to the Lomb-Scargle method, which has the advantage that it can be applied to unevenly-spaced data. Both methods, however, assume that the data are a composite of sine and cosine waves that are globally uniform in time and have infinite spans. The evolutionary Blackman-Tukey method divides the time series into overlapping segments and computes the Fourier transform of these segments. To avoid spectral leakage, the data are multiplied by windows with finite lengths and smooth ends (Chapter 5.3). The higher the temporal resolution of the evolutionary powerspectrum the lower is the accuracy of the result. Moreover, short time windows contain a large number of high-frequency cycles whereas the low-frequency cycles are underrepresented.

In contrast to the Fourier transform, the *wavelet transform* uses base functions (*wavelets*) that have smooth ends *per se* (Lau and Weng 1995, Mackenzie et al. 2001). Wavelets are small packets of waves with a specific frequency that approach zero at both ends. Since wavelets can be stretched and translated with a flexible resolution in both frequency and time, they can easily map changes in the time-frequency domain. Mathematically, a wave-let transformation decomposes a signal $y(t)$ into some elementary functions $\psi_{a,b}(t)$ derived from a *mother wavelet* $\psi(t)$ by dilation and translation,

$$\psi_{a,b} = \frac{1}{(a)^{1/2}} \psi\left(\frac{t-b}{a}\right)$$

where b denotes the position (translation) and a (>0) the scale (dilation) of the wavelet (Lau and Weng 1995). The wavelet transform of the signal $y(t)$ about the mother wavelet $\psi(t)$ is defined as the convolution integral

$$W(b,a) = \frac{1}{(a)^{1/2}} \int \psi*\left(\frac{t-b}{a}\right) y(t)\,dt$$

where $\psi*$ is the complex conjugate of ψ defined on the open time and scale real (b,a) half plane.

There are many mother wavelets available in the literature, such as the the classic *Haar* wavelet, the *Morlet* wavelet and the *Daubechies* wavelet. The most popular wavelet in geosciences is the Morlet wavelet, which is given by

$$\psi_0(\eta) = \pi^{-1/4} \exp(i\omega_0\eta)\exp(-\eta^2/2)$$

where η is the non-dimensional time and ω_0 is the wavenumber (Torrence and Compo 1998). The wavenumber is the number of oscillations within the wavelet itself. We can easily compute a discrete version of the Morlet wavelet `wave` by translating the above equation into MATLAB code where `eta` is the non-dimensional time and `w0` is the wavenumber. Change `w0` to get wavelets with different wave numbers. Note it is important that `i` is not used as index in `for` loops since it is used here as imaginary unit (Fig. 5.15).

```
clear
eta = -10 : 0.1 : 10;
w0 = 6;
wave = pi.^(-1/4) .* exp(i*w0*eta) .* exp(-eta.^2/2);
plot(eta,wave)
xlabel('Position')
ylabel('Scale')
title('Morlet Mother Wavelet')
```

We use a pure sine wave with a period 5 and additive gaussian noise to get familiar with wavelet powerspectra.

```
clear
t = 0 : 0.5 : 50;
y = sin(2*pi*t/5) + randn(size(t));
```

In a first step, we define the number of scales for that the wavelet transform will be computed. The scales define how much a wavelet is stretched or compressed to map the variability of the time series on different wavelengths. Lower scales correspond to higher frequencies and therefore map rapidly-changing details, whereas higher scales map the long-term variations. As an example, we run the wavelet analysis for 120 different `scales` between 1 and 120.

```
scales = 1 : 120;
```

In a second step, we compute the real or complex continuous Morlet wavelet coefficients using the function `cwt` contained in the Wavelet Toolbox.

```
coefs = cwt(y,scales,'morl');
```

The function `scal2frq` converts scales to pseudo-frequencies, using the Morley mother wavelet and the sampling period 0.5.

```
f = scal2frq(scales,'morl',0.5);
```

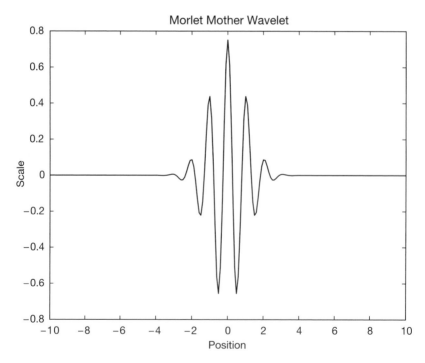

Fig. 5.15 Morlet mother wavelet with wavenumber 6.

We use a filled contour plot to visualize the powerspectrum, i.e., the absolute of the wavelet coefficients (Fig. 5.16).

```
contour(t,f,abs(coefs),'LineStyle','none','LineColor', ...
    [0 0 0],'Fill','on')
xlabel('Time')
ylabel('Frequency')
title('Wavelet Powerspectrum')
```

We apply this concept to the synthetic data from the example to demonstrate the windowed Blackman-Tukey method and load the synthetic data contained in file `series3.txt`. We recall that the data contain periodicities of 100, 40, 20 kyr and additive gaussian noise. The data are unevenly spaced about the time axis.

```
clear
series3 = load('series3.txt');
```

Similar to the Fourier transform and in contrast to the Lomb-Scargle algorithm, the wavelet transform requires evenly-spaced data. Therefore, we

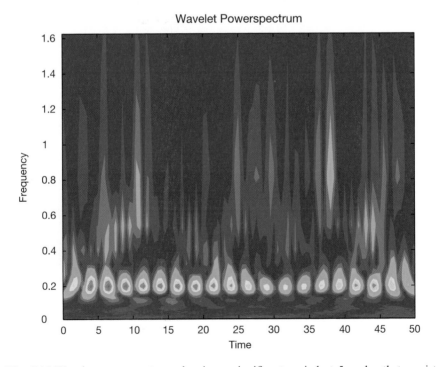

Fig. 5.16 Wavelet powerspectrum showing a significant period at 5 cycles that persists through the full length the time vector.

interpolate the data using `interp1`.

```
t = 0 : 3 : 1000;
y = interp1(series3(:,1),series3(:,2),t,'linear');
```

Similar to above example, we compute the wavelet transform of 120 scales using the function `cwt` and a Morley mother wavelet.

```
scales = 1 : 120;
coefs = cwt(y,scales,'morl');
```

We use `scal2freq` to convert scales to pseudo-frequencies, using the Morley mother wavelet and the sampling period of three.

```
f = scal2frq(scales,'morl',3);
```

We use a filled contour plot to visualize the powerspectrum, i.e., the absolute of the wavelet coefficients (Fig. 5.17).

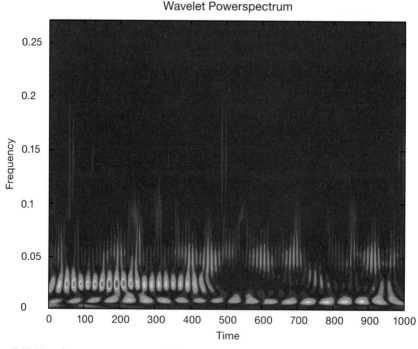

Fig. 5.17 Wavelet powerspectrum of the synthetic data series contained in *series_3.txt*. The plot clearly shows significant periodicities at frequencies of 0.1, 0.025 and 0.05 kyr^{-1} corresponding to the 100, 40 and 20 kyr cycles. The 100 kyr cycle is present through the entire time series, whereas the 40 kyr cycle appears at around 450 kyr before present. The 20 kyr cycle is relatively weak but probably present throughout the full time series.

```
contour(t,f,abs(coefs),'LineStyle', 'none', ...
    'LineColor',[0 0 0],'Fill','on')
xlabel('Time'),ylabel('Frequency')
title('Wavelet Powerspectrum')
```

The graph shows horizontal clusters of peaks at 0.01 and 0.05 kyr^{-1} corresponding to 100 and 20 kyr cycles, although the 20 kyr cycle is not very clear. The powerspectrum also reveals a significant 40 kyr cycle or a frequency of 0.025 kyr^{-1} that appears at ca. 450 kyr before present. Compared to the windowed Blackman-Tukey method, the wavelet powerspectrum clearly shows a much higher resolution on both the time and frequency axis. Instead of dividing the time series into overlapping segments and computing the powerspectrum for each segment, the wavelet transform uses short packets of waves that better map temporal changes in the cyclicities. The disadvantage of both the Blackman-Tukey and the wavelet powerspectral analysis, however, is the requirement of evenly-spaced data. The Lomb-Scargle method overcomes this problem, but has – similar to the Blackman-Tukey method – limited capabilities in mapping temporal changes in the frequency domain.

5.9 Nonlinear Time-Series Analysis (by N. Marwan)

The methods described in the previous sections detect linear relationships in the data. However, natural processes on the Earth often show a more complex and chaotic behavior. Methods based on linear techniques may therefore yield unsatisfying results. In the last decades, new techniques of nonlinear data analysis derived from chaos theory have become increasingly popular. As an example, methods have been employed to describe nonlinear behavior by defining, e.g., scaling laws and fractal dimensions of natural processes (Turcotte 1997, Kantz and Schreiber 1997). However, most methods of nonlinear data analysis need either long or stationary data series. These requirements are often not satisfied in the earth sciences. While most nonlinear techniques work well on synthetic data, these methods fail to describe nonlinear behavior in real data.

In the last decade, *recurrence plots* as a new method of nonlinear data analysis have become very popular in science and engineering (Eckmann 1987). Recurrence is a fundamental property of dissipative dynamical systems. Although small disturbancies of such a system cause exponentially divergence of its state, after some time the system will come back to a state that is arbitrary close to a former state and pass through a similar evolution.

Recurrence plots allow to visualize such a recurrent behavior of dynamical systems. The method is now a widely accepted tool for the nonlinear analysis of short and nonstationary data sets.

Phase Space Portrait

The starting point of most nonlinear data analysis is the construction of the phase space portrait of a system. The state of a system can be described by its state variables $x_1(t)$, $x_2(t)$, ..., $x_d(t)$. As an example, suppose the two variables *temperature* and *pressure* to describe the thermodynamic state of *the Earth's mantle* as a complex system. The d state variables at time t form a vector in a d-dimensional space, the so-called phase space. The state of a system typically changes in time. The vector in the phase space therefore describes a trajectory representing the temporal evolution, i.e., the dynamics of the system. The course of the trajectory provides all important information of the dynamics of the system, such as periodic or chaotic systems having characteristic phase space portraits.

In many applications, the observation of a natural process does not yield all possible state variables, either because they are not known or they cannot be measured. However, due to coupling between the system's components, we can reconstruct a phase space trajectory from a single observation u_i:

$$x_i = \left(u_i, u_{i+\tau}, \ldots, u_{i+(m-1)\tau} \right)^T$$

where m is the embedding dimension and τ is the time delay (index based; the real time delay is $\tau = \Delta t$). This reconstruction of the phase space is called *time delay embedding*. The phase space reconstruction is not exactly the same to the original phase space, but its topological properties are preserved, if the embedding dimension is large enough. In practice, the embedding dimension has to be larger then twice the the dimension of the attractor, or exactly $m > 2d+1$. The reconstructed trajectory is sufficient enough for the subsequent data analysis.

As an example, we now explore the phase space portrait of a harmonic oscillator, like an undamped pendulum. First, we create the position vector `y1` and the velocity vector `y2`

```
x = 0 : pi/10 : 3*pi;
y1 = sin(x);
y2 = cos(x);
```

The phase space portrait

```
plot(y1,y2)
xlabel('y_1')
ylabel('y_2')
```

is a circle, suggesting an exact recurrence of each state after one cycle
(Fig. 5.18). Using the time delay embedding, we can reconstruct this phase
space portrait using only one observation, e.g., the velocity vector, and a
delay of 5, which corresponds to a quarter of the period of our pendulum.

```
t = 5;
plot(y2(1:end-t),y2(1+t:end))
xlabel('y_1')
ylabel('y_2')
```

As we see, the reconstructed phase space is almost the same as the original
phase space. Next, we compare this phase space portrait with the one of a
typical nonlinear system, the Lorenz system (Lorenz 1963). While studying weather patterns, one realizes that weather often does not change as
predicted. In 1963, Edward Lorenz introduced a simple three-dimensional
model to describe turbulence in the atmosphere which exhibits such a chaotic behaviour. Small initial changes cause dramatic divergent weather patterns. This behavior is often referred to as butterfly effect. The Lorenz system consists of three coupled nonlinear differential equations for the three
variables, the two temperature distributions and the velocity.

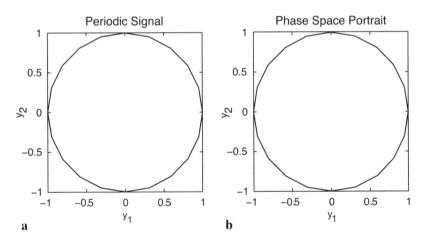

Fig. 5.18 a Original and **b** reconstructed phase space portrait of a periodic system. The
reconstructed phase space is almost the same as the original phase space.

$$\frac{dx}{dt} = s(y(t) - x(t)),$$

$$\frac{dy}{dt} = -x(t)z(t) + rx(t) - y(t),$$

$$\frac{dz}{dt} = x(t)y(t) - bz(t).$$

Integrating the differential equation yields a simple MATLAB code for computing the xyz triplets of the Lorenz system. As system parameters controlling the chaotic behavior we use `s=10`, `r=28` and `b=8/3`, the time delay is `dt=0.01`. The initial values are `x1=8`, `x2=9` and `x3=25`, that can certainly be changed at other values.

```
clear
dt = .01;
s = 10;
r = 28;
b = 8/3;
x1 = 8; x2 = 9; x3 = 25;
for i = 1 : 5000
    x1 = x1 + (-s*x1*dt) + (s*x2*dt);
    x2 = x2 + (r*x1*dt) - (x2*dt) - (x3*x1*dt);
    x3 = x3 + (-b*x3*dt) + (x1*x2*dt);
    x(i,:) = [x1 x2 x3];
end
```

Typical traces of a variable, such as the first variable can be viewed by plotting `x(:,1)` over time in seconds (Fig. 5.19).

```
t = 0.01 : 0.01 : 50;
plot(t,x(:,1))
xlabel('Time')
ylabel('Temperature')
```

We next plot the phase space portrait of the Lorenz system (Fig. 5.20).

```
plot3(x(:,1),x(:,2),x(:,3))
grid, view(70,30)
xlabel('x_1')
ylabel('x_2')
zlabel('x_3')
```

In contrast to the simple periodic system described above, the trajectories of the Lorenz system obviously do not follow the same course again, but it recurs very closely to a previous state. Moreover, if we follow two very close segments of the trajectory, we will see that they run into different regions

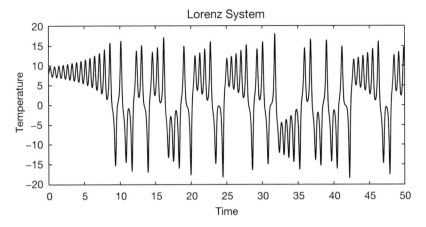

Fig. 5.19 The Lorenz system. As system parameters we use $s=10$, $r=28$ and $b=8/3$, the time delay is $dt=0.01$.

of the phase space with time. The trajectory is obviously circling one fixed point in the phase space – and after some random time period – circling around another. The curious orbit of the phase states around fixed points is known as the Lorenz attractor.

These observed properties are typical of chaotic systems. While small disturbances of such a system cause exponential divergence of its state, the system returns approximately to a previous state through a similar course. The reconstruction of the phase space portrait using only the first state and a delay of six

```
tau = 6;
plot3(x(1:end-2*tau,1),x(1+tau:end-tau,1),x(1+2*tau:end,1))
grid, view([100 60])
xlabel('x_1'), ylabel('x_2'), zlabel('x_3')
```

reveals a similar phase portrait with the two typical ears (Fig. 5.20). The characteristic properties of chaotic systems are also seen in this reconstruction.

The time delay and embedding dimension have to be chosen with a preceding analysis of the data. The delay can be estimated with the help of the autocovariance or autocorrelation function. For our example of a periodic oscillation,

```
x = 0 : pi/10 : 3*pi;
y1 = sin(x);
```

we compute and plot the autocorrelation function

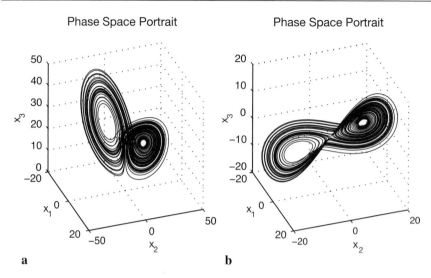

Fig. 5.20 a The phase space portrait of the Lorenz system. In contrast to the simple periodic system, the trajectories of the Lorenz system obviously do not follow the same course again, but it recurs very closely to a previous state. **b** The reconstruction of the phase space portrait using only the first state and a delay of six reveals a topologically similar phase portrait with the two typical ears.

```
for i = 1 : length(y1) - 2
    r = corrcoef(y1(1:end-i),y1(1+i:end));
    C(i) = r(1,2);
end

plot(C)
xlabel('Delay'), ylabel('Autocorrelation')
grid on
```

Now we choose such a delay at which the autocorrelation function equals zero for the first time. In our case this is 5, which is the value that we have already used in our example of phase space reconstruction. The appropriate embedding dimension can be estimated by using the false nearest neighbours method or, simpler, recurrence plots, which are introduced in the next chapter. The embedding dimension is gradually increased until the majority of the diagonal lines are parallel to the line of identity.

The phase space trajectory or its reconstruction is the base of several measures defined in nonlinear data analysis, like *Lyapunov exponents*, *Rényi entropies* or *dimensions*. The book on nonlinear data analysis by Kantz and Schreiber (1997) is recommended for more detailed information on these methods. Phase space trajectories or their reconstructions are also necessary for constructing recurrence plots.

Recurrence Plots

The phase space trajectories of dynamic systems that have more than three dimensions are difficult to visualize. *Recurrence plots* provide a way for analyzing higher dimensional systems. They can be used, e.g., to detect transitions between different regimes or to find interrelations between several systems. The method was first introduced by Eckmann and others (1987). The recurrence plot is a tool that visualizes the recurrences of states in the phase space by a two-dimensional plot.

$$R_{i,j} = \begin{cases} 0 & \left\| x_i - x_j \right\| > \varepsilon \\ 1 & \left\| x_i - x_j \right\| \le \varepsilon \end{cases}$$

If the distance between two states i and j on the trajectory are smaller than a given threshold ε, the value of the recurrence matrix R is one, otherwise zero. This analysis is therefore a pairwise test of all states. For N states we compute N^2 tests. The recurrence plot is then the two-dimensional display of the $N \times N$ matrix, where black pixels represent $R_{i,j}=1$ and white pixels indicate $R_{i,j}=0$ and a coordinate system representing two time axes. Such recurrence plots can help to find a first characterization of the dynamics of data or to find transitions and interrelations of the system (cf. Fig. 5.21).

As a first example, we load the synthetic time series containing 100 kyr, 40 kyr and 20 kyr cycles already used in the previous chapter. Since the data are unevenly spaced, we have to linearly transform it to an evenly-spaced time axis.

```
series1 = load('series1.txt');
t = 0 : 3 : 996;
series1L = interp1(series1(:,1),series1(:,2),t,'linear');
```

We start with the assumption that the phase space is only one-dimensional. The calculation of the distances between all points of the phase space trajectory reveals the distance matrix S.

```
N = length(series1L);
S = zeros(N, N);

for i = 1 : N,
    S(:,i) = abs(repmat(series1L(i), N, 1 ) - series1L(:));
end
```

Now we plot the distance matrix

```
imagesc(t,t,S)
colorbar
xlabel('Time'), ylabel('Time')
```

for the data set, where a colorbar provides a quantitative measure for the distances between states (Fig. 5.22). We apply a threshold ε to the distance matrix to generate the black/white recurrence plot (Fig. 5.23).

```
imagesc(t,t,S<1)
colormap([1 1 1;0 0 0])
xlabel('Time'), ylabel('Time')
```

Both plots reveal periodically occurring patterns. The distances between

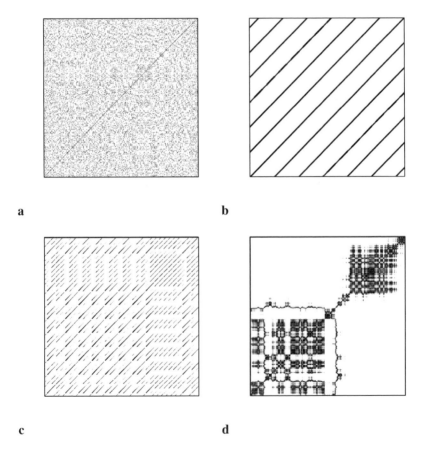

a   b

c   d

Fig. 5.21 Recurrence plots representing typical dynamical behaviours: **a** stationary uncorrelated data (white noise), **b** periodic oscillation, **c** chaotic data (Roessler system) and **d** non-stationary data with abrupt changes.

these periodic patterns represent the cycles contained in the time series. The most significant periodic structures have periods of 200 and 100 kyr. The 200 kyr period is most significant because of the superposition of the 100 and 40 kyr cycles, which are common divisors of 200 kyr. Moreover, there are small substructures in the recurrence plot, which have sizes of 40 and 20 kyr.

As a second example, we apply the method of recurrence plots to the Lorenz system. We again generate *xyz* triplets from the coupled differential equations.

```
clear
dt = .01;
s = 10;
r = 28;
b = 8/3;
x1 = 8; x2 = 9; x3 = 25;
```

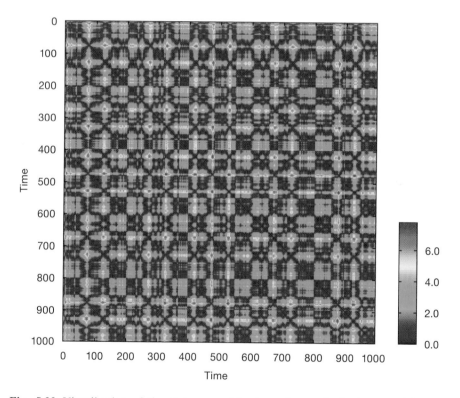

Fig. 5.22 Visualization of the distance matrix from the synthetic data providing a quantitative measure for the distances between states at certain times; blue colors indicate small distances, red colors represent large distances.

```
for i = 1 : 5000
    x1 = x1 + (-s*x1*dt) + (s*x2*dt);
    x2 = x2 + (r*x1*dt) - (x2*dt) - (x3*x1*dt);
    x3 = x3 + (-b*x3*dt) + (x1*x2*dt);
    x(i,:) = [x1 x2 x3];
end
```

We choose the resampled first component of this system and reconstruct a phase space trajectory by using an embedding of $m=3$ and $\tau=2$, which corresponds to a delay of 0.17 sec.

```
t = 0.01 : 0.05 : 50;
y = x(1:5:5000,1);
m = 3; tau = 2;

N = length(y);
N2 = N - tau*(m - 1);
```

The original data series has a length of 5000, after resampling 1000 data points or 50 sec, but because of the time delay method, the reconstructed

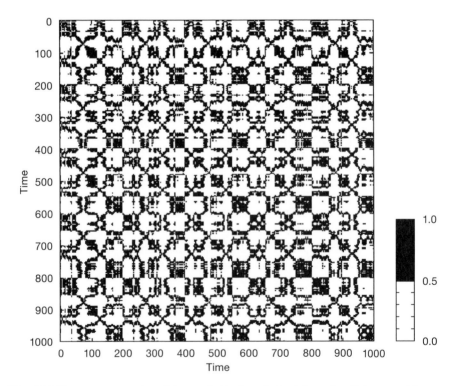

Fig. 5.23 The recurrence plot of the synthetic data derived from the distance matrix as shown in Fig. 5.22 after applying a threshold of $\varepsilon=1$.

phase space trajectory has the length 996. Now we create the phase space trajectory with

```
for mi = 1:m
    xe(:,mi) = y([1:N2] + tau*(mi-1));
end
```

We can accelerate the pair-wise test between each points on the trajectory with a fully vectorized algorithm supported by MATLAB. For that we need to transfer the trajectory vector into two test vectors, whose component-wise test will provide the pair-wise test of the trajectory vector:

```
x1 = repmat(xe,N2,1);
x2 = reshape(repmat(xe(:),1,N2)',N2*N2,m);
```

Using these vectors we calculate the recurrence plot using the Euclidean norm without any FOR loop.

```
S = sqrt(sum((x1 - x2).^ 2,2 ));
S = reshape(S,N2,N2);

imagesc(t(1:N2),t(1:N2),S<10)
colormap([1 1 1;0 0 0])
xlabel('Time'), ylabel('Time')
```

This recurrence plot reveals many short diagonal lines (Fig. 5.24). These lines represent epochs, where the phase space trajectory runs parallel to former or later sequences of this trajectory, i.e., the states and the dynamics are similar at these times. The distances between these diagonal lines, representing the periods of the cycles, differ and are not constant – just as they are in a harmonic oscillation (cp. Fig. 5.21).

The structure of recurrence plots can also be described by a suite of quantitative measures. Several measures are based on the distribution of the lengths of diagonal or vertical lines. These parameters can be used to trace hidden transitions in a process. Bivariate and multivariate extensions of recurrence plots furthermore offer nonlinear correlation tests and synchronization analysis. A detailed introduction to recurrence plot based methods can be found at the web site

```
http://www.recurrence-plot.tk
```

The analysis of recurrence plots has already been applied to many problems in earth sciences. The comparison of the dynamics of modern precipitation data with paleo-rainfall data inferred from annual-layered lake sediments in the northwestern Argentine Andes provides a good example of such anal-

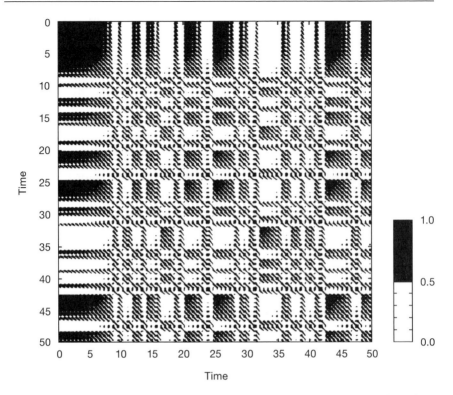

Fig. 5.24 The recurrence plot of the Lorenz system using a threshold of $\varepsilon = 10$. The regions with organized diagonal lines reveal unstable periodic orbits, typical for chaotic systems.

ysis (Marwan et al. 2003). In this example, the method of recurrence plots was applied to red-color intensity transects across ca. 30 kyr-old varved lake sediments shown in Figure 5.1. Comparing the recurrence plots from the sediments with the ones from modern precipitation data revealed that the reddish layers document more intense rainy seasons during the La Niña years. The application of linear techniques was not able to link the increased flux of reddish clays and enhanced precipitation to either the El Niño or La Niña phase of the ENSO. Moreover, recurrence plots helped to prove the hypothesis that a longer rainy seasons, enhanced precipitation and stronger influence of the El Niño/Southern Oscillation has caused enhanced land-sliding at 30 kyrs ago (Marwan et al. 2003, Trauth et al. 2003).

Recommended Reading

Eckmann JP, Kamphorst SO, Ruelle D (1987) Recurrence Plots of Dynamical Systems. Europhysics Letters 5:973-977

Kantz H, Schreiber T (1997) Nonlinear Time Series Analysis. Cambridge University Press, Cambridge

Lau KM, Weng H (1995) Climate Signal Detection Using Wavelet Transform: How to make a Time Series Sing. Bulletin of the American Meteorological Society 76:2391–2402

Lomb NR (1972) Least-Squared Frequency Analysis of Unequally Spaced Data. Astrophysics and Space Sciences 39:447–462

Lorenz EN (1963) Deterministic Nonperiodic Flow. Journal of Atmospheric Sciences 20:130-141

Mackenzie D, Daubechies I, Kleppner D, Mallat S, Meyer Y, Ruskai MB, Weiss G (2001) Wavelets: Seeing the Forest and the Trees. Beyond Discovery, National Academy of Sciences, December 2001, available online at http://www.beyonddiscovery.org

Marwan N, Thiel M, Nowaczyk NR (2002) Cross Recurrence Plot Based Synchronization of Time Series. Nonlinear Processes in Geophysics 9(3/4):325-331

Marwan N, Trauth MH, Vuille M, Kurths J (2003) Nonlinear Time-Series Analysis on Present-Day and Pleistocene Precipitation Data from the NW Argentine Andes. Climate Dynamics 21:317-332

Press WH, Teukolsky SA, Vetterling WT (1992) Numerical Recipes in Fortran 77. Cambridge University Press, Cambridge

Press WH, Teukolsky SA, Vetterling WT, Flannery BP (2002) Numerical Recipes in C++. Cambridge University Press. Cambridge

Romano M, Thiel M, Kurths J, von Bloh W (2004) Multivariate Recurrence Plots. Physics Letters A 330(3-4):214-223

Scargle JD (1981) Studies in Astronomical Time Series Analysis. I. Modeling Random Processes in the Time Domain. The Astrophysical Journal Supplement Series 45:1–71

Scargle JD (1982) Studies in Astronomical Time Series Analysis. II. Statistical Aspects of Spectral Analysis of Unevenly Spaced Data. The Astrophysical Journal 263:835–853

Scargle JD (1989) Studies in Astronomical Time Series Analysis. III. Fourier Transforms, Autocorrelation Functions, and Cross-Correlation Functions of Unevenly Spaced Data.

Schulz M, Stattegger K (1998) SPECTRUM: Spectral Analysis of Unevenly Spaced Paleoclimatic Time Series. Computers & Geosciences 23:929-945

Takens F (1981) Detecting Strange Attractors in Turbulence. Lecture Notes in Mathematics, 898:366-381

The Mathworks (2006) Signal Processing Toolbox User's Guide – For the Use with MATLAB®. The MathWorks, Natick, MA

Torrence C, Compo GP (1998) A Practical Guide to Wavelet Analysis. Bulletin of the American Meteorological Society 79:61-78

Trulla LL, Giuliani A, Zbilut JP, Webber Jr CL (1996) Recurrence Quantification Analysis of the Logistic Equation with Transients. Physics Letters A 223(4):255-260

Turcotte DL (1992) Fractals and Chaos in Geology and Geophysics. Cambridge University Press, Cambridge

Trauth MH, Bookhagen B, Marwan N, Strecker MR (2003) Multiple Landslide Clusters Record Quaternary Climate Changes in the NW Argentine Andes. Palaeogeography Palaeoclimatology Palaeoecology 194:109-121

Weedon G (2003) Time-Series Analysis and Cyclostratigraphy - Examining Stratigraphic Records of Environmental Change. Cambridge University Press, Cambridge

Welch PD (1967) The Use of Fast Fourier Transform for the Estimation of Powerspectra: A Method Based on Time Averaging over Short, Modified Periodograms. IEEE Trans. Audio Electroacoustics AU-15:70-73

6 Signal Processing

6.1 Introduction

Signal processing refers to techniques for manipulating a signal to mini-mize the effects of noise, to correct all kinds of unwanted distortions or to separate various components of interest. Most signal processing algorithms include the design and realization of filters. A *filter* can be described as a system that transforms signals. *System theory* provides the mathematical background for filter design and realization. A filter as a system has an input and an output, where the *output signal* $y(t)$ is modified with respect to the *input signal* $x(t)$ (Fig. 6.1). The *signal transformation* is often called convo-lution or, if filters are applied, filtering.

This chapter is on the design and realization of *digital filters* with the help of a computer. However, many natural processes resemble *analog filters* that act over a range of spatial dimensions. A single rainfall event is not recorded in lake sediments because short and low-amplitude events are smeared over a longer time span. Bioturbation also introduces serious distortions for instance to deep-sea sediment records. Aside from such natural filters, the field collection and sampling of geological data alters and smoothes the data with respect to its original form. For example, a finite size sediment sample integrates over a certain period of time and therefore smoothes the natural signal. Similarly, the measurement of mag-

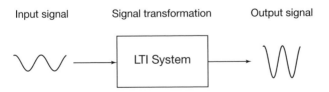

Fig. 6.1 Schematic of a linear time-invariant (LTI) system. The input signal is transformed into an output signal.

netic susceptibility with the help of a loop sensor introduces significant smoothing since the loop integrates over a certain section of the sediment core.

The characteristics of these natural filters are often difficult to determine. Numerical filters, however, are designed with well-defined characteristics. In addition, artificial filters are time invariant in most cases, while natural filters, such as lake mixing or bioturbation, may change with time. An easy way to describe or predict the effect of a filter is to explore the filter output of a simple input signal, such as a sine wave, a square wave, a sawtooth, ramp or step function. Although there is an endless variety of such signals, most systems or filters are described by their impulse response, i.e., the output of a unit impulse.

The chapter starts with a more technical section on generating periodic signals, trends and noise, similar to Chapter 5.2. Chapter 6.3 is on linear time-invariant systems, which provide the mathematical background for filters. The following Chapters 6.4 to 6.9 are on the design, the realization and the application of linear time-invariant filters. Chapter 6.10 then suggests the application of adaptive filters originally developed in telecommunication. Adaptive filters automatically extract noisefree signals from duplicate measurements on the same object. Such filters can be used in a large number of applications, such as noise removal from duplicate paleoceanographic time series or to improve the signal-to-noise ratio of parallel color-intensity transects across varved lake sediments (see Chapter 5, Fig. 5.1). Moreover, such filters are also widley-used in geophysics for noise canceling.

6.2 Generating Signals

MATLAB provides numerous tools to generate basic signals that can be used to illustrate the effects of filters. In Chapter 5, we have generated a signal by adding together three sine waves with different amplitudes and periods. In the following example, the time vector is transposed for the purpose of generating column vectors.

```
t = (1:100)';
x = 2*sin(2*pi*t/50) + sin(2*pi*t/15) + 0.5*sin(2*pi*t/5);

plot(t,x), axis([0 100 -4 4])
```

Frequency-selective filters are very common in earth sciences. They are used for removing certain frequency bands from the data. As an example, we could design a filter that has the capability to suppress the portion of the signal with a periodicity of $\tau=15$, whereas the other two cycles are unaffected. Such simple periodic signals can also be used to predict signal distortions of natural filters.

A *step function* is another basic input signal that can be used for exploring filter characteristics. It describes the transition from a value of one towards zero at a certain time.

```
t = (1:100)';
x = [ones(50,1);zeros(50,1)];

plot(t,x), axis([0 100 -2 2])
```

This signal can be used to study the effects of a filter on a sudden transition. An abrupt climate change could be regarded as an example. Most natural filters tend to smooth such a transition and smear it over a longer time period.

The *unit impulse* is the third important signal that we will use in the following examples. This signal equals zero for all times except for a single data point which equals one.

```
t = (1:100)';
x = [zeros(49,1);1;zeros(50,1)];

plot(t,x), axis([0 100 -4 4])
```

The unit impulse is the most popular synthetic signal for studying the performance of a filter. The output of the filter, the impulse response, describes the characteristics of a filter very well. Moreover, the output of a linear time-invariant filter can be described by the superposition of impulse responses that have been scaled by the amplitude of the input signal.

6.3 Linear Time-Invariant Systems

Filters can be described as systems with an input and output. Therefore, we first describe the characteristics of a more general system before we apply this theory to filters. Important characteristics of a system are

- *Continuity* – A system with continuous inputs and outputs is continuous. Most of the natural systems are continuous. However, after sampling natural signals we obtain discrete data series and model these natural systems as discrete systems, which have discrete inputs and outputs.

- *Linearity* – For linear systems, the output of the linear combination of several input signals

$$x(t) = k_1 x_1(t) + k_2 x_2(t)$$

is the same linear combination of the outputs:

$$y(t) = k_1 y_1(t) + k_2 y_2(t)$$

The important consequence of linearity is scaling and additivity (*superposition*). Input and output can be multiplied by a constant before or after transformation. Superposition allows to extract additive components of the input and transform these separately. Fortunately, many natural systems show a linear behavior. Complex linear signals such as additive harmonic components can be separated and transformed independently. Milankovitch cycles provide an example of linear superposition in paleoclimate records, although there is an ongoing debate about the validity of this assumption. Numerous nonlinear systems exist in nature that do not obey the properties of scaling and additivity. An example of such a linear system is

```
x = (1:100)';
y = 2*x;

plot(x,y)
```

An example of a nonlinear system is

```
x = (-100:100)';
y = x.^2;

plot(x,y)
```

- *Time invariance* – The system output $y(t)$ does not change with a delay of the input $x(t+i)$. The system characteristics are constant with time. Unfortunately, natural systems often change their characteristics with time. For instance, benthic mixing or bioturbation depends on various environmental parameters such as nutrient supply. Therefore, the system's performance varies with time significantly. In such case, the actual input of the system is hard to determine from the output, e.g., to extract the actual climate signal from a bioturbated sedimentary record.

- *Invertibility* – An invertible system is a system where the original input signal can be reproduced from the system's output. This is an important property if unwanted signal distortions have to be corrected. Here, the known system is inverted and applied to the output to reconstruct the undisturbed input. As an example, a core logger measuring the magnetic susceptibility with a loop sensor integrates over a certain core interval with highest sensitivity at the location of the loop and decreasing sensitivity down- and up-core. The above system is also invertible, i.e., we can compute the input signal from the output signal by inverting the system. The inverse system of the above linear system is

```
x = (1:100)';
y = 0.5*x;

plot(t,y)
```

The nonlinear system

```
x = (-100:100)';
y = x.^2;

plot(x,y)
```

is not invertible. Since this system yields equal responses for different inputs, such as $y=+4$ for inputs $x=-2$ and $x=+2$, the input cannot be reconstructed from the output. A similar situation can also occur in linear systems, such as

```
x = (1:100)';
y = 0;

plot(x,y)
```

The output is zero for all inputs. Therefore, the output does not contain any information about the input.

- *Causality* – The system response only depends on present and past inputs $x(0)$, $x(-1)$, ..., whereas future inputs $x(+1)$, $x(+2)$, ... have no effect on the output $y(0)$. All realtime systems, such telecommunication systems, must be causal since they cannot have future inputs available to them. All systems and filters in MATLAB are indexed as causal. In earth sciences, however, numerous non-causal filters are used. Filtering images and signals extracted from sediment cores are examples where the future inputs are available at the time of filtering. Output signals have to be delayed after filtering to compensate the differences between causal and non-causal indexing.

• *Stability* – A system is stable if the output of a finite input is also finite. Stability is critical in filter design, where filters often have the disadvantage of provoking diverging outputs. In such cases, the filter design has to be revised and improved.

Linear time-invariant (LTI) systems as a special type of filters are very popular. Such systems have all the advantages that have been described above. They are easy to design and to use in many applications. The following chapters 6.4 to 6.9 describe the design, realization and application of LTI-type filters to extract certain frequency components of signals. These filters are mainly used to reduce the noise level in signals. Unfortunately, many natural systems do not behave as LTI systems. The signal-to-noise ratio often varies with time. Chapter 6.10 describes the application of adaptive filters that automatically adjust their characteristics in a time-variable environment.

6.4 Convolution and Filtering

The mathematical description of a system transformation is the convolution. Filtering is one application of the convolution process. A running mean of length five provides an example of such a simple filter. The output of an arbitrary input signal is

$$y(t) = \frac{1}{5} \sum_{k=-2}^{2} x(t-k)$$

The output $y(t)$ is simply the average of the five input values $x(t-2)$, $x(t-1)$, $x(t)$, $x(t+1)$ and $x(t+2)$. In other words, all the five consecutive input values are multiplied by a factor of 1/5 and summed to form $y(t)$. In this example, all input values are multiplied by the same factor, i.e., they are equally weighted. The five factors used in the above operation are also called filter weights b_k. The filter can be represented by the vector

```
b = [0.2 0.2 0.2 0.2 0.2]
```

consisting of the identical filter weights. Since this filter is symmetric, it does not shift the signal on the time axis. The only function of this filter is to smooth the signal. Therefore, running means of a given length are often used to smooth signals, mainly for cosmetic reasons. A modern spreadsheet software usually contains running means as a function for smoothing data series. The impact of the smoothing filter increases with increasing filter length.

The weights that a filter of arbitrary length may take can vary. As an example, let us assume an asymmetric filter of five weights.

```
b = [0.05 0.08 0.14 0.26 0.47]
```

The sum of all of the filter weights is one. Therefore, it does not introduce energy to the signal. However, since it is highly asymmetric, it shifts the signal along the time axis, i.e., it introduces a phase shift.

The general mathematical representation of the filtering process is the *convolution*:

$$y(t) = \sum_{k=-N_1}^{N_2} b_k \cdot x(t-k)$$

where b_k is the vector of *filter weights*, N_1+N_2 is the *order of the filter*, which is the length of the filter reduced by one. Filters with five weights have an order of four, as in our example. In contrast to this format, MATLAB uses the engineering standard of indexing filters, i.e., filters are always defined as causal. Therefore, the convolution used by MATLAB is

$$y(t) = \sum_{k=0}^{N} b_k \cdot x(t-k)$$

where N is the order of the filter. A number of frequency-domain tools provided by MATLAB cannot simply be applied to non-causal filters that have been designed for applications in earth sciences. Hence, it is common to carry out phase corrections to simulate non-causality. For example, frequency-selective filters as introduced in Chapter 6.9 can be applied using the function `filtfilt`, which provides zero-phase forward and reverse filtering.

The functions `conv` and `filter` that provide digital filtering with MATLAB are best illustrated in terms of a simple running mean. The n elements of the vector $x(t_1), x(t_2), x(t_3), ..., x(t_n)$ are replaced by the arithmetic means of subsets of the input vector. For instance, a running mean over three elements computes the mean of inputs $x(t_{n-1}), x(t_n), x(t_{n+1})$ to obtain the output $y(t_n)$. We can easily illustrate this by generating a random signal

```
clear
```

```
t = (1:100)';
randn('seed',0);
x1 = randn(100,1);
```

designing a filter that averages three data points of the input signal

```
b1 = [1 1 1]/3;
```

and convolving the input vector with the filter

```
y1 = conv(b1,x1);
```

The elements of b1 are the weights of the filter. In our example, all filter
weights are the same and they equal $1/3$. Note that the conv function yields
a vector that has the length $n+m-1$, where m is the length of the filter.

```
m1 = length(b1);
```

We should explore the contents of our workspace to check for the length of
the input and output of conv. Typing

```
whos
```

yields

Name	Size	Bytes	Class	Attributes
b1	1x3	24	double	
m1	1x1	8	double	
t	100x1	800	double	
x1	100x1	800	double	
y1	102x1	816	double	

Here, we see that the actual input series x1 has a length of 100 data points,
whereas the output y1 has two more elements. Generally, convolution introduces $(m-1)/2$ data points at both ends of the data series. To compare input
and output signal, we cut the output signal at both ends.

```
y1 = y1(2:101,1);
```

A more general way to correct the phase shifts of conv is

```
y1 = y1(1+(m1-1)/2:end-(m1-1)/2,1);
```

which of course works only for an odd number of filter weights. Then, we
can plot both input and output signals for comparison. We also use legend
to display a legend for the plot.

```
plot(t,x1,'b-',t,y1,'r-')
legend('x1(t)','y1(t)')
```

This plot illustrates the effect of the running mean on the original input series. The output `y1` is significantly smoother than the input signal `x1`. If we
increase the length of the filter, we obtain an even smoother signal.

```
b2 = [1 1 1 1 1]/5;
m2 = length(b2);

y2 = conv(b2,x1);
y2 = y2(1+(m2-1)/2:end-(m2-1)/2,1);

plot(t,x1,'b-',t,y1,'r-',t,y2,'g-')
legend('x1(t)','y1(t)','y2(t)')
```

The next chapter introduces a more general description of filters.

6.5 Comparing Functions for Filtering Data Series

A very simple example of a *nonrecursive filter* was described in the previous section. The filter output $y(t)$ depends only on the filter input $x(t)$ and
the filter weights b_k. Prior to introducing a more general description for
linear time-invariant filters, we replace the function `conv` by `filter` that
can be used also for *recursive filters*. In this case, the output $y(t_n)$ depends
on the filter input $x(t)$, but also on previous elements of the output $y(t_{n-1})$,
$y(t_{n-2})$, $y(t_{n-3})$ and so on (Chapter 6.6). First, we use `filter` for nonrecursive filters.

```
clear

t = (1:100)';
randn('seed',0);
x3 = randn(100,1);
```

We design a filter that averages five data points of the input signal.

```
b3 = [1 1 1 1 1]/5;
m3 = length(b3);
```

The input vector can be convolved with the function `conv`. The output is
again corrected for the length of the data vector.

```
y3 = conv(b3,x3);
y3 = y3(1+(m3-1)/2:end-(m3-1)/2,1);
```

Although the function `filter` yields an output vector with the same length as the input vector, we have to correct the output as well. Here, the function `filter` assumes that the filter is causal. The filter weights are indexed n, $n-1$, $n-2$ and so on. Therefore, no future elements of the input vector, such as $x(n+1)$, $x(n+2)$ etc. are needed to compute the output $y(n)$. This is of great importance in electrical engineering, the classic field of application of MATLAB, where filters are often applied in real time. In earth sciences, however, in most applications the entire signal is available at the time of processing the data. Filtering the data series is done by

```
y4 = filter(b3,1,x3);
```

and afterwards the phase correction is carried out using

```
y4 = y4(1+(m3-1)/2:end-(m3-1)/2,1);
y4(end+1:end+m3-1,1) = zeros(m3-1,1);
```

which works only for an odd number of filter weights. This command simply shifts the output by $(m-1)/3$ towards the lower end of the t-axis, then fills the end of the data series by zeros. Comparing the ends of both outputs illustrates the effect of this correction, where

```
y3(1:5,1)
y4(1:5,1)
```

yields

```
ans =
     0.3734
     0.4437
     0.3044
     0.4106
     0.2971

ans =
     0.3734
     0.4437
     0.3044
     0.4106
     0.2971
```

This was the lower end of the output. We see that both vectors `y3` and `y4` contain the same elements. Now we explorer the upper end of the data vector, where

```
y3(end-5:end,1)
y4(end-5:end,1)
```

causes the output

```
ans =
     0.2268
     0.1592
     0.3292
     0.2110
     0.3683
     0.2414

ans =
     0.2268
     0.1592
          0
          0
          0
          0
```

The vectors are identical up to element `y(end-m3+1)`, then the second vector `y4` contains zeros instead of true data values. Plotting the results with

```
subplot(2,1,1), plot(t,x3,'b-',t,y3,'g-')
subplot(2,1,2), plot(t,x3,'b-',t,y4,'g-')
```

or in one single plot,

```
plot(t,x3,'b-',t,y3,'g-',t,y4,'r-')
```

shows that the results of `conv` and `filter` are identical except for the upper end of the data vector. These observations are important for our next steps in signal processing, particularly if we are interested in leads and lags between various components of signals.

6.6 Recursive and Nonrecursive Filters

Now we expand the nonrecursive filters by a recursive component, i.e., the output $y(t_n)$ depends on the filter input $x(t)$, but also on previous output values $y(t_{n-1}), y(t_{n-2}), y(t_{n-3})$ and so on. This filter requires the nonrecursive filter weights b_i, but also the recursive filters weights a_i (Fig. 6.2). This filter can be described by the *difference equation*:

$$y(t) = \sum_{k=-N_1}^{N_2} b_k \cdot x(t-k) - \sum_{k=1}^{M} a_k \cdot y(t-k)$$

Whereas this is a non-causal version of the difference equation, MATLAB uses the causal indexing again,

Input signal x(t)

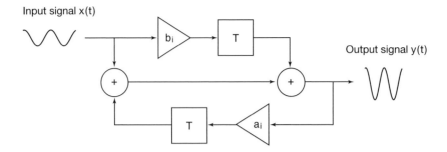

Output signal y(t)

Fig. 6.2 Schematic of a linear time-invariant filter with an input $x(t)$ and an output $y(t)$. The filter is characterized by its weights a_i and b_i, and the delay elements T. Nonrecursive filters only have nonrecursive weights b_i, whereas the recursive filter also requires the recursive filters weights a_i.

$$y(t) = \sum_{k=0}^{N} b_k \cdot x(t-k) - \sum_{k=1}^{M} a_k \cdot y(t-k)$$

with the known problems in the design of zero-phase filters. The larger of the two quantities M and $N_1 + N_2$ or N is the order of the filter.

We use the same synthetic input signal as in the previous example to illustrate the performance of a recursive filter.

```
clear
t = (1:100)';
randn('seed',0);
x5 = randn(100,1);
```

We filter this input using a recursive filter with a set of weights a5 and b5,

```
b5 = [0.0048    0.0193    0.0289    0.0193    0.0048];
a5 = [1.0000    -2.3695   2.3140    -1.0547   0.1874];

m5 = length(b5);

y5 = filter(b5,a5,x5);
```

and correct the output for the phase

```
y5 = y5(1+(m5-1)/2:end-(m5-1)/2,1);
y5(end+1:end+m5-1,1) = zeros(m5-1,1);
```

Now we plot the results.

```
plot(t,x5,'b-',t,y5,'r-')
```

Obviously, this filter changes the signal dramatically. The output contains only low-frequency components, whereas all higher frequencies are eliminated. The comparison of the periodograms of the input and the output reveals that all frequencies above $f = 0.1$ corresponding to a period of $\tau = 10$ are suppressed.

```
[Pxx,F] = periodogram(x5,[],128,1);
[Pyy,F] = periodogram(y5,[],128,1);

plot(F,abs(Pxx),F,abs(Pyy))
```

Hence, we have now designed a frequency-selective filter, i.e., a filter that eliminates certain frequencies whereas other periodicities are relatively unaffected. The next chapter introduces tools to characterize a filter in the time and frequency domain that help to predict the effect of a frequency-selective filter on arbitrary signals.

6.7 Impulse Response

The impulse response is a very convenient way of describing the filter characteristics (Fig. 6.3). A useful property of the impulse response h in LTI systems involves the convolution of the input signal $x(t)$ with h to obtain the output signal $y(t)$.

$$y(t) = \sum_{k=-N_1}^{N_2} h_k \cdot x(t-k)$$

It can be shown that the impulse response h is identical to the filter weights in the case of nonrecursive filters, but is different for recursive filters. Alternatively, the convolution is often written in a short form:

$$y(t) = h(t) * x(t)$$

In many examples, the convolution in the time domain is replaced by a simple multiplication of the Fourier transforms $H(f)$ and $X(f)$ in the frequency domain.

$$Y(f) = H(f) \cdot X(f)$$

The output signal $y(t)$ in the time domain is then obtained by a reverse

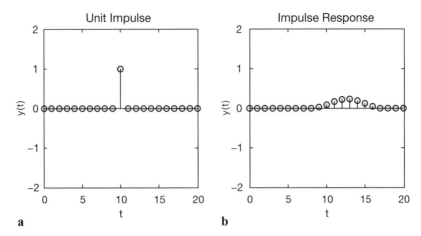

Fig. 6.3 Transformation of **a** a unit impulse to compute **b** the impulse response of a system. The impulse response is often used to describe and predict the performance of a filter.

Fourier transformation of $Y(f)$. The signals are often convolved in the frequency domain for simplicity of the multiplication as compared to a convolution in the time domain. However, the Fourier transformation itself introduces a number of artifacts and distortions and therefore, convolution in the frequency domain is not without problems. In the following examples we apply the convolution only in the time domain.

First, we generate an unit impulse:

```
clear
t = (0:20)';
x6 = [zeros(10,1);1;zeros(10,1)];

stem(t,x6), axis([0 20 -4 4])
```

The function `stem` plots the data sequence `x6` as stems from the x-axis terminated with circles for the data value. This might be a better way to plot digital data than using the continuous lines generated by `plot`. We now feed this to the filter and explore the output. The impulse response is identical to the weights of nonrecursive filters.

```
b6 = [1 1 1 1 1]/5;
m6 = length(b6);

y6 = filter(b6,1,x6);
```

We correct this for the phase shift of the function `filter` again, although this might not be important in this example.

```
y6 = y6(1+(m6-1)/2:end-(m6-1)/2,1);
y6(end+1:end+m6-1,1) = zeros(m6-1,1);
```

We obtain an output vector y6 of the same length and phase as the input vector x6. We plot the results for comparison.

```
stem(t,x6)
hold on
stem(t,y6,'filled','r')
axis([0 20 -2 2])
```

In contrast to plot, the function stem accepts only one data series. There-fore, the second series y6 is overlaid on the same plot using the function hold. The effect of the filter is clearly seen on the plot. It averages the unit impulse over a length of five elements. Furthermore, the values of the output equal the filter weights of a6, in our example 0.2 for all elements of a6 and y6.

For a recursive filter, the output y6 does not agree with the filter weights. Again, an impulse is generated first.

```
clear
t = (0:20)';
x7 = [zeros(10,1);1;zeros(10,1)];
```

Subsequently, an arbitrary recursive filter with weights of a7 and b7 is de-signed.

```
b7 = [0.0048    0.0193    0.0289    0.0193    0.0048];
a7 = [1.0000   -2.3695    2.3140   -1.0547    0.1874];

m7 = length(b7);

y7 = filter(b7,a7,x7);

y7 = y7(1+(m7-1)/2:end-(m7-1)/2,1);
y7(end+1:end+m7-1,1) = zeros(m7-1,1);
```

The stem plot of the input x2 and the output y2 shows an interesting im-pulse response:

```
stem(t,x7)
hold on
stem(t,y7,'filled','r')
axis([0 20 -2 2])
```

The signal is again smeared over a wider area. It is also shifted towards the right. Therefore, this filter not only affects the amplitude of the signal, but also shifts the signal towards lower or higher values. Phase shifts are usu-ally unwanted characteristics of filters, although in some applications shifts along the time axis might be of particular interest.

6.8 Frequency Response

Next, we investigate the frequency response of a filter, i.e., the effect of
a filter on the amplitude and phase of a signal (Fig. 6.4). The frequency
response $H(f)$ of a filter is the Fourier transform of the impulse response
$h(t)$. The absolute of the complex frequency response $H(f)$ is the magnitude response of the filter $A(f)$.

$$A(f) = |H(f)|$$

The argument of the complex frequency response $H(f)$ is the phase response of the filter.

$$\Phi(f) = \arg\left(H(f)\right)$$

Since MATLAB filters are all causal it is difficult to explore the phase of
signals using the corresponding functions included in the Signal Processing
Toolbox. The user's guide for this toolbox simply recommends to delay the
filter output in the time domain by a fixed number of samples, as we have
done it in the previous examples. As an example, a sine wave with a period
of 20 and an amplitude of 2 is used as an input signal.

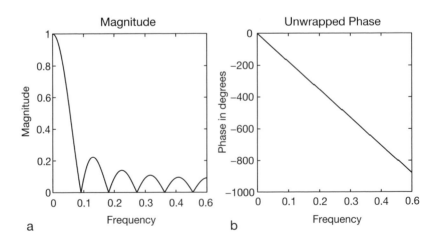

Fig. 6.4 a Magnitude and **b** phase response of a running mean over eleven elements.

```
clear
t = (1:100)';
x8 = 2*sin(2*pi*t/20);
```

A running mean over eleven elements is designed and this filter is applied to the input signal.

```
b8 = ones(1,11)/11;
m8 = length(b8);

y8 = filter(b8,1,x8);
```

The phase is corrected for causal indexing.

```
y8 = y8(1+(m8-1)/2:end-(m8-1)/2,1);
y8(end+1:end+m8-1,1) = zeros(m8-1,1);
```

Both input and output of the filter are plotted.

```
plot(t,x8,t,y8)
```

The filter obviously reduces the amplitude of the sine wave. Whereas the input signal has an amplitude of 2, the output has an amplitude of

```
max(y8)

ans =
    1.1480
```

The filter reduces the amplitude of a sine with a period of 20 by

```
1-max(y8(40:60))/2

ans =
    0.4260
```

i.e., approximately 43%. The elements 40 to 60 are used for computing the maximum value of y8 to avoid edge effects. On the other hand, the filter does not affect the phase of the sine wave, i.e., both input and output are in phase.

The same filter, however, has a different impact on a different signal. Let us design another sine wave with a similar amplitude, but with a different period of 15.

```
clear
t = (1:100)';
x9 = 2*sin(2*pi*t/15);
```

Applying a similar filter and correcting the output for the phase shift of the function filter yields

```
b9 = ones(1,11)/11;
m9 = length(b9);

y9 = filter(b9,1,x9);

y9 = y9(1+(m9-1)/2:end-(m9-1)/2,1);
y9(end+1:end+m9-1,1) = zeros(m9-1,1);
```

The output is again in phase with the input, but the amplitude is dramatically reduced as compared to the input.

```
plot(t,x9,t,y9)

1-max(y9(40:60))/2

ans =
    0.6768
```

The running mean over eleven elements reduces the amplitude of this signal by 67%. More generally, the filter response obviously depends on the frequency of the input. The frequency components of a more complex signal containing multiple periodicities are affected in a different way. The frequency response of a filter

```
clear
b10 = ones(1,11)/11;
```

can be computed using the function freqz.

```
[h,w] = freqz(b10,1,512);
```

The function freqz returns the complex frequency response h of the digital filter b10. The frequency axis is normalized to π. We transform the frequency axis to the true frequency values. The true frequency values are w times the sampling frequency, which is one in our example, divided by 2*pi.

```
f = 1*w/(2*pi);
```

Next, we calculate the magnitude of the frequency response and plot the magnitude over the frequency.

```
magnitude = abs(h);

plot(f,magnitude)
xlabel('Frequency'), ylabel('Magnitude')
title('Magnitude')
```

This plot can be used to predict the magnitude of the filter for any frequency of an input signal. An exact value of the magnitude can also be obtained by simple interpolation of the magnitude,

```
1-interp1(f,magnitude,1/20)

ans =
    0.4260
```

which is the expected ca. 43% reduction of the amplitude of a sine wave with period 20. The sine wave with period 15 experiences an amplitude reduction of

```
1-interp1(f,magnitude,1/15)

ans =
    0.6751
```

i.e., around 68% similar to the value observed at the beginning. The frequency response can be calculated for all kinds of filters. It is a valuable tool to predict the effects of a filter on signals in general. The phase response can also be calculated from the complex frequency response of the filter (Fig. 6.4):

```
phase = 180*angle(h)/pi;

plot(f,phase)
xlabel('Frequency'), ylabel('Phase in degrees')
title('Phase')
```

The phase angle is plotted in degrees. We observe frequent 180° jumps in this plot that are an artifact of the arctangent function inside the function angle. We can unwrap the phase response to eliminate the 180° jumps using the function unwrap.

```
plot(f,unwrap(phase))
xlabel('Frequency'), ylabel('Phase in degrees')
title('Phase')
```

Since the filter has a linear phase response, no shifts of the frequency components of the signal occur relative to each other. Therefore, we would not expect any distortions of the signal in the frequency domain. The phase shift of the filter can be computed using

```
interp1(f,unwrap(phase),1/20) * 20/360

ans =
   -5.0000
```

and

```
interp1(f,unwrap(phase),1/15) * 15/360

ans =
   -5.0000
```

respectively. Since MATLAB uses causal indexing for filters, the phase needs to be corrected, similar to the delayed output of the filter. In our example, we used a filter of the length eleven. We have to correct the phase by $(11-1)/2=5$. This suggests a zero phase shift of the filter for both frequencies.

This also works for recursive filters. Assume a simple sine wave with period 8 and the previously employed recursive filter.

```
clear
t = (1:100)';
x11 = 2*sin(2*pi*t/8);

b11 = [0.0048    0.0193    0.0289    0.0193    0.0048];
a11 = [1.0000   -2.3695    2.3140   -1.0547    0.1874];

m11 = length(b11);

y11 = filter(b11,a11,x11);
```

Correct the output for the phase shift introduced by causal indexing and plot both input and output signals.

```
y11= y11(1+(m11-1)/2:end-(m11-1)/2,1);
y11(end+1:end+m11-1,1) = zeros(m11-1,1);

plot(t,x11,t,y11)
```

The magnitude is reduced by

```
1-max(y11(40:60))/2

ans =
   0.6465
```

which is also supported by the magnitude response

```
[h,w] = freqz(b11,a11,512);

f = 1*w/(2*pi);

magnitude = abs(h);

plot(f,magnitude)
xlabel('Frequency'), ylabel('Magnitude')
title('Magnitude Response')
```

```
1-interp1(f,magnitude,1/8)

ans =
    0.6462
```

The phase response

```
phase = 180*angle(h)/pi;

f = 1*w/(2*pi);

plot(f,unwrap(phase))
xlabel('Frequency'), ylabel('Phase in degrees')
title('Magnitude Response')

interp1(f,unwrap(phase),1/8) * 8/360

ans =
    -5.0144
```

must again be corrected for causal indexing. The sampling interval was one, the filter length is five. Therefore, we have to add $(5-1)/2=2$ to the phase shift of -5.0144. This suggests a corrected phase shift of -3.0144, which is exactly the delay seen on the plot.

```
plot(t,x11,t,y11), axis([30 40 -2 2])
```

The next chapter gives an introduction to the design of filters with a desired frequency response. These filters can be used to amplify or suppress different components of arbitrary signals.

6.9 Filter Design

Now we aim to design filters with a desired frequency response. Firstly, a synthetic signal with two periods, 50 and 15, is generated. The power-spectrum of the signal shows the expected peaks at the frequencies 0.02 and ca. 0.07.

```
t = 0 : 1000;
x12 = 2*sin(2*pi*t/50) + sin(2*pi*t/15);

plot(t,x12), axis([0 200 -4 4])

[Pxx,f] = periodogram(x12,[],1024,1);

plot(f,abs(Pxx))
xlabel('Frequency')
ylabel('Power')
```

We add some gaussian noise with amplitude one and explore the signal and its periodogram.

```
xn12 = x12 + randn(1,length(t));

plot(t,xn12), axis([0 200 -4 4])

[Pxx,f] = periodogram(xn12,[],1024,1);

plot(f,abs(Pxx))
xlabel('Frequency')
ylabel('Power')
```

The Butterworth filter design technique is a widely-used method to create filters of any order with a lowpass, highpass, bandpass and bandstop configuration (Fig. 6.5). In our example, we like to design a five-order lowpass filter with a cutoff frequency of 0.08. The inputs of the function `butter` are the order of the filter and the cutoff frequency normalized to the Nyquist frequency, which is 0.5 in our example, that is half of the sampling frequency.

```
[b12,a12] = butter(5,0.08/0.5);
```

The frequency characteristics of the filter show a relatively smooth transition from the passband to the stopband, but the advantage of the filter is its low order.

```
[h,w] = freqz(b12,a12,1024);
f = 1*w/(2*pi);

plot(f,abs(h)), grid
xlabel('Frequency')
ylabel('Magnitude')
```

We can again apply the filter to the signal by using the function `filter`. However, frequency selective filters such as lowpass, highpass, bandpass and bandstop are designed to suppress certain frequency bands, whereas phase shifts should be avoided. The function `filtfilt` provides zero-phase forward and reverse digital filtering. After filtering in the forward direction, the filtered sequence is reversed and it runs back through the filter. The magnitude of the signal is not affected by this operation, since it is either 0 or 100% of the initial amplitude, depending on the frequency. In contrast, all phase shifts introduced by the filter are zeroed by the forward and reverse application of the same filter. This function also helps to overcome the problems with causal indexing of filters in MATLAB. It eliminates the phase differences of the causal vs. non-causal versions of the same filter.

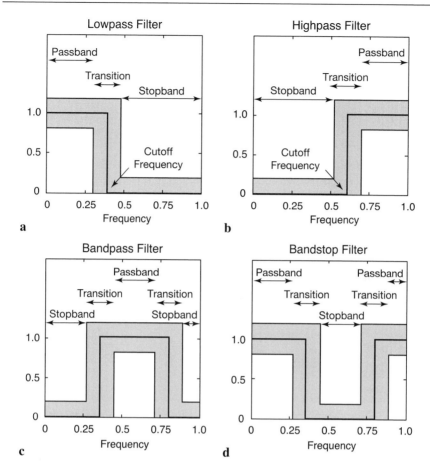

Fig. 6.5 Frequency response of the fundamental types of frequency-selective filters.
a Lowpass filter to suppress the high-frequency component of a signal. In earth sciences,
such filters are often used to suppress high-frequency noise in a low-frequency signal.
b Highpass filter are employed to remove all low frequencies and trends in natural data.
c-d Bandpass and bandstop filters extract or suppress a certain frequency band. Whereas
the solid line in all graphs depicts the ideal frequency response of a frequency-selective
filter, the gray band shows the tolerance for a low-order design of such a filter. In practice,
the frequency response lies within the gray band.

Filtering and plotting the results clearly illustrates the effects of the filter.

```
xf12 = filtfilt(b12,a12,xn12);

plot(t,xn12,'b-',t,xf12,'r-')
axis([0 200 -4 4])
```

One might now wish to design a new filter with a more rapid transition from passband to stopband. Such a filter needs a higher order. It needs to have a larger number of filter weights. We now create a 15-order Butterworth filter as an alternative to the above filter.

```
[b13,a13] = butter(15,0.08/0.5);

[h,w] = freqz(b13,a13,1024);

f = 1*w/(2*pi);

plot(f,abs(h)), grid
xlabel('Frequency')
ylabel('Magnitude')
```

The frequency response is clearly improved. The entire passband is relatively flat at a value of 1.0, whereas the stopband is approximately zero everywhere. Next, we modify our input signal by introducing a third period of 5. This signal is then used to illustrate the operation of a Butterworth bandstop filter.

```
x14 = 2*sin(2*pi*t/50) + sin(2*pi*t/15) + 0.5*sin(2*pi*t/5);
plot(t,x14), axis([0 200 -4 4])

[Pxx,f] = periodogram(x14,[],1024,1);

plot(f,abs(Pxx))
```

The new Butterworth filter is a bandstop filter. The stopband of the filter is between the frequencies 0.06 and 0.08. It can therefore be used to suppress the period of 15 corresponding to a frequency of approximately 0.07.

```
xn14 = x14 + randn(1,length(t));

[b14,a14] = butter(5,[0.06 0.08]/0.5,'stop');
xf14 = filtfilt(b14,a14,x14);

[Pxx,f] = periodogram(xf14,[],1024,1);

plot(f,abs(Pxx))

plot(t,xn14,'b-',t,xf14,'r-'), axis([0 200 -4 4])
```

The plots show the effect of this filter. The frequency band between 0.06 and 0.08, and therefore also the frequency of 0.07 was successfully removed from the signal.

6.10 Adaptive Filtering

The fixed filters used in the previous chapters make the basic assumption that the signal degradation is known and it does not change with time. In most applications, however, an *a priori* knowledge of the signal and noise statistical characteristics is usually not available. In addition, both the noise level and the variance of the genuine signal can be highly nonstationary with time, e.g., stable isotope records during the glacial-interglacial transition. Fixed filters thus cannot be used in a nonstationary environment without a knowledge of the signal-to-noise ratio.

In contrast, adaptive filters widely used in the telecommunication industry could help to overcome these problems. An adaptive filter is an inverse modeling process, which iteratively adjusts its own coefficients automatically without requiring any *a priori* knowledge of signal and noise. The operation of an adaptive filter includes, (1) a filtering process, the purpose of which is to produce an output in response to a sequence of data, and (2) an adaptive process providing a mechanism for the adaptive control of the filter weights (Haykin 1991).

In most practical applications, the adaptive process is oriented towards minimizing an error signal or cost function e. The estimation error e at an instant i is defined by the difference between some desired response d_i and the actual filter output y_i, that is the filtered version of a signal x_i, as shown by

$$e_i = d_i - y_i$$

where $i = 1, 2, \ldots, N$ and N is the length of the input data vector. In the case of a nonrecursive filter characterized by the vector of filter weights W with f elements, the filter output y_i is given by the inner product of the transposed vector W and the input vector X_i.

$$y_i = W^T \cdot X_i$$

The selection of the desired response d that is used in the adaptive process depends the application. Traditionally, d is a combined signal that contains a signal s and random noise n_0. The signal x contains a noise n_1 uncorrelated with the signal s but correlated in some unknown way to the noise n_0. In noise canceling systems, the practical objective is to produce a system output y that is a best fit in the least-squares sense to the signal d.

Different approaches have been developed to solve this multivariate minimum error optimization problem (e.g., Widrow and Hoff 1960, Widrow et al. 1975, Haykin 1991). Selection of one algorithm over another is influenced by various factors: the rate of convergence (number of adaptive steps required for the algorithm to converge close enough to an optimum solution), misadjustment (measure of the amount by which the final value of the mean-squared error deviates from the minimum squared error of an optimal filter, e.g., Wiener 1945, Kalman and Bucy 1961), and tracking (the capability of the filter to work in a nonstationary environment, i.e., to track changing statistical characteristics of the input signal) (Haykin 1991).

The simplicity of the least-mean-squares (LMS) algorithm, originally developed by Widrow and Hoff (1960), has made it the benchmark against which other adaptive filtering algorithms are tested. For applications in earth sciences, we use this filter to extract the noise from two signals S and X, both containing the same signal s, but uncorrelated noise n_1 and n_2 (Hattingh 1988). As an example, consider a simple duplicate set of measurements on the same material, e.g., two parallel stable isotope records from the same foraminifera species. What you will expect are two time-series with N elements containing the same desired signal overlain by different uncorrelated noise. The first record is used as the primary input S

$$S = (s_1, s_2, ..., s_N)$$

and the second record is the reference input X.

$$X = (x_1, x_2, ..., x_N)$$

As demonstrated by Hattingh (1988), the required noise-free signal can be extracted by filtering the reference input X using the primary input S as the desired response d. The minimum error optimization problem is solved by the norm least-mean-square. The mean-squared error e_i^2 is a second-order function of the weights in the nonrecursive filter. The dependence of e_i^2 on the unknown weights may be seen as a multidimensional paraboloid with a uniquely defined minimum point. The weights corresponding to the minimum point of this error performance surface define the optimum Wiener solution (Wiener 1945). The value computed for the weight vector W using the LMS algorithm represents an estimator whose expected value approaches the Wiener solution as the number of iterations approaches infinity (Haykin 1991). Gradient methods are used to reach the minimum point of the error performance surface. For simplification of the optimization problem, Widrow and Hoff (1960) developed an approximation for the required gradient function that can be computed directly from the data. This leads to a simple relation for updating the filter-weight vector W.

$$W_{i+1} = W_i + 2 \cdot u \cdot e_i \cdot X_i$$

The new parameter estimate W_{i+1} is based on the previous set of filter weights W_i plus a term, which is the product of a bounded step size u, a function of the input state X_i and a function of the error e_i. In other words, error e_i calculated from the previous step is fed back to the system to update filter coefficients for the next step (Fig. 6.6). The fixed convergence factor u regulates the speed and stability of adaption. A small value ensures a higher accuracy, but more data are needed to teach the filter to reach the optimum solution. In the modified version of the LMS algorithm by Hattingh (1988), this problem is overcome by feeding the data back so that the canceler can have another chance to improve its own coefficients and adapt to the changes in the data.

In the following function `canc`, each of these loops is called an iteration since many of these loops are required to achieve optimal results. This algorithm extracts the noise-free signal from two vectors x and s containing the correlated signal and uncorrelated noise. As an example, we generate two signals containing the same sine wave, but different gaussian noise.

```
x = 0 : 0.1 : 100;
y = sin(x);
yn1 = y + 0.2*randn(size(y));
yn2 = y + 0.2*randn(size(y));

plot(x,yn1,x,yn2)
```

Save the following code in a text file *canc.m* and include it into the search path. The algorithm `canc` formats both signals, feeds them into the filter loop,

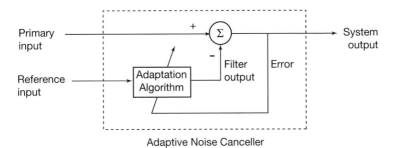

Adaptive Noise Canceller

Fig. 6.6 Schematic of an adaptive filter. Each iteration involves a new estimate of the filter weights W_{i+1} based on the previous set of filter weights W_i plus a term which is the product of a bounded step size u, a function of the filter input X_i, and a function of the error e_i. In other words, error e_i calculated from the previous step is fed back to the system to update filter coefficients for the next step (modified from Trauth 1998).

corrects the signals for phase shifts and formats the signals for the output.

```
function [zz,yy,ee] = canc(x,s,u,l,iter)
% CANC Correlated Adaptive Noise Canceling
[n1,n2] = size(s); n = n2; index = 0;          % Formatting
if n1 > n2
    s = s'; x = x'; n = n1; index = 1;
end
w(1:l) = zeros(1,l); e(1:n) = zeros(1,n);       % Initialization
xx(1:l) = zeros(1,l); ss(1:l) = zeros(1,l);
z(1:n) = zeros(1,n); y(1:n) = zeros(1,n);
ors = s; ms(1:n) = mean(s) .* ones(size(1:n));
s = s - ms; x = x - ms; ors = ors - ms;
for it = 1 : iter                               % Iterations
    for I = (l+1) : (n+1)                        % Filter loop
        for k = 1 : l
            xx(k) = x(I-k); ss(k) = s(I-k);
        end
        for J = 1 : l
            y(I-1) = y(I-1) + w(J) .* xx(J);
            z(I-1) = z(I-1) + w(J) .* ss(J);
        end
        e(I-1) = ors(I-1-(fix(l/2)))-y(I-1);
        for J = 1 : l
            w(J) = w(J) + 2.*u.*e(I-1).*xx(J);
        end
    end                                         % End filter loop
    for I = 1 : n                               % Phase correction
        if I <= fix(l/2)
            yy(I) = 0; zz(I) = 0; ee(I) = 0;
        elseif I > n-fix(l/2)
            yy(I) = 0; zz(I) = 0; ee(I) = 0;
        else
            yy(I) = y(I+fix(l/2));
            zz(I) = z(I+fix(l/2));
            ee(I) = abs(e(I+fix(l/2)));
        end
        yy(I) = yy(I) + ms(I);
        zz(I) = zz(I) + ms(I);
    end                                         % End phase correction
    y(1:n) = zeros(size(1:n));
    z(1:n) = zeros(size(1:n));
    mer(it) = mean(ee((fix(l/2)):(n-fix(l/2))).^2);
end                                             % End iterations
if index == 1                                   % Reformatting
    zz = zz'; yy = yy'; ee = ee';
end
```

The required inputs are the signals x and s, the step size u, the filter length l and the number of iterations iter. In our example, the two noisy signals are yn1 and yn2. For instance, we choose a filter with l=5 filter weights. A value of u in the range of $0 < u < 1/\lambda_{max}$ where λ_{max} is the largest eigenvalue of the autocorrelation matrix of the reference input, leads to reasonable results (Haykin 1991) (Fig. 6.7). The value of u is computed by

```
k = kron(yn1,yn1');
u = 1/max(eig(k))
```

which yields

```
u =
    0.0019
```

We now run the adaptive filter canc for 20 iterations and use the above
value of u.

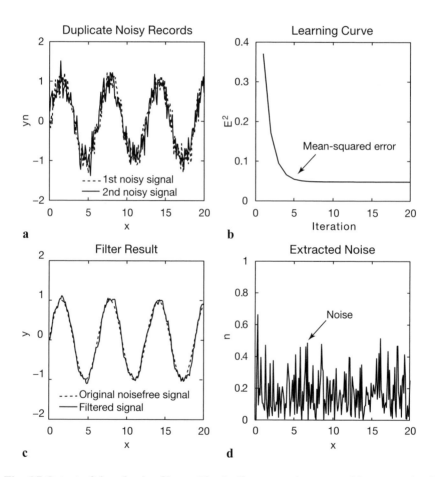

Fig. 6.7 Output of the adaptive filter. **a** The duplicate records corrupted by uncorrelated
noise are fed into the adaptive filter with 5 weights with a convergence factor of 0.0019.
After 20 iterations, the filter yields the **b** learning curve, **c** the noisefree record and **d** the
noise extracted from the duplicate records.

```
[z,e,mer] = canc(yn1,yn2,0.0019,5,20);
```

The evolution of the mean-squared error

```
plot(mer)
```

illustrates the performance of the adaptive filter, although the chosen step size u=0.0019 obviously leads to a relatively fast convergence. In most examples, a smaller step size decreases the rate of convergence, but increases the quality of the final result. We therefore reduce u by one order of magnitude and run the filter again with more iterations.

```
[z,e,mer] = canc(yn1,yn2,0.0001,5,20);
```

The plot of the mean-squared error against the iterations

```
plot(mer)
```

now convergences after around six iterations. We now compare the filter output with the original noise-free signal.

```
plot(x,y,'b',x,z,'r')
```

This plot shows that the noise level of the signal has been reduced dramatically by the filter. Finally, the plot

```
plot(x,e,'r')
```

shows the noise extracted from the signal. In practice, the user should vary the parameters u and l to obtain the optimum result.

The application of this algorithm has been demonstrated on duplicate oxygen-isotope records from ocean sediments (Trauth 1998). The work by Trauth (1998) illustrates the use of the modified LMS algorithm, but also another type of adaptive filters, the recursive least-squares (RLS) algorithm (Haykin 1991) in various environments.

Recommended Reading

Alexander ST (1986) Adaptive Signal Processing: Theory and Applications. Springer, Berlin Heidelberg New York
Buttkus B (2000) Spectral Analysis and Filter Theory in Applied Geophysics. Springer, Berlin Heidelberg New York
Cowan CFN, Grant PM (1985) Adaptive Filters. Prentice Hall, Englewood Cliffs, New Jersey

Grünigen DH (2004) Digitale Signalverarbeitung, mit einer Einführung in die konti-
    nuierlichen Signale und Systeme, Dritte bearbeitete und erweiterte Auflage. Fach-
    buchverlag Leipzig, Leipzig
Hattingh M (1988) A new Data Adaptive Filtering Program to Remove Noise from
    Geophysical Time- or Space Series Data. Computers & Geosciences 14(4):467–480
Haykin S (2003) Adaptive Filter Theory. Prentice Hall, Englewood Cliffs, New Jersey
Kalman R, Bucy R (1961) New Results in Linear Filtering and Prediction Theory. ASME
    Tans. Ser. D Jour. Basic Eng. 83:95–107
Sibul LH (1987) Adaptive Signal Processing. IEEE Press
The Mathworks (2006) Signal Processing Toolbox User's Guide – For the Use with
    MATLAB®. The MathWorks, Natick, MA
Trauth MH (1998) Noise Removal from Duplicate Paleoceanographic Time-Series: The
    Use of adaptive Filtering Techniques. Mathematical Geology 30(5):557–574
Widrow B, Hoff Jr. M (1960) Adaptive Switching Circuits. IRE WESCON Conv. Rev.
    4:96–104
Widrow B, Glover JR, McCool JM, Kaunitz J, Williams CS, Hearn RH, Zeidler JR, Dong E,
    Goodlin RC (1975) Adaptive Noise Cancelling: Principles and Applications. Proc. IEEE
    63(12):1692–1716
Wiener N (1949) Extrapolation, Interpolation and Smoothing of Stationary Time Series,
    with Engineering Applications. MIT Press, Cambridge, Mass (reprint of an article
    originally issued as a classified National Defense Research Report, February, 1942)

7 Spatial Data

7.1 Types of Spatial Data

Most data in earth sciences are spatially distributed, either as vector data, (points, lines, polygons) or as raster data (gridded topography). Vector data are generated by digitizing map objects such as drainage networks or outlines of lithologic units. Raster data can be obtained directly from a satellite sensor output, but in most cases grid data can be interpolated from irregularly-distributed samples from the field (*gridding*).

The following chapter introduces the use of vector data by using coastline data as an example (Chapter 7.2). Subsequently, the acquisition and handling of raster data are illustrated with help of digital topography data (Chapters 7.3 to 7.5). The availability and use of digital elevation data has increased considerably since the early 90's. With 5 arc minutes resolution, the ETOPO5 was one of the first data sets for topography and bathymetry. In October 2001, it was replaced by the ETOPO2 that has a resolution of 2 arc minutes. In addition, there is a data set for topography called GTOPO30 completed in 1996 that has a horizontal grid spacing of 30 arc seconds (approximately 1 km). Most recently, the 30 and 90 m resolution data from the Shuttle Radar Topography Mission (SRTM) have replaced the older data sets in most scientific studies.

The second part of the chapter deals with surface estimates from irregular-spaced data and statistics on spatial data (Chapters 7.6 to 7.8). In earth sciences, most data are collected in an irregular pattern. Access to rock samples is often restricted to natural outcrops such as shoreline cliffs and the walls of a gorge, or anthropogenic outcrops such as road cuts and quarries. Clustered and traversed data are a challenge for all gridding techniques. The corresponding chapters illustrate the use of the most important gridding routines and outline the potential pitfalls while using these methods. Chapters 7.9 to 7.11 introduce various methods to analyse spatial data, including the application of statistical tests to point distributions (Chapter 7.9), the spatial analysis of digital elevation models (Chapter 7.10) and an overview of geostatistics and kriging (Chapter 7.10).

This chapter requires the Mapping Toolbox although most graphics routines used in our examples can be easily replaced by standard MATLAB functions. An alternative and useful mapping toolbox by Rich Pawlowicz (Earth and Ocean Sciences at the Unversity of British Columbia) is available from

```
http://www2.ocgy.ubc.ca/~rich
```

The handling and processing of large spatial data sets also requires a powerful computing system with at least 1 GB physical memory.

7.2 The GSHHS Shoreline Data Set

The global self-consistent, hierarchical, high-resolution shoreline data base GSHHS is amalgamated from two public domain data bases by Paul Wessel (SOEST, University of Hawaii, Honolulu, HI) and Walter Smith (NOAA Laboratory for Satellite Altimetry, Silver Spring, MD). On the web page of the US National Geophysical Data Center (NGDC)

```
http://www.ngdc.noaa.gov/mgg/shorelines/shorelines.html
```

the coastline vector data can be downloaded as MATLAB vector data. First, we define the geographic range of interest as decimal degrees with West and South denoted by a negative sign. For example, the East African coast would be displayed on the latitude between 0 and +15 degrees and longitude of +35 to +55 degrees. Subsequently, it is important to choose the coastline data base from which the data is to be extracted. As an example, the *World Data Bank II* provides maps at the scale 1 : 2,000,000. Finally, the compression method is set to *None* for the ASCII data that have been extracted. The data format is set to be *MATLAB* and *GMT Preview* is enabled. The resulting GMT map and a link to the raw text data can be displayed by pressing the *Submit-Extract* button at the end of the web page. By opening the 430 KB large text file on a browser, the data can be saved onto a new file called *coastline.txt*. The two columns in this file represent the *longitude/latitude* coordinates of NaN-separated polygons or coastline segments.

```
NaN         NaN
42.892067   0.000000
42.893692   0.001760
NaN         NaN
42.891052   0.001467
42.898093   0.007921
```

```
42.904546   0.013201
42.907480   0.016721
42.910414   0.020828
42.913054   0.024642
42.915987   0.028749
42.918921   0.032562
42.922441   0.035789
(cont'd)
```

The NaN's perform two functions: they provide a means for identifying break points in the data. They also serve as pen-up commands when the Mapping Toolbox plots vector maps. The shorelines can be displayed by using

```
data = load('coastline.txt');

plot(data(:,1),data(:,2),'k'), axis equal
xlabel('Longitude'), ylabel('Latitude')
```

More advanced plotting functions are contained in the Mapping Toolbox, which allow to generate an alternative version of this plot (Fig. 7.1):

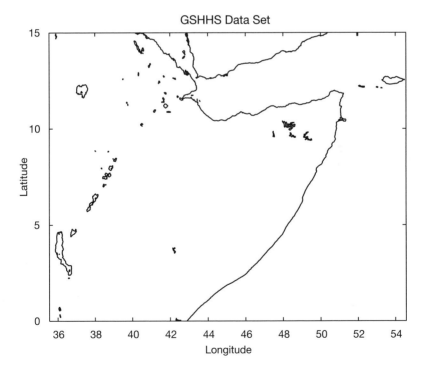

Fig. 7.1 Display of the GSHHS shoreline data set. The map shows an area between 0° and 15° northern latitude, 40° and 50° eastern longitude. Simple map using the function plot and equal axis aspect ratios.

```
axesm('MapProjection','mercator', ...
      'MapLatLimit',[0 15], ...
      'MapLonLimit',[35 55], ...
      'Frame','on', ...
      'MeridianLabel','on', ...
      'ParallelLabel','on');
plotm(data(:,2),data(:,1),'k');
```

Note that the input for `plotm` is given in the order *longitude*, followed by the *latitude*. The second column of the data matrix is entered first. In contrast, the function `plot` requires an *xy* input. The first column is entered first. The function `axesm` defines the map axis and sets various map properties such as the map projection, the map limits and the axis labels.

7.3 The 2-Minute Gridded Global Elevation Data ETOPO2

ETOPO2 is a global data base of topography and bathymetry on a regular 2-minute grid. It is a compilation of data from a variety of sources. It can be downloaded from the US National Geophysical Data Center (NGDC) web page

```
http://www.ngdc.noaa.gov/mgg/fliers/01mgg04.html
```

From the menu bar *Free online* we select *Make custom grids* which is linked to the *GEODAS Grid Translator*. First, we choose a Grid ID (e.g., *grid01*), the Grid Data Base (e.g., *ETOPO2 2-minute Global Relief*), our computer system (e.g., *Macintosh*) and the Grid Format (e.g., *ASCII* for both the data and the header). Next we define the *longitude* and *latitude* bounds. For example, the latitude (*lat*) from −20 to +20 degrees and a longitude (*lon*) between +30 and +60 degrees corresponds to the East African coast. The selected area can be transformed into a digital elevation matrix by pressing *Design–a–grid*. this matrix may be downloaded from the web page by pressing *Download your Grid Data, Compress and Retrieve* and *Retrieve compressed file* in the subsequent windows. Decompressing the file *grid01. tgz* creates a directory *grid01_data*. This directory contains various data and help files. The subdirectory *grid01* contains the ASCII raster grid file *grid01.asc* that has the following content:

```
NCOLS     901
NROWS     1201
XLLCORNER   30.00000
YLLCORNER  -20.00000
CELLSIZE 0.03333333
NODATA_VALUE   -32768
270    294    278    273    262    248    251    236    228    223 ...
```

```
280    278    278    264    254    253    240    234    225    205 ...
256    266    267    283    257    273    248    228    215    220 ...
272    273    258    258    254    264    232    218    229    210 ...
259    263    268    275    242    246    237    219    211    209 ...
(cont'd)
```

The header documents the size of the data matrix (e.g., 901 columns and 1201 rows in our example), the coordinates of the lower-left corner (e.g., $x=30$ and $y=-20$), the cell size (e.g., $0.033333 = 1/30$ degree latitude and longitude) and the -32768 flag for data voids. We comment the header by typing % at the beginning of the first six lines

```
%NCOLS    901
%NROWS    1201
%XLLCORNER   30.00000
%YLLCORNER  -20.00000
%CELLSIZE 0.03333333
%NODATA_VALUE   -32768
270    294    278    273    262    248    251    236    228    223 ...
280    278    278    264    254    253    240    234    225    205 ...
256    266    267    283    257    273    248    228    215    220 ...
272    273    258    258    254    264    232    218    229    210 ...
259    263    268    275    242    246    237    219    211    209 ...
(cont'd)
```

and load the data into the workspace.

```
ETOPO2 = load('grid01.asc');
```

We flip the matrix up and down. Then, the -32768 flag for data voids has to be replaced by the MATLAB representation for Not-a-Number NaN.

```
ETOPO2 = flipud(ETOPO2);
ETOPO2(find(ETOPO2 == -32768)) = NaN;
```

Finally, we check whether the data are now correctly stored in the workspace by printing the minimum and maximum elevations of the area.

```
max(ETOPO2(:))
min(ETOPO2(:))
```

In this example, the maximum elevation of the area is 5199 m and the minimum elevation is −5612 m. The reference level is the sea level at 0 m. We now define a coordinate system using the information that the lower-left corner is *s20e30*, i.e., 20° southern latitude and 30° eastern longitude. The resolution is 2 arc minutes corresponding to 1/30 degrees.

```
[LON,LAT] = meshgrid(30:1/30:60,-20:1/30:20);
```

Now we generate a colored surface from the elevation data using the function `surf`.

```
surf(LON,LAT,ETOPO2)
shading interp
axis equal, view(0,90)
colorbar
```

This script opens a new figure window and generates a colored surface. The surface is highlighted by a set of color shades on an overhead view (Fig. 7.2). More display methods will be described in the chapter on SRTM elevation data.

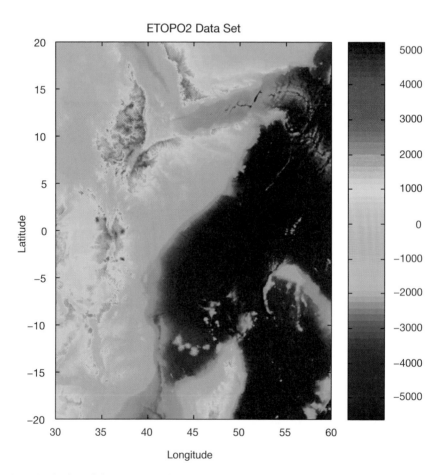

Fig. 7.2 Display of the ETOPO2 elevation data set. The map uses the function `surf` for generating a colored surface. The colorbar provides an information on the colormap used to visualize topography and bathymetry.

7.4 The 30-Arc Seconds Elevation Model GTOPO30

The 30 arc second (approximately 1 km) global digital elevation data set GTOPO30 only contains elevation data, not bathymetry. The data set has been developed by the Earth Resources Observation System Data Center and is available from the web page

```
http://edcdaac.usgs.gov/gtopo30/gtopo30.html
```

The model uses a variety of international data sources. However, it is mainly based on raster data from the Digital Terrain Elevation Model (DTEM) and vector data from the Digital Chart of the World (DCW). The GTOPO30 data set has been divided into 33 pieces or tiles. The tile names refer to the longitude and latitude of the upper-left (northwest) corner of the tile. The tile name *e020n40* refers to the upper-left corner of the tile. In our example, the coordinates of the upper-left corner are 20 degrees eastern longitude and 40 degrees northern latitude. As example, we select and download the tile *e020n40* provided as a 24.9 MB compressed *tar* file. After decompressing the *tar* file, we obtain eight files containing the raw data and header files in various formats. Moreover, the file provides a GIF image of a shaded relief display of the data.

Importing the GTOPO30 data into the workspace is simple. The Mapping Toolbox provides an import routine `gtopo30` that reads the data and stores it onto a regular data grid. We import only a subset of the original matrix:

```
latlim = [-5 5]; lonlim = [30 40];
GTOPO30 = gtopo30('E020N40',1,latlim,lonlim);
```

This script reads the data from the tile *e020n40* (without file extension) in full resolution (scale factor = 1) into the matrix GTOPO30 of the dimension 1200x1200 cells. The coordinate system is defined by using the *lon/lat* limits as listed above. The resolution is 30 arc seconds corresponding to 1/120 degrees.

```
[LON,LAT] = meshgrid(30:1/120:40-1/120,-5:1/120:5-1/120);
```

We have to reduce the limits by 1/120 to obtain a matrix of similar dimension as the matrix GTOPO30. A grayscale image can be generated from the elevation data by using the function `surf`. The fourth power of the colormap `gray` is used to darken the map at higher levels of elevation. Subsequently, the colormap is flipped vertically in order to obtain dark colors for high elevations and light colors for low elevations.

```
figure
surf(LON,LAT,GTOPO30)
shading interp
colormap(flipud(gray.^4))
axis equal, view(0,90)
colorbar
```

This script opens a new figure window, generates the gray surface using
interpolated shading in an overhead view (Fig. 7.3).

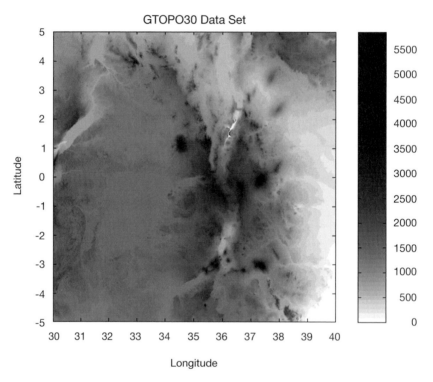

Fig. 7.3 Display of the GTOPO30 elevation data set. The map uses the function `surf` for
generating a gray surface. We use the colormap `gray` to power of four in order to darken
the colormap with respect to the higher elevation. In addition, we flip the colormap in
up/down direction using `flipud` to obtain dark colors for high elevations and light colors
for low elevations.

7.5 The Shuttle Radar Topography Mission SRTM

The Shuttle Radar Topography Mission (SRTM) incorporates a radar system that flew onboard the Space Shuttle *Endeavour* during an 11-day mission in February 2000. SRTM is an international project spearheaded by the National Geospatial-Intelligence Agency (NGA) and the National Aeronautics and Space Administration (NASA). Detailed info on the SRTM project including a gallery of images and a users forum can be accessed on the NASA web page:

```
http://www2.jpl.nasa.gov/srtm/
```

The data were processed at the Jet Propulsion Laboratory. They are being distributed through the United States Geological Survey's (USGS) EROS Data Center by using the Seamless Data Distribution System.

```
http://seamless.usgs.gov/
```

Alternatively, the raw data files can be downloaded via FTP from

```
ftp://e0srp01u.ecs.nasa.gov/srtm
```

This directory contains zipped files of SRTM-3 DEM's from various areas of the world, processed by the SRTM global processor and sampled at 3 arc seconds or 90 meters. As an example, we download the 1.7 MB large file *s01e036.hgt.zip* containing the SRTM data. All elevations are in meters referenced to the WGS84 EGM96 geoid as documented at

```
http://earth-info.nga.mil/GandG/wgs84/index.html
```

The name of this file refers to the longitude and latitude of the lower-left (southwest) pixel of the tile, i.e., one degree southern latitude and 36 degrees eastern longitude. SRTM-3 data contain 1201 lines and 1201 samples with similar overlapping rows and columns. After having downloaded and unzipped the file, we save *s01e036.hgt* in our working directory. The digital elevation model is provided as 16-bit signed integer data in a simple binary raster. Bit order is Motorola (*big-endian*) standard with the most significant bit first. The data are imported into the workspace using

```
fid = fopen('S01E036.hgt','r');
SRTM = fread(fid,[1201,inf],'int16','b');
fclose(fid);
```

This script opens the file *s01e036.hgt* for read access using `fopen`, defines the file identifier `fid`, which is then used for reading the binaries from the file using `fread`, and writing it into the matrix `SRTM`. Function `fclose` closes the file defined by `fid`. First, the matrix needs to be transposed and flipped vertically.

```
SRTM = SRTM'; SRTM = flipud(SRTM);
```

The –*32768* flag for data voids can be replaced by `NaN`, which is the MATLAB representation for Not-a-Number.

```
SRTM(find(SRTM == -32768)) = NaN;
```

Finally, we check whether the data are now correctly stored in the workspace by printing the minimum and maximum elevations of the area.

```
max(SRTM(:))

ans =
    3992

min(SRTM(:))

ans =
    1504
```

In our example, the maximum elevation of the area is 3992 m, the minimum altitude is 1504 m above sea level. A coordinate system can be defined by using the information that the lower-left corner is *s01e036*. The resolution is 3 arc seconds corresponding to 1/1200 degrees.

```
[LON,LAT] = meshgrid(36:1/1200:37,-1:1/1200:0);
```

A shaded grayscale map can be generated from the elevation data using the function `surfl`. This function displays a shaded surface with simulated lighting.

```
figure
surfl(LON,LAT,SRTM)
shading interp
colormap gray
view(0,90)
colorbar
```

This script opens a new figure window, generates the shaded-relief map using interpolated shading and a gray colormap in an overhead view. Since SRTM data contain much noise, we first smooth the data using an arbitrary

9×9 pixel moving average filter. The new matrix is stored in the matrix
`SRTM_FILTERED`.

```
B = 1/81 * ones(9,9);
SRTM_FILTERED = filter2(B,SRTM);
```

The corresponding shaded-relief map is generated by

```
figure
surfl(LON,LAT,SRTM_FILTERED)
shading interp
colormap gray
view(0,90)
colorbar
```

After having generated the shaded-relief map (Fig. 7.4), the graph has to be exported onto a graphics file. For instance, the figure may be written onto a JPEG format with 70% quality level and a 300 dpi resolution.

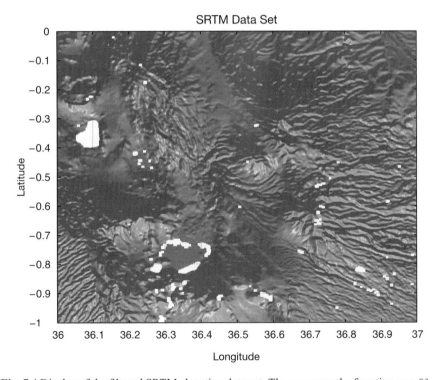

Fig. 7.4 Display of the filtered SRTM elevation data set. The map uses the function `surfl` for generating a shaded-relief map with simulated lighting using interpolated shading and a gray colormap in an overhead view. Note that the SRTM data set contains a lot of gaps, in particular in the lake areas.

```
print -djpeg70 -r300 srtmimage
```

The new file *srtmimage.jpg* has a size of 300 KB. The decompressed image
has a size of 16.5 MB. This file can now be imported to another software
package such as Adobe® Photoshop®.

7.6 Gridding and Contouring Background

The previous data sets were all stored in evenly-spaced two-dimensional
arrays. Most data in earth sciences, however, are obtained on an irregular
sampling pattern. Therefore, irregular-spaced data have to be interpolated,
i.e., we compute a smooth and continuous surface from our measurements
in the field. *Surface estimation* is typically carried out in two major steps.
Firstly, the number of *control points* needs to be selected. Secondly, the
grid points have to be estimated. Control points are irregularly-spaced field
measurements, such as the thicknesses of sandstone units at different outcrops or the concentrations of a chemical tracer in water wells. The data are
generally represented as *xyz* triplets, where *x* and *y* are spatial coordinates,
and *z* is the variable of interest. In such cases, most gridding methods require continuous and unique data. However, the spatial variables in earth
sciences are often discontinuous and spatially nonunique. As an example,
the sandstone unit may be faulted or folded. Furthermore, gridding requires
spatial autocorrelation. In other words, the neighboring data points should
be correlated with each other by a certain relationship. It is not sensible to
use random *z* variable for the surface estimation if the data are not autocorrelated. Having selected the control points, the calculation of the *z* values at
the evenly-spaced grid points varies from method to method.

Various techniques exist for selecting the control points (Fig. 7.5a). Most
methods make arbitrary assumptions on the autocorrelation of the *z* variable. The *nearest-neighbor criterion* includes all control points within a
circular neighborhood of the grid point, where the radius of the circle is
specified by the user. Since the spatial autocorrelation is likely to decrease
with increasing distance from the grid point, considering too many distant
control points is likely to lead to erroneous results while computing the grid
points. On the other hand, small circular areas limit the calculation of the
grid points to a very small number of control points. Such an approach leads
to a noisy estimate of the modeled surface.

It is perhaps due to these difficulties that *triangulation* is often used as an
alternative method for selecting the control points (Fig. 7.5b). In this tech-

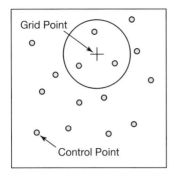
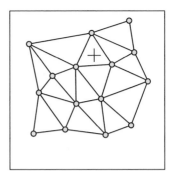

a   b

Fig. 7.5 Methods to select the control points for estimating the grid points. **a** Construction of a circle around the grid point (plus sign) with a radius defined by the spatial autocorrelation of the z-values at the control points (circles). **b** Triangulation. The control points are selected from the apices of the triangles surrounding the grid point and optional also the apices of the adjoining triangles.

nique, all control points are connected to a triangular net. Every grid point is located in a triangular area of three control points. The z value of the grid point is computed from the z values of the grid points. In a modification of such gridding, the three points at the apices of the three adjoining triangles are also used. The *Delauney triangulation* uses the triangular net where the acuteness of the triangles is minimized, i.e., the triangles are as close as possible to equilateral.

Kriging introduced in Chapter 7.9 is an alternative approach of selecting control points. It is often regarded as *the* method of gridding. Some people even use the term *geostatistics* synonymous with kriging. Kriging is a method for determining the spatial autocorrelation and hence the circle dimension. More sophisticated versions of kriging use an elliptical area which includes the control points.

The second step of surface estimation is the actual computation of the z values of the grid points. The *arithmetic mean* of the z values at the control points

$$\overline{z} = \frac{1}{N} \sum_{i=1}^{N} z_i$$

provides the easiest way of computing the grid points. This is a particularly useful method if there are only a limited number of control points. If the study area is well covered by control points and the distance between these points is highly variable, the z values of the grid points should be computed by a *weighted mean*. The z values at the control points are weighted by the inverse distance d_i from the grid points.

$$\overline{z} = \frac{\displaystyle\sum_{i=1}^{N}(z_i / d_i)}{\displaystyle\sum_{i=1}^{N}(1 / d_i)}$$

Depending on the spatial scaling relationship of the parameter z, the inverse square or the root of distance may also be used instead of weighing the z values by the inverse of distance. The fitting of 3D *splines* to the control points provides another method for computing the grid points that is commonly used in the earth sciences. Most routines used in surface estimation involve *cubic polynomial splines*, i.e., a third-degree 3D polynomial is fitted to at least six adjacent control points. The final surface consists of a composite of pieces of these splines. MATLAB also provides interpolation with biharmonic splines generating very smooth surfaces (Sandwell, 1987).

7.7 Gridding Example

MATLAB provides a biharmonic spline interpolation since the beginnings. This interpolation method was developed by Sandwell (1987). This specific gridding method produces smooth surfaces that are particularly suited for noisy data sets with irregular distribution of control points.

As an example, we use synthetic *xyz* data representing the vertical distance of an imaginary surface of a stratigraphic horizon from a reference surface. This lithologic unit was displaced by a normal fault. The foot wall of the fault shows roughly horizontal strata, whereas the hanging wall is characterized by the development of two large sedimentary basins. The *xyz* data are irregularly distributed and have to be interpolated onto a regular grid. Assume that the *xyz* data are stored as a three-column table in a file named *normalfault.txt*.

```
4.32e+02    7.46e+01    0.00e+00
4.46e+02    7.21e+01    0.00e+00
4.51e+02    7.87e+01    0.00e+00
4.66e+02    8.71e+01    0.00e+00
4.65e+02    9.73e+01    0.00e+00
4.55e+02    1.14e+02    0.00e+00
4.29e+02    7.31e+01    5.00e+00
(cont'd)
```

The first and second column contains the coordinates x (between 420 and 470 of an arbitrary spatial coordinate system) and y (between 70 and 120), whereas the third column contains the vertical z values. The data are loaded using

```
data = load('normalfault.txt');
```

Initially, we wish to create an overview plot of the spatial distribution of the control points. In order to label the points in the plot, numerical z values of the third column are converted into string representation with maximum two digits.

```
labels = num2str(data(:,3),2);
```

The 2D plot of our data is generated in two steps. Firstly, the data are displayed as empty circles by using the plot command. Secondly, the data are labeled by using the function text(x,y,'string') which adds text contained in string to the xy location. The value 1 is added to all x coordinates as a small offset between the circles and the text.

```
plot(data(:,1),data(:,2),'o')
hold on
text(data(:,1)+1,data(:,2),labels);
hold off
```

This plot helps us to define the axis limits for gridding and contouring, xlim = [420 470] and ylim = [70 120]. The function meshgrid transforms the domain specified by vectors x and y into arrays XI and YI. The rows of the output array XI are copies of the vector x and the columns of the output array YI are copies of the vector y. We choose 1.0 as grid intervals.

```
x = 420:1:470; y = 70:1:120;
[XI,YI] = meshgrid(x,y);
```

The biharmonic spline interpolation is used to interpolate the irregular-spaced data at the grid points specified by XI and YI.

```
ZI = griddata(data(:,1),data(:,2),data(:,3),XI,YI,'v4');
```

The option v4 depicts the biharmonic spline interpolation, which was the sole gridding algorithm until MATLAB4 was replaced by MATLAB5. MATLAB provides various tools for the visualization of the results. The simplest way to display the gridding results is a contour plot using contour. By default, the number of contour levels and the values of the contour levels are chosen automatically. The choice of the contour levels depends on the minimum and maximum values of z.

```
contour(XI,YI,ZI)
```

Alternatively, the number of contours can be chosen manually, e.g., ten contour levels.

```
contour(XI,YI,ZI,10)
```

Contouring can also be performed at values specified in a vector v. Since the maximum and minimum values of z is

```
min(data(:,3))

ans =
   -25

max(data(:,3))

ans =
   20
```

we choose

```
v = -30 : 10 : 20;
```

The command

```
[c,h] = contour(XI,YI,ZI,v);
```

returns contour matrix c and a handle h that can be used as input to the function clabel, which labels contours automatically.

```
clabel(c,h)
```

Alternatively, the graph is labeled manually by selecting the manual option in the function clabel. This function places labels onto locations that have been selected with the mouse. Labeling is terminated by pressing the return key.

```
[c,h] = contour(XI,YI,ZI,v);
clabel(c,h,'manual')
```

Filled contours are an alternative to the empty contours used above. This function is used together with colorbar displaying a legend for the graph. In addition, we plot the locations and z values of the true data points (black empty circles, text labels) (Fig. 7.6).

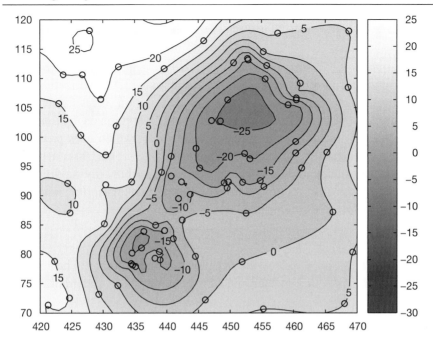

Fig. 7.6 Contour plot of the locations and z-values of the true data points (black empty circles, text labels).

```
contourf(XI,YI,ZI,v), colorbar
hold on
plot(data(:,1),data(:,2),'ko')
text(data(:,1)+1,data(:,2),labels);
hold off
```

A pseudocolor plot is generated by using the function `pcolor`. Black contours are also added at the same levels as in the above example.

```
pcolor(XI,YI,ZI), shading flat
hold on
contour(XI,YI,ZI,v,'k')
hold off
```

The third dimension is added to the plot by using the `mesh` command. We use this example also to introduce the function `view(az,el)` for a viewpoint specification. Herein, `az` is the azimuth or horizontal rotation and `el` is the vertical elevation (both in degrees). The values `az = −37.5` and `el = 30` define the default view of all 3D plots,

```
mesh(XI,YI,ZI), view(-37.5,30)
```

whereas $az = 0$ and $el = 90$ is directly overhead and the default 2D view

```
mesh(XI,YI,ZI), view(0,90)
```

The function `mesh` represents only one of the many 3D visualization methods. Another commonly used command is the function `surf`. Furthermore, the figure may be rotated by selecting the *Rotate 3D* option on the *Edit Tools* menu. We also introduce the function `colormap`, which uses predefined pseudo colormaps for 3D graphs. Typing `help graph3d` lists a number of builtin colormaps, although colormaps can be arbitrarily modified and generated by the user. As an example, we use the colormap *hot*, which is a *black-red-yellow-white* colormap.

```
surf(XI,YI,ZI), colormap('hot'), colorbar
```

Here, *Rotate 3D* only rotates the 3D plot, not the colorbar. The function `surfc` combines both a surface and a 2D contour plot in one graph.

```
surfc(XI,YI,ZI)
```

The function `surfl` can be used to illustrate an advanced application of 3D visualization. It generates a 3D colored surface with interpolated shading and lighting. The axis labeling, ticks and background can be turned off by typing `axis off`. In addition, black 3D contours may be added to the surface plot. The grid resolution is increased prior to data plotting to obtain smooth surfaces (Fig. 7.7).

```
[XI,YI] = meshgrid(420:0.25:470,70:0.25:120);
ZI = griddata(data(:,1),data(:,2),data(:,3),XI,YI,'v4');

surf(XI,YI,ZI), shading interp, light, axis off
hold on
contour3(XI,YI,ZI,v,'k');
hold off
```

The biharmonic spline interpolation described in this chapter provides a solution to most gridding problems. Therefore, it was the only gridding method that came with MATLAB for quite a long time. However, different applications in earth sciences require different methods for interpolation, but there is no method without problems. The next chapter compares biharmonic splines with other gridding methods and summarizes their strengths and weaknesses.

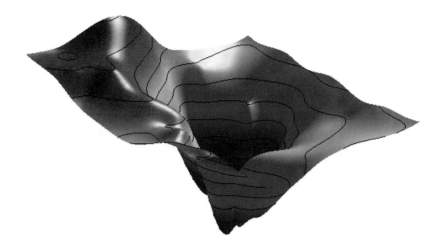

Fig. 7.7 Three-dimensional colored surface with interpolated shading and simulated lighting. The axis labeling, ticks and background are turned off. In addition, the graph contains black 3D contours.

7.8 Comparison of Methods and Potential Artifacts

The first example illustrates the use of the *bilinear interpolation* technique for gridding irregular-spaced data. Bilinear interpolation is an extension of the one-dimensional linear interpolation. In the two-dimensional case, linear interpolation is performed in one direction first, then in the other direction. Intuitively, the bilinear method is one of the simplest interpolation techniques. One would not expect serious artifacts and distortions of the data. On the contrary, this method has a number of disadvantages and therefore other methods are used in many applications.

The sample data used in the previous chapter can be loaded to study the performance of a bilinear interpolation.

```
data = load('normalfault.txt');
labels = num2str(data(:,3),2);
```

We now choose the option `linear` while using the function `griddata` to interpolate the data.

```
[XI,YI] = meshgrid(420:0.25:470,70:0.25:120);
ZI = griddata(data(:,1),data(:,2),data(:,3),XI,YI,'linear');
```

The results are plotted as contours. The plot also includes the location of the control points.

```
contourf(XI,YI,ZI), colorbar, hold on
plot(data(:,1),data(:,2),'o'), hold off
```

The new surface is restricted to the area that contains control points. By default, bilinear interpolation does not extrapolate beyond this region. Furthermore, the contours are rather angular compared to the smooth outline of the contours of the biharmonic spline interpolation. The most important character of the bilinear gridding technique, however, is illustrated by a projection of the data in a vertical plane.

```
plot(XI,ZI,'k'), hold on
plot(data(:,1),data(:,3),'ro')
text(data(:,1)+1,data(:,3),labels)
title('Linear Interpolation'), hold off
```

This plot shows the projection of the estimated surface (vertical lines) and the labeled control points. The z-values at the grid points never exceed the z-values of the control points. Similar to the linear interpolation of time series (Chapter 5), bilinear interpolation causes significant smoothing of the data and a reduction of the high-frequency variation.

Biharmonic splines are sort of the other extreme in many ways. They are often used for extremely irregular-spaced and noisy data.

```
[XI,YI] = meshgrid(420:0.25:470,70:0.25:120);
ZI = griddata(data(:,1),data(:,2),data(:,3),XI,YI,'v4');

contourf(XI,YI,ZI), colorbar, hold on
plot(data(:,1),data(:,2),'o'), hold off
```

The contours suggest an extremely smooth surface. In many applications, this solution is very useful, but the method also produces a number of artifacts. As we can see from the next plot, the estimated values at the grid points are often out of the range of the measured z-values.

```
plot(XI,ZI,'k'), hold on
plot(data(:,1),data(:,3),'o')
text(data(:,1)+1,data(:,3),labels);
title('Biharmonic Spline Interpolation'), hold off
```

This sometimes makes much sense and does not smooth the data in the way bilinear gridding does. However, introducing very close control points with different z-values can cause serious artifacts.

```
data(79,:) = [450 105 5];
```

```
data(80,:) = [450 104.5 -5];
labels = num2str(data(:,3),2);
ZI = griddata(data(:,1),data(:,2),data(:,3),XI,YI,'v4');

contourf(XI,YI,ZI), colorbar, hold on
plot(data(:,1),data(:,2),'ko')
text(data(:,1)+1,data(:,2),labels)
```

The extreme gradient at the location (450,105) results in a paired *low* and *high* (Fig. 7.8). In such cases, it is recommended to delete one of the two control points and replace the z-value of the remaining control point by the arithmetic mean of both z-values.

Extrapolation beyond the area supported by control points is a common feature of splines (see also Chapter 5). Extreme local trends combined with large areas with no data often cause unrealistic estimates. To illustrate these edge effects we eliminate all control points in the upper-left corner.

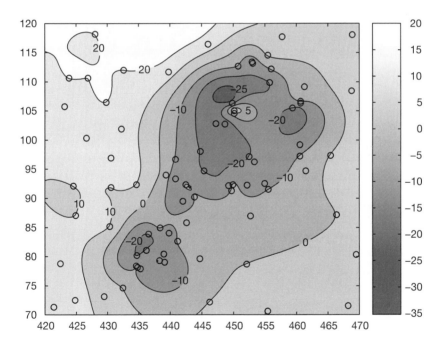

Fig. 7.8 Contour plot of a data set gridded using a biharmonic spline interpolation. At the location (450,105), very close control points with different z-values have been introduced. Interpolation causes a paired low and high, which is a common artefact of spline interpolation of noisy data.

```
[i,j] = find(data(:,1)<435 & data(:,2)>105);
data(i,:) = [];

labels = num2str(data(:,3),2);

plot(data(:,1),data(:,2),'ko')
hold on
text(data(:,1)+1,data(:,2),labels);
hold off
```

We again employ the biharmonic spline interpolation technique.

```
[XI,YI] = meshgrid(420:0.25:470,70:0.25:120);
ZI = griddata(data(:,1),data(:,2),data(:,3),XI,YI,'v4');

v = -40 : 10 : 40;
contourf(XI,YI,ZI,v)
caxis([-40 40])
colorbar
hold on
plot(data(:,1),data(:,2),'ko')
```

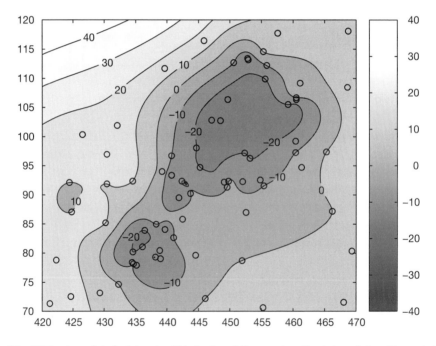

Fig. 7.9 Contour plot of a data set gridded using a biharmonic spline interpolation. No control points are available in the upper left corner. The spline interpolation then extrapolates beyond the area with control points using gradients at the map edges causing unrealistic z estimates at the grid points.

```
text(data(:,1)+1,data(:,2),labels)
hold off
```

As we can see from the plot, this method extrapolates beyond the area with control points using gradients at the map edges (Fig. 7.9). Such effect is particular undesired in the case of gridded closed data, such as percentages, or data that have only positive values. In such cases, it is recommended to replace the estimated z values by NaN. For instance, we erase the areas with z values larger than 20, which is regarded as an unrealistic value. The corresponding plot now contains a sector with no data.

```
ZID = ZI;
ZID(find(ZID > 20)) = NaN;

contourf(XI,YI,ZID,v)
caxis([-40 40])
colorbar
hold on
plot(data(:,1),data(:,2),'ko')
text(data(:,1)+1,data(:,2),labels)
hold off
```

Alternatively, we can eliminate a rectangular area with no data.

```
ZID = ZI;
ZID(131:201,1:71) = NaN;

contourf(XI,YI,ZID,v)
caxis([-40 40])
colorbar
hold on
plot(data(:,1),data(:,2),'ko')
text(data(:,1)+1,data(:,2),labels)
hold off
```

In some examples, the area with no control points is simply eliminated by putting a legend on this part of the map.

Another very useful MATLAB gridding method are *splines with tension* by Wessel and Bercovici (1998). The *tsplines* use biharmonic splines in tension t, where the parameter t can vary between 0 and 1. A value of $t=0$ corresponds to a standard cubic spline interpolation. Increasing t reduces undesirable oscillations between data points, e.g., the paired *lows* and *highs* observed in one of the above examples. The limiting situation $t \rightarrow 1$ corresponds to linear interpolation.

7.9 Statistics of Point Distributions

This chapter is about the statistical distribution of points in an area, which may help understand the relationship between these objects and properties of the area. For instance, the spatial concentration of handaxes in an archaeological site suggests that a larger population of hominins lived in that part of the area. The clustered occurrence of fossils may document environmental conditions that are favourable to the corresponding organisms. Volcano alignments often help to map tectonic structures in the deeper and shallower subsurface.

The following text introduces methods for the statistical analysis of point distributions. First, the spatial distribution of objects is tested for uniform and random distribution. Then, a simple test for clustered distributions of objects is presented.

Test for Uniform Distribution

We compute synthetic data to illustrate the test for uniform distributions. The function rand computes uniformly-distributed pseudo-random numbers drawn from a uniform distribution on the unit interval. We compute xy data using rand and multiply the data by ten to obtain data on the interval [0,10].

```
rand('seed',0)
data = 10 * rand(100,2);
```

We use the χ^2–test introduced in Chapter 3.8 to test the hypothesis that the data have a uniform distribution. The xy data are now organized in 25 classes that are square subareas of the size 2-by-2. We display the data as blue points in a plot y versus x. The square areas are outlined by red lines (Fig. 7.10).

```
plot(data(:,1),data(:,2),'o')
hold on
x = 0:10; y = ones(size(x));
for i = 1:4, plot(x,2*i*y,'r-'), end
for i = 1:4, plot(2*i*y,x,'r-'), end
hold off
```

The three-dimensional version of histogram hist3 is used to display the spatial data organized in classes (Fig. 7.11).

```
hist3(data,[5 5]), view(30,70)
```

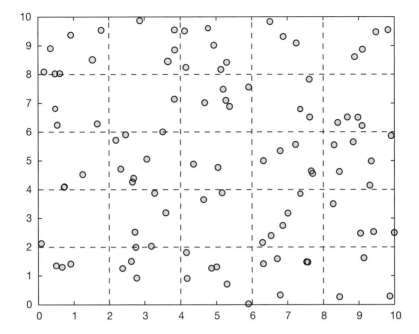

Fig. 7.10 Two-dimensional plot of a point distribution. The distribution of objects in the field are tested for uniform distribution using the χ^2-test. The xy data are organized in 25 classes that are square subareas of the size 2-by-2.

Equivalent to the two-dimensional function, the function `hist3` can be used to compute the frequency distribution `n_exp` of the data.

```
n_exp = hist3(data,[5 5]);
n_exp = n_exp(:);
```

For a uniform distribution, the theoretical frequencies for the classes are identical. The expected number of objects in each square area is the size of the total area $10 \times 10 = 100$ divided by the 25 subareas or classes, which comes to be four. To compare the theoretical frequency distribution with the actual distribution of objects, we generate an 5-by-5 array with identical elements four.

```
n_syn = 4 * ones(25,1);
```

The χ^2-test explores the squared differences between the observed and expected frequencies (Chapter 3.8). The quantity χ^2 is defined as the sum of the squared differences divided by the expected frequencies.

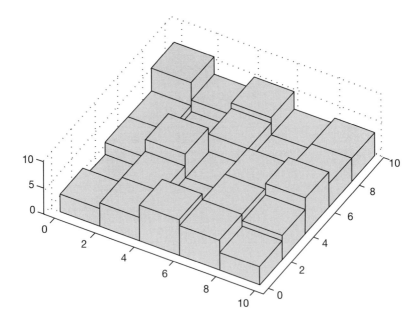

Fig. 7.11 Three-dimensional histogram displaying the numbers of objects for each subarea. The histogram was created using `hist3`.

```
chi2_data = sum((n_exp - n_syn).^2 ./n_syn)

chi2 =
    14
```

The critical χ^2 can be calculated by using `chi2inv`. The χ^2-test requires the degrees of freedom Φ. In our example, we test the hypothesis that the data are uniformly distributed, i.e., we estimate only one parameter (Chapter 3.4). Therefore, the number of degrees of freedom is $\Phi = 25 - (1+1) = 23$. We test the hypothesis on a $p = 95\%$ significance level. The function `chi2inv` computes the inverse of the χ^2 CDF with parameters specified by Φ for the corresponding probabilities in p.

```
chi2_theo = chi2inv(0.95,25-1-1)

ans =
    35.1725
```

The critical χ^2 of 35.1725 is well above the measured χ^2 of 14. Therefore, we cannot reject the null hypothesis and conclude that our data follow a uniform distribution.

Test for Random Distribution

The following example illustrates the test for randomly-distributed objects in an area. We use the uniformly-distributed data generated in the previous example and display the point distribution.

```
clear
rand('seed',0)
data = 10 * rand(100,2);
plot(data(:,1),data(:,2),'o')
hold on
x = 0:10; y = ones(size(x));
for i = 1:9, plot(x,i*y,'r-'), end
for i = 1:9, plot(i*y,x,'r-'), end
hold off
```

We generate the three-dimensional histogram and use the function `hist3` to count the objects per class. In contrast to the previous test, we now count the subareas containing a certain number of observations. The number of subareas is usually larger than it would be used for the previous test. In our example, we use 49 subareas or classes.

```
hist3(data,[7 7])
view(30,70)

counts = hist3(data,[7 7]);
counts = counts(:);
```

The frequency distribution of subareas with a certain number of objects follows a Poisson distribution (Chapter 3.4) if the objects are randomly distributed. First, we compute a frequency distribution of subareas with N objects. In our example, we count the subareas with 0, ..., 5 objects. We also display the histogram of the frequency distribution as a two-dimensional histogram using `hist` (Fig. 7.12).

```
N = 0 : 5;

[n_exp,v] = hist(counts,N);

hist(counts,N)
title('Histogram')
xlabel('Number of observations N')
ylabel('Subareas with N observations')
```

The expected number of subareas E_j with a certain number of objects j can be computed using

$$E_j = Te^{-n/T} \frac{(n/T)^j}{j!}$$

where n is the total number of objects and T is the number of subareas. For $j=0$, $j!$ is taken to be 1. We compute the theoretical frequency distribution using the equation shown above,

```
for i = 1 : 6
    n_syn(i) = 49*exp(-100/49)*(100/49)^N(i)/factorial(N(i));
end
n_syn = sum(n_exp)*n_syn/sum(n_syn);
```

and display both the empirical and theoretical frequency distributions in one plot.

```
h1 = bar(v,n_exp);
hold on
h2 = bar(v,n_syn);
hold off

set(h1,'FaceColor','none','EdgeColor','r')
set(h2,'FaceColor','none','EdgeColor','b')
```

The χ^2-test is again employed to compare the empirical and theoretical distributions. The test is performed on a $p=95\%$ significance level. The Poisson distribution is defined by only one parameter (Chapter 3.4). Therefore, the number of degrees of freedom is $\Phi=6-(1+1)=4$. The measured χ^2 of

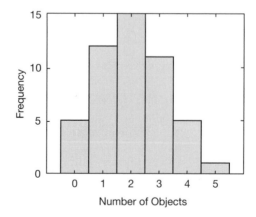

Fig. 7.12 Frequency distribution of subareas with N objects. In our example, we count the subareas with 0, ..., 5 objects. We display the histogram of the frequency distribution as a two-dimensional histogram using `hist`.

```
chi2 = sum((n_exp - n_syn).^2 ./n_syn)

chi2 =
    1.4357
```

is well below the critical χ^2, which is

```
chi2inv(0.95,6-1-1)

ans =
    9.4877
```

Therefore, we cannot reject the null hypothesis and conclude that our data follow a Poission distribution. Therfore, the point distribution is random.

Test for Clustering

Point distributions in geosciences are often clustered. We use a *nearest-neighbor criterion* to test a spatial distribution for clustering. Davis (2002) published an excellent summary of the nearest-neighbor analysis, summarizing the work of a number of other authors. Swan and Sandilands (1996) presented a simplified description of this analysis. The test for clustering computes the distances d_i of all possible pairs of nearest points in the field. The *observed mean nearest-neighbor distance* is

$$\bar{d} = \frac{1}{n}\sum_{i=1}^{n}d_i$$

where n is the total number of points or objects in the field. The arithmetic mean of all distances is related to the area of the map. This relationship is expressed by the *expected mean nearest-neighbor distance*, which is

$$\bar{\delta} = \frac{1}{2}\sqrt{A/n}$$

where A is the map area. Small values of this ratio then suggest significant clustering, whereas larger values indicate regularity or uniformity. The test uses a Z statistic (Chapter 3.4), which is

$$Z = \frac{\bar{d} - \bar{\delta}}{s_e}$$

where s_e is the standard error of the mean nearest-neighbor distance, which is defined as

$$s_e = \frac{0.26136}{\sqrt{n^2 / A}}$$

The null hypothesis *randomness* is tested against two alternative hypotheses, *clustering* and *uniformity or regularity*. The Z statistic has critical values of 1.96 and -1.96 at a significance level of 95%. If $-1.96 < Z < +1.96$, we accept the null hypothesis that the data are randomly distributed. If $Z < -1.96$, we reject the null hypothesis and accept the first alternative hypothesis of clustering. If $Z > +1.96$, we also reject the null hypothesis, but accept the alternative hypothesis of uniformity or regularity.

As an example, we use the synthetic data analyzed in the previous examples again.

```
clear
rand('seed',0)
data = 10 * rand(100,2);
plot(data(:,1),data(:,2),'o')
```

We first compute the pairwise Euclidian distance between all pairs of observations using the function `pdist` (Chapter 9.4). The resulting distance matrix is then reformatted between upper triangular and square form using `squareform`.

```
distances = pdist(data,'Euclidean');
distmatrix = squareform(distances);
```

The following `for` loop finds the nearest neighbors, stores the corresponding distances and computes the mean distance.

```
for i = 1 : 5
    distmatrix(i,i) = NaN;
    k = find(distmatrix(i,:) == min(distmatrix(i,:)));
    nearest(i) = distmatrix(i,k(1));
end
observednearest = mean(nearest)

observednearest =
    0.5471
```

In our example, the mean nearest distance `observednearest` comes to be 0.5471. Next, we calculate the area of the map. The expected mean nearest-neighbor distance is half the squareroot of the map area divided by the number of observations.

```
maparea = (max(data(:,1)-min(data(:,1)))) ...
          *(max(data(:,2)-min(data(:,2))));
expectednearest = 0.5 * sqrt(maparea/length(data))

expectednearest =
    0.4940
```

In our example, the expected mean nearest distance `expectednearest` is 0.4940. Finally, we compute the standard error of the mean nearest-neighbor distance `se`

```
se = 0.26136/sqrt((length(data).^2/maparea))

se =
    0.0258
```

and the test statistic `z`.

```
z = (observednearest - expectednearest)/se

z =
    2.0561
```

In our example, `z` is 2.0561. Since `z`>+1.96, we reject the null hypothesis and conclude that the data are uniformly or regularly distributed, but not clustered.

7.10 Analysis of Digital Elevation Models (by R. Gebbers)

Digital elevation models (DEM) and their derivatives (e.g., slope and aspect) can indicate surface processes like lateral water flow, solar irradiation or erosion. The simplest derivatives of a DEM are the slope and the aspect. The *slope* (or *gradient*) describes the measurement of the steepness, the incline or the grade of a surface measured in percentages or degrees. The *aspect* (or *exposure*) generally refers to the direction to which a mountain slope faces.

We use the SRTM data set introduced in Chapter 7.5 to illustrate the analysis of a digital elevation model for slopes, aspects and other derivatives. The data are loaded by

```
fid = fopen('S01E036.hgt','r');
SRTM = fread(fid,[1201,inf],'int16','b');
fclose(fid);

SRTM = SRTM';
SRTM = flipud(SRTM);
SRTM(find(SRTM==-32768)) = NaN;
```

These data are elevation values in meters above sea level sampled at a 3-arc-second or 90 meter grid. The SRTM data contain small-scale spatial disturbances and noise that could cause problems when computing a consistent drainage pattern. Therefore, we lowpass-filter the data using a two-dimensional moving-average filter using the function `filter2`. The filter used here is a spatial running mean of 3×3 elements. We use only the subset `SRTM(400:600,650:850)` of the original data set to reduce computation time. We also remove the data at the edges of the DEM to eliminate filter artifacts.

```
F = 1/9 * ones(3,3);
SRTM = filter2(F, SRTM(750:850,700:800));
SRTM = SRTM(2:99,2:99);
```

The DEM is displayed as a pseudocolor plot using `pcolor` and the colormap `demcmap` included in the Mapping Toolbox. This colormap creates and assigns a colormap appropriate for elevation data since it provides land and sea colors in proportion to topography and bathymetry.

```
h = pcolor(SRTM);
demcmap(SRTM), colorbar
set(h,'LineStyle','none')
axis equal
title('Elevation [m]')
[r c] = size(SRTM);
axis([1 c 1 r])
set(gca,'TickDir','out');
```

The DEM is characterized by a horseshoe-shaped mountain range surrounding a valley descending towards the Southeast (Fig. 7.15a).

The SRTM subset is now analyzed for slopes and aspects. While we are working with DEMs on a regular grid, slope and aspect can be estimated as local derivatives by using centered finite differences in a local 3×3 neighborhood. Figure 7.13 shows the local neighborhood using the cell indexing convention of MATLAB. For calculating slope and aspect, we need two finite differences of the DEM elements z in x and y direction:

$$z_x = \frac{z_{r,c-1} - z_{r,c+1}}{2h}$$

and

$$z_y = \frac{z_{r-1,c} - z_{r+1,c}}{2h}$$

Z(1)	Z(4)	Z(7)
Z(2)	Z(5)	Z(8)
Z(3)	Z(6)	Z(9)

Fig. 7.13 Local neighborhood showing cell number convention of MATLAB.

where h is the cell size, which has the same unit as the elevation. Using the finite differences, the dimensionless slope is then calculated by

$$SLP_{DF} = \sqrt{z_x^2 + z_y^2}$$

Other primary relief attributes such as the *aspect*, the *plan*, the *profile* and the *tangential curvature* can be derived in a similar way using finite differences (Wilson and Galant 2000). The function `gradientm` contained in the Mapping Toolbox calculates slope and aspect of a data grid `z` in units of degrees clockwise from North and up from the horizontal. Function `gradientm(z,refvec)` requires a three-element referencing vector `refvec`. The reference vector contains the number of cells per degree as well as the latitude and longitude of the upper-left (northwest) element of the data array. Since the SRTM digital elevation model is sampled at a 3-arc-second grid, $60 \times 60/3 = 1200$ elements of the DEM correspond to one degree longitude or latitude. For simplicity, we ignore the actual coordinates of the SRTM subset in this example and use the indices of the DEM elements instead.

```
refvec = [1200 0 0];
[asp, slp] = gradientm(SRTM, refvec);
```

We display a pseudocolor map of the slope (in degrees) of the DEM (Fig 7.15b).

```
h = pcolor(slp);
colormap(jet), colorbar
set(h,'LineStyle','none')
```

```
axis equal
title('Slope [°]')
[r c] = size(slp);
axis([1 c 1 r])
set(gca,'TickDir','out');
```

Flat areas can be found everywhere on the summits and the valley bottoms. The southeastern and south-southwestern sectors are relatively flat. Steeper slopes are concentrated in the center and the southwestern sector. Next, a pseudocolor map of the aspect is generated (Fig. 7.15c).

```
h = pcolor(asp);
colormap(hsv), colorbar
set(h,'LineStyle','none')
axis equal
title('Aspect')
[r c] = size(asp);
axis([1 c 1 r])
set(gca,'TickDir','out');
```

This plot displays the aspect in units of degrees clockwise from North. For instance, mountain slopes facing North are displayed in red colors, whereas green areas depict East-facing slopes.

The aspect changes abruptly along the ridges of the mountain ranges where neighboring drainage basins are divided by *watersheds*. The Image Processing Toolbox includes the function watershed to detect the drainage divides and to label individual watershed regions or catchments by integer values, where the first watershed region is labeled 1, the elements labeled 2 belong to the second catchment, and so on.

```
watersh = watershed(SRTM);
```

The watershed regions are displayed by a pseudocolor plot where the labels of the regions are assigned by colors given in the color table hsv (Fig 7.15d).

```
h = pcolor(watersh);
colormap(hsv), colorbar
set(h,'LineStyle','none')
axis equal
title('Watershed')
[r c] = size(watersh);
axis([1 c 1 r])
set(gca,'TickDir','out');
```

The watersheds are displayed as series of red pixels. The largest catchment corresponds to the medium blue region in the center of the map. To the Northwest, this large catchment seems to be neighbored by three catchments (represented by green colors) without an outlet. As in this example, `watershed` often generates unrealistic results as watershed algorithms are sensitive to local minima that act as spurious sinks. We can detect such sinks in the SRTM data using the function `imregionalmin`. The output of this function is a binary image that has the value 1 corresponding to the elements of the DEM that belong to regional minima and the value of 0 otherwise.

```
sinks = 1*imregionalmin(SRTM);

h = pcolor(sinks);
colormap(gray)
set(h,'LineStyle','none')
axis equal
title('Sinks')
[r c] = size(sinks);
axis([1 c 1 r])
set(gca,'TickDir','out');
```

The pseudocolor plot of the binary image exhibits twelve local sinks represented by white pixels that are potentially the locations of non-outlet catchments and should be kept in mind while computing the following hydrological DEM attributes.

Flow accumulation (specific catchment area, upslope contributing area) is defined as the number of cells, or area, which contribute to runoff of a given cell (Fig. 7.14). In contrast to the local parameters slope and aspect, flow accumulation can only be determined from the global neighborhood. The principal operation is to add cell outflows iteratively to lower neighbors. Before cascading the cell outflows, we have to determine the individual gradients to each neighbor indexed by N. The array N contains indices for the eight neighboring cells according to the MATLAB convention as shown in Figure 17.3. We make use of the `circshift` function to access the neighboring cells. In the case of a two-dimensional matrix Z, the function `circshift(Z, [r c])` circularly shifts the values in the matrix Z by an amount of rows and columns given by `r` and `c`, respectively. For example, `circshift(Z, [1 1])` will circularly shift Z one row down and one column to the right. The individual gradients are calculated by

$$grad = \frac{z_{r+y,c+x} - z_{r,c}}{h}$$

for the eastern, southern, western, and northern neighbors (the so-called *rook's case*) and by

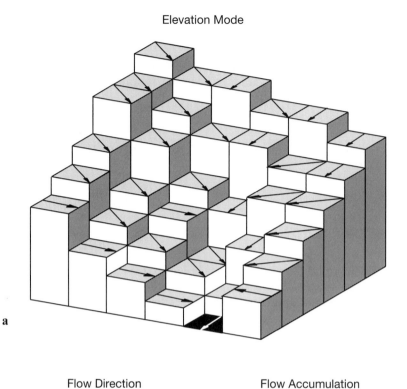

Fig. 7.14 Schematic of calculation of flow accumulation by the D8 method

$$grad = \frac{z_{r+y,c+x} - z_{r,c}}{\sqrt{2h}}$$

for the diagonal neighbors (*bishop's case*). Herein, h is the cell size, $z_{r,c}$ is the elevation of the center cell and $z_{r+y,c+x}$ is the elevation of a neighbor. The cell indices x and y are obtained from the matrix N. The gradients are stored in a three-dimensional matrix grads, where grads(:,:,1) contains the gradients towards the neighbors in the East, grads(:,:,2) contains the gradients towards the neighbors in the Southeast, and so on. Negative gradients indicate outflow from the center to the respective neighbor. To obtain relative surface flow gradients are transformed by inverse tangent divided by 0.5π.

```
N = [0 -1;-1 -1;-1 0;+1 -1;0 +1;+1 +1;+1 0;-1 +1];
[a b] = size(SRTM);
grads = zeros(a,b,8);
for c = 2 : 2 : 8
    grads(:,:,c) = (circshift(SRTM,[N(c,1) N(c,2)]) ...
        -SRTM)/sqrt(2*90);
end
for c = 1 : 2 : 7
    grads(:,:,c) = (circshift(SRTM,[N(c,1) N(c,2)]) ...
        -SRTM)/90;
end
grads = atan(grads)/pi*2;
```

Since a center cell can have several downslope neighbors, water can flow in several directions. This phenomenon is called *divergent flow*. Early flow accumulation algorithms were based on the single-flow-direction method (D8 method, Fig. 7.14), which allows flow to only one of the cell's eight neighbors. This method cannot model divergence in ridge areas and tends to produce parallel flow lines in some examples. Here, we are illustrating the use of a multiple-flow-direction method, which allows flow from a cell to multiple neighbors. The flow to another neighbor corresponds to the individual gradient and is a fraction of the total outflow. Even though multiple-flow methods reveal more realistic results in most examples, they tend to cause dispersion in valleys where the flow should be more concentrated. Thus, a weighting factor w is introduced, which controls the relation of the outflows.

$$flow_i = \frac{grad_i^w}{\sum\limits_{i=1}^{8} grad_i^w} \quad \text{for} \quad grad_i^w < 0$$

A recommended value for w is 1.1. Higher values will concentrate the flow in the direction of the steepest slope, while $w=0$ would cause an extreme dispersion. In the following sequence of commands, we first select the gradients less than zero and multiply the result with the weight.

```
w = 1.1;
flow = (grads.*(-1*grads<0)).^w;
```

Then we are summing up the upslope gradients, i.e., the third dimension of flow. We replace values of 0 by the value of 1 that avoids the problems with division by zero.

```
upssum = sum(flow,3);
upssum(upssum==0) = 1;
```

We divide the flows by upssum to obtain fractional weights summing up to one. In our code, this is done separately for each layer of the 3D flow array by a for loop:

```
for i=1:8
    flow(:,:,i) = flow(:,:,i).*(flow(:,:,i)>0)./upssum;
end
```

The 2D matrix inflowsum will store the intermediate sums of inflows for each step of the iteration. The inflows are summed up to the total flow accumulation flowac at the end of each iteration. Initial values of inflowsum and flowac are provided by upssum.

```
inflowsum = upssum;
flowac = upssum;
```

Another 3D matrix inflow is now needed to store the intermediate inflow achieved by all neighbors:

```
inflow = grads*0;
```

Flow accumulation is terminated when there is no inflow, or translated into MATLAB code, we use a conditional while loop that terminates if sum(inflowsum(:)) == 0. The number of non-zero entries in inflow-sum will decrease during each loop iteration. This is achieved by alternately updating inflow and inflowsum. Here, inflowsum is updated with the intermediate inflow of the neighbor(s) weighted by flow under the condition that the neighbors are contributing cells, i.e., where grads are positive. Since not all neighbors are contributing cells, the intermediate inflow-sum, and also inflow is reduced. Flow accumulation flowac is increasing through the consecutive summation of the intermediate `inflowsum`.

```
while sum(inflowsum(:))>0
    for i = 1:8
        inflow(:,:,i) = circshift(inflowsum,[N(i,1) N(i,2)]);
    end
    inflowsum = sum(inflow.*flow.*grads>0,3);
    flowac = flowac + inflowsum;
end
```

We display the result as a pseudocolor map with log-scaled values
(Fig 7.15 e).

```
h = pcolor(log(1+flowac));
colormap(flipud(jet)), colorbar
set(h,'LineStyle','none')
axis equal
title('Flow accumulation')
[r c] = size(flowac);
axis([1 c 1 r])
set(gca,'TickDir','out');
```

The plot displays areas with high flow accumulation in blue colors, whereas
areas with low flow accumulation are displayed in red colors usually corresponding to ridges. We used a logarithmic scaling for mapping the flow
accumulation to obtain a better representation of the results. The simplified
algorithm to calculate flow accumulation introduced here can be used to analyze DEMs representing a sloping terrain. In flat terrains, where the slope
becomes zero, no flow direction can be generated by our algorithm and
thus flow accumulation stops. Such examples require more sophisticated
algorithms to perform the analysis of DEMs. Furthermore, more advanced
algorithms also include sink-filling routines to avoid spurious sinks that in-
terrupt flow accumulation. Small depressions can be filled by smoothing as
we have done it at the beginning of this chapter.

The first part of this chapter was about primary relief attributes.
Secondary attributes of a DEM are functions of two or more primary attributes. Examples for secondary attributes are the wetness index and the
stream power index. The *wetness index* is the log of the ratio of the specific
catchment area and tangent of slope:

$$weti = \log\left(\frac{1 + flowac}{\tan(slp)}\right)$$

The term $1 + flowac$ avoids the problems with calculating the logarithm of
zero when `flowac=0`. The wetness index is used to predict the soil water

content (*saturation*) due to the lateral water movement. The potential for water logging is usually high at lower elevations of a catchment with small slopes. Flat areas having a large upslope area have a high wetness index as compared with steep areas with small catchments. The wetness index `weti` is computed and displayed by

```
weti = log((1+flowac)./tand(slp));

h = pcolor(weti);
colormap(flipud(jet)), colorbar
set(h,'LineStyle','none')
axis equal
title('Wetness index')
[r c] = size(weti);
axis([1 c 1 r])
set(gca,'TickDir','out');
```

In this graph, blue colors indicate high values of the wetness index, whereas red colors display low values (Fig. 7.15f). In our example, soils in the Southeast most likely have high water content due to the runoff from the large central valley and the terrain flatness.

The *stream power index* is another important secondary relief attribute which is frequently used in hillslope hydrology, geomorphology, soil science and related disciplines. As a measure of stream power it indicates sediment transport and erosion by water. It is defined as the product of the specific catchment area and tangent of the slope:

$$spi = flowac \cdot \tan{(slp)}$$

The potential for erosion is high when large quantities of water (calculated by the flow accumulation) are fast flowing due to an extreme slope. The following series of commands compute and display the stream power index:

```
spi = flowac.*tand(slp);

h = pcolor(log(1+spi));
colormap(jet), colorbar
set(h,'LineStyle','none')
axis equal
title('Stream power index')
[r c] = size(spi);
axis([1 c 1 r])
set(gca,'TickDir','out');
```

The wetness and stream power indices are particularly useful in large-scale terrain analysis, i.e., digital elevation models sampled on intervals of less

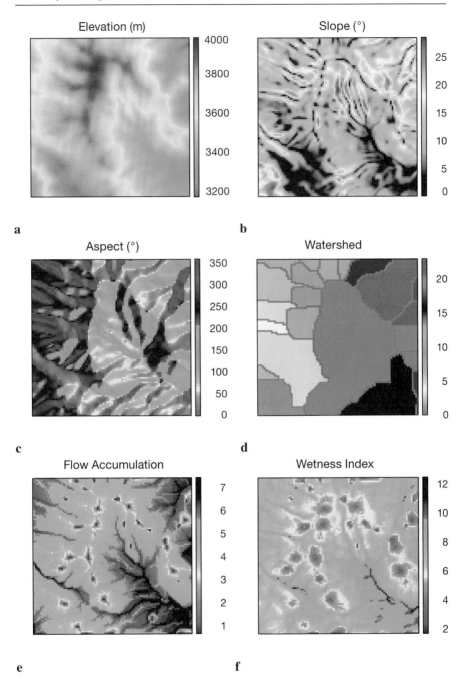

Fig. 7.15 Display of a subset of the SRTM data set used in Chapter 7.5 and primary and secondary attributes of the digital elevation model; **a** elevation, **b** slope, **c** aspect, **d** watershed, **e** flow accumulation and **f** wetness index.

than 30 meters. Though we have calculated `weti` and `spi` from a medium-scale DEM, we have to expect scale dependency of these attributes in our terrain analysis example.

This chapter has illustrated the use of basic tools to analyze digital elevation models. More detailed introductions to digital terrain modelling are given by the book by Wilson & Galant (2002). Furthermore, the article by Freeman (1991) provides a comprehensive summary and introduction to advanced algorithms for flow accumulation.

7.11 Geostatistics and Kriging (by R. Gebbers)

Geostatistics describes the autocorrelation of one or more variables in the 1D, 2D, and 3D space or even in 4D space-time, to make predictions at unobserved locations, to give information about the accuracy of prediction and to reproduce spatial variability and uncertainty. The shape, the range, and the direction of the spatial autocorrelation are described by the *variogram*, which is the main tool in linear geostatistics. The origins of geostatistics can be dated back to the early 50's when the South African mining engineer Daniel G. Krige first published an interpolation method based on spatial dependency of samples. In the 60's and 70's, the French mathematician George Matheron developed the *theory of regionalized variables* which provides the theoretical foundations of Kriges's more practical methods. This theory forms the basis of several procedures for the analysis and estimation of spatially dependent variables, which Matheron called *geostatistics*. Matheron as well coined the term *kriging* for spatial interpolation by geostatistical methods.

Theorical Background

A basic assumption in geostatistics is that a spatiotemporal process is composed of deterministic and stochastic components (Fig. 7.16). The deterministic components can be global and local trends (sometimes called *drifts*). The stochastic component is formed by a purely random and an autocorrelated part. An autocorrelated component implies that on average, closer observations are more similar than more distant observations. This behavior is described by the *variogram* where squared differences between observations are plotted against their separation distances. The fundamental idea of D. Krige was to use the variogram for interpolation as means to determine the magnitude of influence of neighboring observations when predicting

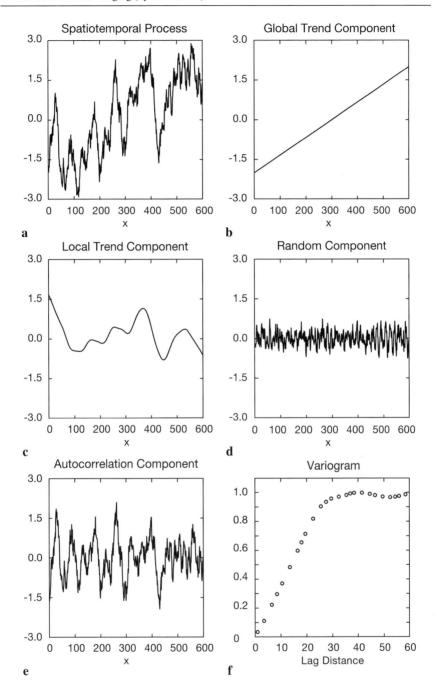

Fig. 7.16 Components of a spatiotemporal process and the variogram. The variogram (**f**) should only be derived from the autocorrelated component.

values at unobserved locations. Basic linear geostatistics includes two main procedures: variography for modeling the variogram and kriging for interpolation.

Preceding Analysis

Because linear geostatistics as presented here is a parametric method, the underlying assumptions have to be checked by a preceding analysis. As other parametric methods, linear geostatistics is sensitive to outliers and deviations from normal distribution. First, after opening the data file *geost_dat.mat* containing *xyz* data triplets we plot the sampling locations. Doing this, we can check point distribution and detect gross errors on the data coordinates *x* and *y*.

```
load geost_dat.mat

plot(x,y,'.')
```

Checking of the limits of the observations *z* can be done by

```
min(z)

ans =
    3.7199

max(z)

ans =
    7.8460
```

For linear geostatistics, the observations *z* should be gaussian distributed. In most cases, this is only tested by visual inspection of the histogram because statistical tests are often too sensitive if the number of samples exceed ca. 100. In addition, one can calculate skewness and kurtosis of the data.

```
hist(z)

skewness(z)

ans =
    0.2568

kurtosis(z)

ans =
    2.5220
```

A flat-topped or multiple peaks distribution suggests that there is more than one population in your data set. If these populations can be related to continuous areas they should be treated separately. Another reason for multiple peaks can be preferential sampling of areas with high and/or low values. This happens usually due to some a priori knowledge and is called cluster effect. Handling of the cluster effect is described in Deutsch and Journel (1998) and Isaaks and Srivastava (1998).

Most problems arise from positive skewness (long upper tail). According to Webster and Oliver (2001), one should consider root transformation if skewness is between 0.5 and 1, and logarithmic transformation if skewness exceeds 1. A general formula of transformation is:

$$z^* = \begin{cases} \dfrac{(z+m)^k - 1}{k} & \text{for } k \neq 0 \\ \log(z+m) & \text{for } k = 0 \end{cases}$$

for $\min(z) + m > 0$. This is the so called Box-Cox transform with the special case $k=0$ when a logarithm transformation is used. In the logarithm transformation, m should be added when z values are zero or negative. Interpolation results of power-transformed values can be backtransformed directly after kriging. The backtransformation of log-transformed values is slightly more complicated and will be explained later. The procedure is known as *lognormal kriging*. It can be important because lognormal distributions are not unusual in geology.

Variography with the Classical Variogram

The variogram describes the spatial dependency of referenced observations in a one or multidimensional space. While usually we do not know the true variogram of the spatial process we have to estimate it from observations. This procedure is called variography. Variography starts with calculating the *experimental variogram* from the raw data. In the next step, the experimental variogram is summarized by the variogram estimator. Variography finishes with fitting a variogram model to the *variogram estimator*. The *experimental variogram* is calculated as the difference between pairs of the observed values depending on the *separation vector h* (Fig. 7.17). The classical experimental variogram is given by the *semivariance*,

$$\gamma(h) = 0.5 \cdot (z_x - z_{x+h})^2$$

where z_x is he observed value at location x and z_{x+h} is he observed value at another point within a distance h. The length of the separation vector h is

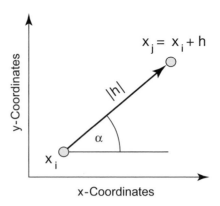

x-Coordinates

Fig. 7.17 Separation vector *h* between two points.

called *lag distance* or simply *lag*. The correct term for $\gamma(h)$ is *semivariogram* (or *semivariance*), where *semi* refers to the fact that it is half of the variance of the difference between z_x and z_{x+h}. It is, nevertheless, the variance per point when points are considered as in pairs (Webster and Oliver, 2001). Conventionally, $\gamma(h)$ is termed *variogram* instead of semivariogram and so we do at the end of this chapter. To calculate the experimental variogram we first have to build pairs of observations. This is done by typing

```
[X1,X2] = meshgrid(x);
[Y1,Y2] = meshgrid(y);
[Z1,Z2] = meshgrid(z);
```

The matrix of separation distances D between the observation points is

```
D = sqrt((X1 - X2).^2 + (Y1 - Y2).^2);
```

where `srqt` is the square root of the data. Then we get the experimental variogram G as half the squared differences between the observed values:

```
G = 0.5*(Z1 - Z2).^2;
```

We used the MATLAB capability to vectorize commands instead of using *for* loops to run faster. However, we have computed n_2 pairs of observations although only $n(n-1)/2$ pairs are required. For large data sets, e.g., more than 3000 data points, the software and physical memory of the computer may become a limiting factor. For such cases, a more efficient way of programming is described in the user manual of the software SURFER (2002). The plot of the experimental variogram is called the *variogram cloud* (Fig. 7.18). We get this after extracting the lower triangular portions of the D and G arrays.

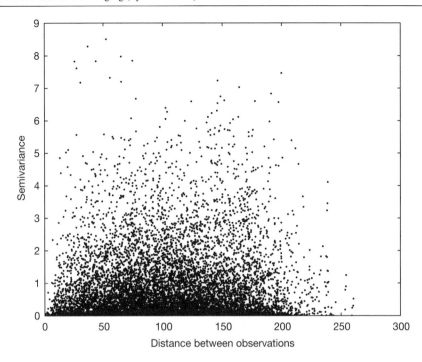

Fig. 7.18 Variogram cloud: Plot of the experimental variogram (half squared difference between pairs of observations) versus the lag distance (separation distance of the pairs).

```
indx = 1:length(z);
[C,R] = meshgrid(indx);
I = R > C;

plot(D(I),G(I),'.')
xlabel('lag distance')
ylabel('variogram')
```

The variogram cloud gives you an impression of the dispersion of values at the different lags. It might be useful to detect outliers or anomalies, but it is hard to judge from it whether there is any spatial correlation, what form it might have, and how we could model it (Webster and Oliver, 2001). To obtain a clearer view and to prepare variogram modeling the experimental variogram is replaced by the variogram estimator in the next section.

The *variogram estimator* is derived from the experimental variograms to summarize their central tendency (similar to the descriptive statistics derived from univariate observations, Chapter 3.2). The classical variogram estimator is the averaged empirical variogram within certain distance classes or bins defined by multiples of the lag interval. The classification of separation distances is visualized in Figure 7.19.

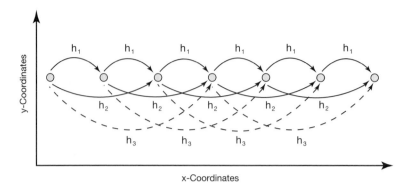

Fig. 7.19 Classification of separation distances in the case of equally spaced observations along a line. The lag interval is h_1 and h_2, h_3 etc. are multiples of the lag interval.

The variogram estimator is calculated by:

$$\gamma_E(h) = \frac{1}{2 * N(h)} \cdot \sum_{i=1}^{N(h)} (z_{xi} - z_{xi+h})^2$$

where $N(h)$ is the number of pairs within the lag interval h.

First, we need an idea about a suitable lag interval h. If you have sampled on a regular grid, you can use the length of a grid cell. If the samples have irregular spacings, as in our case, the mean minimum distance of pairs is a good starting point for the lag interval (Webster and Oliver 2001). To calculate the mean minimum distance of pairs we have to replace the diagonal of the lag matrix D zeros with NaN's, otherwise the minimum distance will be zero:

```
D2 = D.*(diag(x*NaN)+1);
lag = mean(min(D2))

lag =
     8.0107
```

While the estimated variogram values tend to become more erratic with increasing distances, it is important to define a maximum distance which limits the calculation. As a rule of thumb, the half maximum distance is suitable range for variogram analysis. We obtain the half maximum distance and the maximum number of lags by:

```
hmd = max(D(:))/2

hmd =
    130.1901
```

```
max_lags = floor(hmd/lag)

max_lags =
    16
```

Then the separation distances are classified and the classical variogram estimator is calculated:

```
LAGS = ceil(D/lag);

for i = 1 : max_lags
    SEL = (LAGS == i);
    DE(i) = mean(mean(D(SEL)));
    PN(i) = sum(sum(SEL == 1))/2;
    GE(i) = mean(mean(G(SEL)));
end
```

where SEL is the selection matrix defined by the lag classes in LAG, DE is the mean lag, PN is the number of pairs and GE is the variogram estimator. Now we can plot the classical variogram estimator (variogram versus mean separation distance) together with the population variance:

```
plot(DE,GE,'.' )
var_z = var(z);
b = [0 max(DE)];
c = [var_z var_z];

hold on

plot(b,c, '--r')
yl = 1.1 * max(GE);
ylim([0 yl])
xlabel('Averaged distance between observations')
ylabel('Averaged semivariance')

hold off
```

The variogram in Figure 7.20 shows a typical behavior. Values are low at small separation distances (near the origin), they are increasing with increasing distances, than reaching a plateau (*sill*) which is close to the population variance. This indicates that the spatial process is correlated over short distances while there is no spatial dependency over longer distances. The length of the spatial dependency is called the *range* and is defined by the separation distance where the variogram reaches the sill.

The *variogram model* is a parametric curve fitted to the variogram estimator. This is similar to frequency distribution fitting (see Chapter 3.5), where the frequency distribution is modeled by a distribution type and its parameters (e.g., a normal distribution with its mean and variance). Due to

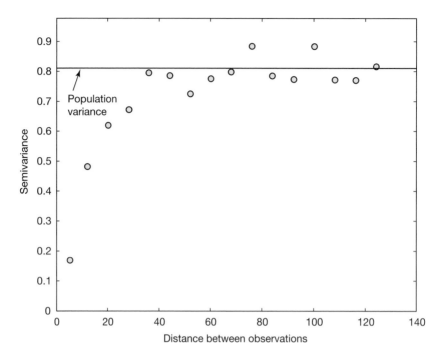

Fig. 7.20 The classical variogram estimator (gray circles) and the population variance (solid line).

theoretical reasons, only functions with certain properties should be used as variogram models. Common *authorized models* are the spherical, the exponential and the linear model (more models can be found in the literature).

Spherical model:

$$
\gamma_{\text{sph}}(h) = \begin{cases} c \cdot \left(1.5 \cdot \dfrac{h}{a} - 0.5 \left(\dfrac{h}{a} \right)^3 \right) & \text{for } 0 \leq h \leq a \\ c & \text{for } h > a \end{cases}
$$

Exponential model:

$$
\gamma_{\text{exp}}(h) = c \cdot \left(1 - \exp\left(-3 \cdot \dfrac{h}{a} \right) \right)
$$

Linear model:

$$\gamma_{\text{lin}}(h) = b \cdot h$$

where c is the sill, a is the range, and b is the slope (in the case of the linear model). The parameters c and a or b have to be modified when a variogram model is fitted to the variogram estimator. The so called *nugget effect* is a special type of variogram model. In practice, when extrapolating the variogram towards separation distance zero, we often observe a positive intercept on the ordinate. This is called the nugget effect and it is explained by measurement errors and by small scale fluctuations (*nuggets*), which are not captured due to too large sampling intervals. Thus, we sometimes have expectations about the minimum nugget effect from the variance of repeated measurements in the laboratory or other previous knowledge. More details about the nugget effect can be found in Cressie (1993) and Kitanidis (1997). If there is a nugget effect, it can be added to the variogram model. An exponential model with a nugget effect looks like this:

$$\gamma_{\text{exp+nug}}(h) = c_0 + c \cdot \left(1 - \exp\left(-3 \cdot \frac{h}{a}\right)\right)$$

where c_0 is the nugget effect.

We can even combine more variogram models, e.g., two spherical models with different ranges and sills. These combinations are called *nested models*. During variogram modeling the components of a nested model are regarded as spatial structures which should be interpreted as the results of geological processes. Before we discuss further aspects of variogram modeling let us just fit some models to our data. We are beginning with a spherical model without nugget, than adding an exponential and a linear model, both with nugget variance:

```
plot(DE,GE,'o','MarkerFaceColor',[.6 .6 .6])
var_z = var(z);
b = [0 max(DE)];
c = [var_z var_z];
hold on
plot(b,c,'--r')
xlim(b)
yl = 1.1*max(GE);
ylim([0 yl])

% Spherical model with nugget
nugget = 0;
sill = 0.803;
```

```
range = 45.9;
lags = 0:max(DE);
Gsph = nugget + (sill*(1.5*lags/range - 0.5*(lags/...
    range).^3).*(lags<=range) + sill*(lags>range));
plot(lags,Gsph,':g')

% Exponential model with nugget
nugget = 0.0239;
sill = 0.78;
range = 45;
Gexp = nugget + sill*(1 - exp(-3*lags/range));
plot(lags,Gexp,'-.b')

% Linear model with nugget
nugget = 0.153;
slope = 0.0203;
Glin = nugget + slope*lags;
plot(lags,Glin,'-m')
xlabel('Distance between observations')
ylabel('Semivariance')
legend('Variogram estimator','Population variance',...
'Sperical model','Exponential model','Linear model')
hold off
```

Variogram modeling is very much a point of discussion. Some advocate *objective* variogram modeling by automated curve fitting, using a weighted least squares, maximum likelihood or maximum entropy method. Contrary to this it is often argued that the geological knowledge should be included in the modeling process and thus, fitting by eye is recommended. In many cases the problem in variogram modeling is much less the question of the appropriate procedure but a question of the quality of the experimental variogram. If the experimental variogram is good, both procedures will yield similar results.

Another question important for variogram modeling is the intended use of the model. In our case, the linear model seems not to be appropriate (Fig. 7.21). At a closer look we can see that the linear model fits reasonably well over the first three lags. This can be sufficient when we use the variogram model only for kriging, because in kriging the nearby points are the most important for the estimate (see discussion of kriging below). Thus, different variogram models with similar fits near the origin will yield similar kriging results when sampling points are regularly distributed. If you are interested in describing the spatial structures it is another case. Then it is important to find a suitable model over all lags and to determine the sill and the range accurately. A collection of geologic case studies in Rendu and Readdy (1982) show how process knowledge and variography can be linked. Good guidelines to variogram modeling are given by Gringarten

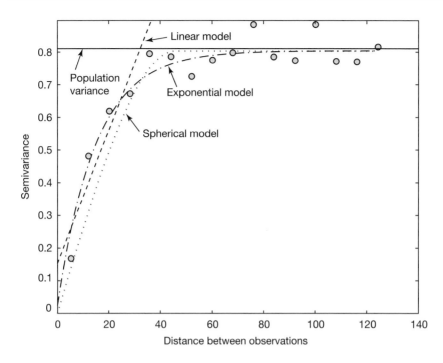

Fig. 7.21 Variogram estimator (gray circles), population variance (solid line), spherical, exponential, and linear models (dashed lines).

and Deutsch (2001) and Webster and Oliver (2001). We will now briefly discuss some more aspects of variography.

- *Sample size* – As in any statistical procedure you need as large a sample as possible to get a reliable estimate. For variography it is recommended to have more than 100 to 150 samples (Webster and Oliver 2001). If you have less, you should consider computing a maximum likelihood variogram (Pardo-Igúzquiza and Dowd 1997).

- *Sampling design* – To get a good estimation at the origin of the variogram sampling design should include observations over small distances. This can be done by a nested design (Webster and Oliver 2001). Other designs were evaluated by Olea (1984).

- *Anisotropy* – Thus far now we have assumed that the structure of spatial correlation is independent of direction. We have calculated *omnidirectional variograms* ignoring the direction of the separation vector *h*. In a more thorough analysis, the variogram should not only be discretized in distance but also in direction (directional bins). Plotting *directional variograms*, usually in four directions, we sometimes can observe different ranges (*geometric anisotropy*), different scales (*zonal anisotropy*), and different shapes (indicating a trend). The treatment of anisotropy needs a highly interactive graphical user interface, e.g., VarioWin by Panatier (1996) which is beyond the scope of this book.

- *Number of pairs and the lag interval* – In the calculation of the classical variogram estimator it is recommended to use more than 30 to 50 pairs of points per lag interval (Webster and Oliver 2001). This is due to the sensitivity to outliers. If there are fewer pairs, the lag interval should be enlarged. The lag spacing has not necessarily to be uniform, it can be chosen individually for each distance class. It is also an option to work with overlapping classes, in this case the *lag width* (*lag tolerance*) has to be defined. On the other hand, increasing the lag width can cause unnecessary smoothing and detail is lost. Thus, the separation distance and the lag width have to be chosen with care. Another option is to use a more robust variogram estimator (Cressie 1993, Deutsch and Journel 1998).

- *Calculation of separation distance* – If your observations are covering a large area, let us say more than 1000 km^2, spherical distances should be calculated instead of the Pythagorean distances from a plane cartesian coordinate system.

Kriging

Now we will interpolate the observations on a regular grid by *ordinary point kriging* which is the most popular kriging method. Ordinary point kriging uses a weighted average of the neighboring points to estimate the value of an unobserved point:

$$\hat{z}_{x0} = \sum_{i}^{N} \lambda_i \cdot z_{xi}$$

where λ_i are the weights which have to be estimated. The sum of the weights should be one to guarantee that the estimates are unbiased:

$$\sum_{i}^{N} \lambda_i = 1$$

The expected (average) error of the estimation has to be zero. That is:

$$E(\hat{z}_{x0} - z_{x0}) = 0$$

where z_{x0} is the true, but unknown value. After some algebra, using the preceding equations, we can compute the mean-squared error in terms of the variogram:

$$E\left((\hat{z}_{x0} - z_{x0})^2\right) = 2\sum_{i=1}^{N}\lambda_i \gamma(x_i, x_0) - \sum_{i=1}^{N}\sum_{j=1}^{N}\lambda_i \lambda_j \gamma(x_i, x_j)$$

where E is the estimation or *kriging variance*, which has to be minimized, $\gamma(x_i, x_0)$ is the variogram (semivariance) between the data point and the unobserved, $\gamma(x_i, x_j)$ is the variogram between the data points x_i and x_j, and λ_i and λ_j are the weights of the ith and jth data point.

For kriging we have to minimize this equation (quadratic objective function) satisfying the condition that the sum of weights should be one (linear constraint). This optimization problem can be solved using a Lagrange multiplier v resulting in the *linear kriging system* of $N+1$ equations and $N+1$ unknowns:

$$\sum_{i=1}^{N}\lambda_i \gamma(x_i, x_j) + v = \gamma(x_i, x_0)$$

After obtaining the weights λ_i, the kriging variance is given by

$$\sigma^2(x_0) = \sum_{i=1}^{N}\lambda_i \gamma(x_i, x_0) + v(x_0)$$

The kriging system can be presented in a matrix notation:

$$G\_mod \cdot E = G\_R$$

where

$$G\_mod = \begin{bmatrix} 0 & \gamma(x_1, x_2) & \cdots & \gamma(x_1, x_N) & 1 \\ \gamma(x_2, x_1) & 0 & \cdots & \gamma(x_2, x_N) & 1 \\ \vdots & \vdots & \vdots & \vdots & \vdots \\ \gamma(x_N, x_1) & \gamma(x_N, x_2) & \cdots & 0 & 1 \\ 1 & 1 & \cdots & 1 & 0 \end{bmatrix}$$

is the matrix of the coefficients, these are the modeled variogram values for the pairs of observations. Note that on the diagonal of the matrix, where separation distance is zero, the value of γ vanishes.

$$E = \begin{bmatrix} \lambda_1 \\ \lambda_2 \\ \vdots \\ \lambda_N \\ v \end{bmatrix}$$

is the vector of the unknown weights and the Lagrange multiplier.

$$G\_R = \begin{bmatrix} \gamma(x_1, x_0) \\ \gamma(x_2, x_0) \\ \vdots \\ \gamma(x_N, x_0) \\ 1 \end{bmatrix}$$

is the right-hand-side vector. To obtain the weights and the Lagrange multiplier the matrix G_mod is inverted:

$$E = G\_\mathrm{mod}^{-1} \cdot G\_R$$

The kriging variance is given by

$$\sigma^2 = G\_R^{-1} \cdot E$$

For our calculations with MATLAB we need the matrix of coefficients derived from the distance matrix D and a variogram model. D was calculated in the variography section above and we use the exponential variogram model with a nugget, sill and range from the previous section:

```
G_mod = (nugget + sill*(1 - exp(-3*D/range))).*(D>0);
```

Then we get the number of observations and add a column and row vector of all ones to the G_mod matrix and a zero at the lower left corner:

```
n = length(x);
G_mod(:,n+1)   = 1;
G_mod(n+1,:)   = 1;
G_mod(n+1,n+1) = 0;
```

Now the G_mod matrix has to be inverted:

```
G_inv = inv(G_mod);
```

A grid with the locations of the unknown values is needed. Here we use a grid cell size of five within a quadratic area ranging from 0 to 200 in x and y direction. The coordinates are created in matrix form by:

```
R = 0 : 5 : 200;
[Xg1,Xg2] = meshgrid(R,R);
```

and converted to vectors by:

```
Xg = reshape(Xg1,[],1);
Yg = reshape(Xg2,[],1);
```

Then we allocate memory for the kriging estimates Zg and the kriging variance s2_k by:

```
Zg = Xg * NaN;
s2_k = Xg * NaN;
```

Now we are kriging the unknown at each grid point:

```
for k = 1 : length(Xg)
    DOR = ((x - Xg(k)).^2 + (y - Yg(k)).^2).^0.5;
    G_R = (nugget + sill*(1 - exp(-3*DOR/range))).*(DOR>0);
    G_R(n+1) = 1;
    E = G_inv * G_R;
    Zg(k) = sum(E(1:n,1).*z);
    s2_k(k) = sum(E(1:n,1).*G_R(1:n,1))+E(n+1,1);
end
```

Here, the first command computes the distance between the grid points (Xg,Yg) and the observation points (x,y). Then we build the right-hand-side vector of the kriging system by using the variogram model G_R and add one to the last row. We next obtain the matrix E with the weights and the lagrange multiplier. The estimate Zg at each point k is the weighted sum of the observations z. Finally, the kriging variance s2_k of the grid point is computed. We plot the results. First, we create a grid of the kriging estimate and the kriging variance:

```
r = length(R);
Z = reshape(Zg,r,r);
SK = reshape(s2_k,r,r);
```

A subplot on the left presents the kriged values:

```
subplot(1,2,1)
h = pcolor(Xg1,Xg2,Z);
set(h,'LineStyle','none')
```

```
axis equal
ylim([0 200])
title('Kriging Estimate')
xlabel('x-Coordinates')
ylabel('y-Coordinates')
colorbar
```

The left subplot presents the kriging variance:

```
subplot(1,2,2)
h = pcolor(Xg1,Xg2,SK);
set(h,'LineStyle','none')
axis equal
ylim([0 200])
title('Kriging Variance')
xlabel('x-Coordinates')
ylabel('y-Coordinates')
colorbar
hold on
```

and we are overlaying the sampling positions:

```
plot(x,y,'ok')
hold off
```

The kriged values are shown in Figure 7.22a. The kriging variance depends only on the distance from the observations and not on the observed values (Fig. 7.22b). Kriging reproduces the population mean when observations are beyond the range of the variogram, at the same time kriging variance increases (lower right corner of the maps in Figure 7.22). The kriging variance can be used as a criterion to improve sampling design and it is needed for backtransformation in lognormal kriging. Back-transformation for lognormal kriging is done by:

$$y(x_0) = \exp(z(x_0) + 0.5 \cdot \sigma^2(x_0) - \nu)$$

Discussion of Kriging

Point kriging as presented here is an exact interpolator. It reproduces exactly the values at an observation point, even though a variogram with a nugget effect is used. Smoothing can be caused by including the variance of the measurement errors (see Kitanidis 1997) and by *block kriging* which averages the observations within a certain neighborhood (block). While kriging variance depends only on the distance between the observed and the unobserved locations it is primary a measure of density of information (Wackernagel 2003). The accuracy of kriging is better evaluated by cross-validation using

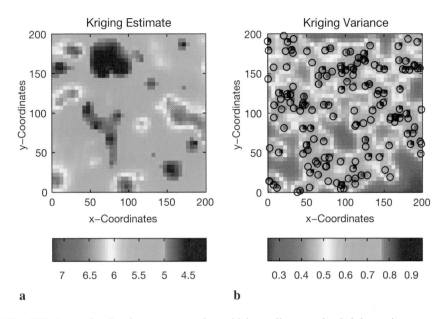

Fig. 7.22 Interpolated values on a regular grid by ordinary point kriging using **a** an exponential variogram model; **b** kriging variance as a function of the distance from the observations (empty circles).

a resampling method or surrogate test (Chapter 4.6 and 4.7). The influence of the neighboring observations on the estimation depends on their configuration. Webster and Oliver (2001) summarize: Near points carry more weight than more distant ones; the relative weight of a point decreases when the number of points in the neighborhood increases; clustered points carry less weight individually than isolated ones at the same distance; data points can be screened by ones lying between them and the target. Sampling design for kriging is different from the design which might be optimal for variography. A regular grid, triangular or quadratic, can be regarded as optimum.

The MATLAB code presented here is a straightforward implementation of the kriging system presented in the formulas above. In professional programs the number of data points entering the *G_mod* matrix are restricted as well as the inversion of *G_mod* is avoided by working with the covariances instead of the variograms (Webster and Oliver 2001, Kitanidis 1997). For those who are interested in programming and in a deeper understanding of algorithms, Deutsch and Journel (1992) is a must. The best internet source is the homepage of AI-GEOSTATISTICS:

```
http://www.ai-geostats.org
```

Recommended Reading

Cressie N (1993) Statistics for Spatial Data, Revised Edition. John Wiley & Sons, New York

Davis JC (2002) Statistics and Data Analysis in Geology, third edition. John Wiley and Sons, New York

Deutsch CV, Journel AG (1998) GSLIB – Geostatistical Software Library and User's Guide, Second edition. Oxford University Press, Oxford

Freeman TG (1991) Calculating Catchment Area with Divergent Flow Based on a Regular Grid. Computers and Geosciences 17:413–422

Gringarten E, Deutsch CV (2001) Teacher's Aide Variogram Interpretation and Modeling. Mathematical Geology 33:507–534

Isaaks E, Srivastava M (1989) An Introduction to Applied Geostatistics. Oxford University Press, Oxford

Gringarten E, Deutsch CV (2001) Teacher's Aide Variogram Interpretation and Modeling. Mathematical Geology 33:507–534

Kitanidis P (1997) Introduction to Geostatistics – Applications in Hydrogeology. Cambridge University Press, Cambridge

Olea RA (1984) Systematic Sampling of Spatial Functions. Kansas Series on Spatial Analysis 7, Kansas Geological Survey, Lawrence, KS

Pannatier Y (1996) VarioWin – Software for Spatial Data Analysis in 2D, Springer, Berlin Heidelberg New York

Pardo-Igúzquiza E, Dowd PA (1997) AMLE3D: A Computer Program for the Interference of Spatial Covariance Parameters by Approximate Maximum Likelihood Estimation. Computers and Geosciences 23:793–805

Rendu JM, Readdy L (1982) Geology and Semivariogram – A Critical Relationship. In: Johnson TB, Barns RJ (eds) Application of Computer & Operation Research in the Mineral Industry. 17th Intern. Symp. American Institute of Mining. Metallurgical and Petroleum Engineers, New York, pp. 771–783

Sandwell DT (1987) Biharmonic Spline Interpolation of GEOS-3 and SEASAT Altimeter data. Geophysical Research Letters 2:139–142

Swan ARH, Sandilands M (1995) Introduction to Geological Data Analysis. Blackwell Sciences, Oxford

The Mathworks (2006) Mapping Toolbox User's Guide – For the Use with MATLAB®. The MathWorks, Natick, MA

Golden Software, Inc. (2002) Surfer 8 (Surface Mapping System). Golden, Colorado

Wackernagel H. (2003) Multivariate Geostatistics: An Introduction with Applications. Third, completely revised edition. Springer, Berlin Heidelberg New York

Webster R, Oliver MA (2001) Geostatistics for Environmental Scientists. John Wiley & Sons, New York

Wessel P, Bercovici D (1998) Gridding with Splines in Tension: A Green Function Approach. Mathematical Geology 30:77–93

Wilson JP, Gallant JC (2000) Terrain Analysis, Principles and Applications. John Wiley and Sons, New York

8 Image Processing

8.1 Introduction

Computer graphics are stored and processed either as vector or raster data. Most data types that were encountered in the previous chapter were vector data, i.e., points, lines and polygons. Drainage networks, the outline of geologic units, sampling locations and topographic contours are examples of vector data. In Chapter 7, coastlines are stored in the vector format while bathymetric and topographic data are saved in the raster format. Vector and raster data are often combined in one data set, for instance, the course of a river is displayed on a satellite image. Raster data are often converted to vector data by digitizing points, lines or polygons. On the other hand, vector data are sometimes transformed to raster data.

Images are generally represented as raster data, i.e., as a 2D array of color intensities. Images are everywhere in geosciences. Field geologists use aerial photos and satellite images to identify lithologic units, tectonic structures, landslides and other features in a study area. Geomorphologists use such images for the analysis of drainage networks, river catchments, vegetation and soil types. The analysis of images from thin sections, automated identification of objects and the measurement of varve thicknesses employ a great variety of image processing methods.

This chapter is about the analysis and display of image data. Firstly, the various ways that raster data can be stored on the computer are explained (Chapter 8.2). Subsequently, the main tools for importing, manipulating and exporting image data are presented (Chapter 8.3). This knowledge is then used to process and to georeference satellite images (Chapter 8.4 and 8.5). Finally, on-screen digitization techniques are discussed (Chapter 8.6). The Image Processing Toolbox is used for the specific examples throughout this chapter. Whereas the MATLAB User's Guide to the Image Processing Toolbox is an excellent introduction to the analysis of images in generally, this chapter provides an overview of typical applications in earth sciences.

8.2 Data Storage

Vector and raster graphics are the two fundamental methods for storing pictures. The typical format for storing *vector data* was already introduced in the previous chapter. In the following example, the two columns in the file *coastline.txt* represent the the longitudes and the latitudes of the points of a polygon.

```
NaN          NaN
42.892067    0.000000
42.893692    0.001760
NaN          NaN
42.891052    0.001467
42.898093    0.007921
42.904546    0.013201
42.907480    0.016721
42.910414    0.020828
42.913054    0.024642
(cont'd)
```

The NaN's help to identify break points in the data (Chapter 7.2).

The *raster data* are stored as 2D arrays. The elements of the array represent the altitude of a grid point above sea level, annual rainfall or, in the case of an image, color intensity values.

```
174  177  180  182  182  182
165  169  170  168  168  170
171  174  173  168  167  170
184  186  183  177  174  176
191  192  190  185  181  181
189  190  190  188  186  183
```

In all cases, raster data can be visualized as 3D plot. The x and y are the indices of the 2D array or any other reference frame, and z is the numerical value of the elements of the array (see also Chapter 7). Alternatively, the numerical values contained in the 2D array can be displayed as pseudo-color plot, which is a rectangular array of cells with colors determined by a colormap. A colormap is a m-by-3 array of real number between 0.0 and 1.0. Each row defines a red, green, blue (RGB) color. An example is the above array that could be interpreted as grayscale intensities ranging from 0 (black) to 255 (white). More complex examples include satellite images that are stored in 3D arrays.

As discussed before, a computer stores data as bits, which have one out of two states, one and zero (Chapter 2). If the elements of the 2D array represent the color intensity values of the *pixels* (short for *picture elements*) of an image, 1-bit arrays contains only ones and zeros.

```
0    0    1    1    1    1
1    1    0    0    1    1
1    1    1    1    0    0
1    1    1    1    0    1
0    0    0    0    0    0
0    0    0    0    0    0
```

This 2D array of ones and zeros can be simply interpreted as a white-and-black image, where the value of one represents white and zero corresponds to black. Alternatively, the 1-bit array could be used to store an image consisting of two different colors only, such as red and blue.

In order to store more complex types of data, the bits are joined to larger groups, such as bytes consisting of eight bits. The earliest computers could only send eight bits at a time and early computer code was written in sets of eight bits, which came to be called a byte. Hence, each element of the 2D array or pixel contains a vector of eight ones or zeros.

```
1    0    1    0    0    0    0    1
```

These 8 bits or 1 byte allows $2^8=256$ possible combinations of the eight ones or zeros. Therefore, 8 bits are enough to represent 256 different intensities such as grayscales. The 8 bits can be read in the following way. The bits are read from the right to the left. A single bit represents two numbers, two bits give four numbers, three bits show eight numbers, and so forth up to a byte, or eight bits, which represents 256 numbers. Each added bit doubles the count of numbers. Here is a comparison of the binary and the decimal representation of the number 161.

```
128    64    32    16    8    4    2    1       (value of the bit)
  1     0     1     0    0    0    0    1       (binary)

128 +   0 + 32   + 0 +  0 +  0 +  0 +  1 = 161  (decimal)
```

The end members of the binary representation of grayscales are

```
0    0    0    0    0    0    0    0
```

which is black, and

```
1    1    1    1    1    1    1    1
```

which is pure white. In contrast to the above 1-bit array, the one-byte array allows to store a grayscale image of 256 different levels. Alternatively, the 256 numbers could be interpreted as 256 different discrete colors. In any case, the display of such an image requires an additional source of information about how the 256 intensity values are converted into colors. Numerous global colormaps for the interpretation of 8-bit color images exist that allow the cross-platform exchange of raster images, whereas local colormaps are often embedded in a graphics file.

The disadvantage of 8-bit color images is that the 256 discrete colorsteps are not enough to simulate smooth transitions for the human eye. Therefore, in many applications a 24-bit system is used with 8 bits of data for each RGB channel giving a total of $256^3=16{,}777{,}216$ colors. Such a 24-bit image is stored in three 2D arrays or one 3D array of intensity values between 0 and 255.

```
195  189  203  217  217  221
218  209  187  192  204  206
207  219  212  198  188  190
203  205  202  202  191  201
190  192  193  191  184  190
186  179  178  182  180  169

209  203  217  232  232  236
234  225  203  208  220  220
224  235  229  214  204  205
223  222  222  219  208  216
209  212  213  211  203  206
206  199  199  203  201  187

174  168  182  199  199  203
198  189  167  172  184  185
188  199  193  178  168  172
186  186  185  183  174  185
177  177  178  176  171  177
179  171  168  170  170  163
```

Compared to the 1-bit and 8-bit representation of raster data, the 24-bit storage certainly requires a lot more computer memory. In the case of very large data sets such as satellite images and digital elevation models the user should therefore carefully think about the suitable way to store the data. The default data type in MATLAB is the 64-bit array which allows to store the sign of a number (first bit), the exponent (bits 2 to 12) and roughly 16 significant decimal digits in the range of roughly 10^{-308} and 10^{+308} (bits 13 to 64). However, MATLAB also works with other data types such as 1-bit, 8-bit and 24-bit raster data to save memory.

The memory required for storing an image depends on the data type and the raster dimension. The dimension of an image can be described by the numbers of pixels, which is the number of rows multiplied by the number of columns of the 2D array. Assume an image of 729×713 pixels, as the one we will use in the following chapter. If each pixel needs 8 bits to store an gray-scale value, the memory required by the data is $729 \times 713 \times 8 = 4,158,216$ bits or $4,158,216/8 = 519,777$ bytes. This number is exactly what we obtain by typing whos in the command window. Common prefixes for bytes are kilobyte, megabyte, gigabyte and so forth.

```
bit = 1 or 0 (b)
8 bits = 1 byte (B)
1024 bytes = 1 kilobyte (KB)
1024 kilobytes = 1 megabyte (MB)
1024 megabytes = 1 gigabyte (GB)
1024 gigabytes = 1 terabyte (TB)
```

Note that in data communication 1 kilobit = 1,000 bits, while in data storage 1 kilobyte = 1,024 bytes. A 24-bit or *true color image* then requires three times the memory needed to store a 8-bit image, or 1,559,331 bytes $= 1,559,331/1,024$ kilobytes (KB) $\approx 1,523$ KB $\approx 1,559,331/1,024^2 = 1.487$ megabytes (MB).

However, the dimension of an image is often not given by the total number of pixels, but the length and height of the picture and its resolution. The resolution of an image is the number of *pixels per inch* (ppi) or *dots per inch* (dpi). The standard resolution of a computer monitor is 72 dpi although modern monitors often have a higher resolution such as 96 dpi. For instance, a 17 inch monitor with 72 dpi resolution displays $1,024 \times 768$ pixels. If the monitor is used to display images at a different (lower, higher) resolution, the image is resampled to match the monitor's resolution. For scanning and printing, a resolution of 300 or 600 dpi is enough in most applications. However, scanned images are often scaled for large printouts and therefore have higher resolutions such as 2,400 dpi. The image used in the next chapter has a width of 25.2 cm (or 9.92 inch) and a height of 25.7 cm (10.12 inch). The resolution of the image is 72 dpi. The total number of pixels is $72 \times 9,92 \approx 713$ in horizontal direction, the vertical number of pixels is $72 \times 10,12 \approx 729$ as expected.

Numerous formats are available to save vector and raster data into a file. All these formats have their advantages and disadvantages. Choosing one format over another in an application depends on the way the images are used in a project and if images are to be analyzed quantitatively. The most popular formats for storing vector and raster data are:

- *Compuserve Graphics Interchange Format* (GIF) – This format was developed in 1987 for raster images using a fixed colormap of 256 colors. The GIF format uses compression without loss of data. It was designed for fast transfer rates in the internet. The limited number of colors makes it not the right format for smooth color transitions that occur in aerial photos or stellite images. In contrast, it is often used for line art, maps, cartoons and logos (http://www.compuserve.com/).

• *Microsoft Windows Bitmap Format* (BMP) – This is the native bitmap format for computers running Microsoft Windows as the operating system. However, numerous converters exist to read and write BMP files also on other platforms. Various modifications of the BMP format are available, some of them without compressions, others with effective and fast compression (http://www.microsoft.com/).

• *Tagged Image File Format* (TIFF) – This format was designed by the Aldus Corporation and Microsoft in 1986 to become an industry standard for image-file exchange. A TIFF file includes an image file header, a directory and the data in all available graphics and image file formats. Some TIFF files even contain vector and raster versions of the same picture, and images in different resolution and colormap. The most important advantage of TIFF was portability. TIFF should perform on all computer platforms. Unfortunately, numerous modifications of TIFF evolved in the following years, causing incompatibilities. Therefore, TIFF is often called *Thousands of Incompatible File Formats*.

• *PostScript* (PS) and *Encapsulated PostScript* (EPS) – The PS format has been developed by John Warnock at Parc, the research institute of Xerox. J. Warnock was co-founder of Adobe Systems, where the EPS format has been created. The vector format PostScript would have never become an industry standard without Apple Computers. In 1985, Apple needed a typesetter-quality controller for the new printer apple LaserWriter and the operating system Macintosh. The third partner in the history of PostScript was the company Aldus, the developer of the software PageMaker and now a part of Adobe Systems. The combination of Aldus PageMaker, the PS format and the Apple LaserWriter were the founders of Desktop Publishing. The EPS format was then developed by Adobe Systems as a standard file format for importing and exporting PS files. Whereas the PS file generally is a single-page format, containing an illustration of a text, the purpose of an EPS file is to be included in other pages, i.e., it can contain any combination of text, graphics and images (http://www.adobe.com/).

- In 1986, the *Joint Photographic Experts Group* (JPEG) was founded for the purpose of developing various standards for image compression. Although JPEG stands for the committee, it is now widely used as the name for an image compression and format. This compression consists of grouping pixel values into 8×8 blocks and transforming each block with a discrete cosine transform. Subsequently, all unnecessary high-frequency information is eased. Such practice makes the compression method irreversible. The advantage of the JPEG format is the availability of a three-channel 24-bit true color version. This allows to store images with smooth color transitions. The new JPEG-2000 format uses a Wavelet transform instead of the cosine transform (Chapter 5.8) (http://www.jpeg.org/).

- *Portable Document Format* (PDF) – The PDF designed by Adobe Systems is now a true self-contained cross-platform document. The PDF files contain the complete formatting of vector illustrations, raster images and text, or a combination of all these, including all necessary fonts. These files are highly compressed, allowing a fast internet download. Adobe Systems provides the free-of-charge Acrobat Reader for all computer platforms to read PDF files (http://www.adobe.com/).

- The PICT format was developed by Apple Computers in 1984 as the native format for Macintosh graphics. The PICT format can be used for raster images and vector illustrations. PICT uses various methods for compressing data. The PICT 1 format only supports monochrome graphics, but PICT 2 supports a color depth of up to 32-bit. The PICT format is not supported on other platforms although some PC software tools can work with PICT files (http://www.apple.com).

8.3 Importing, Processing and Exporting Images

Firstly, we learn how to read an image from a graphics file into the workspace. As an example, we use a satellite image showing a 10.5 km by 11 km subarea in northern Chile:

```
http://asterweb.jpl.nasa.gov/gallery/images/unconform.jpg
```

The file *unconform.jpg* is a processed TERRA-ASTER satellite image that can be downloaded free-of-charge from the NASA web page. We save this image in the working directory. The command

```
unconform1 = imread('unconform.jpg');
```

reads and decompresses the JPEG file, imports the data as 24-bit RGB image array and stores the data in a variable `unconform1`. The command

```
whos
```

shows how the RGB array is stored in the workspace:

```
Name                Size                      Bytes  Class     Attributes
unconform1          729x713x3                 1559331 uint8
```

The details indicate that the image is stored as a 729×713×3 array representing a 729×713 array for each of the colors red, green and blue. The listing of the current variables in the workspace also gives the information *uint8 array*, i.e., each array element representing one pixel contains 8-bit integers. These integers represent intensity values between 0 (minimum intensity) and 255 (maximum). As example, here is a sector in the upper-left corner of the data array for red:

```
unconform1(50:55,50:55,1)

ans =
    174 177 180 182 182 182
    165 169 170 168 168 170
    171 174 173 168 167 170
    184 186 183 177 174 176
    191 192 190 185 181 181
    189 190 190 188 186 183
```

Next, we can view the image using the command

```
imshow(unconform1)
```

which opens a new Figure Window showing an RGB composite of the image (Fig. 8.1).

In contrast to the RGB image, a grayscale image only needs one single array to store all necessary information. We convert the RGB image into a grayscale image using the command `rgb2gray` (RGB to gray):

```
unconform2 = rgb2gray (unconform1);
```

The new workspace listing now reads

```
Name                Size                      Bytes  Class     Attributes
ans                 6x6                           36  uint8
unconform1          729x713x3                 1559331 uint8
unconform2          729x713                    519777 uint8
```

where you can see the difference between the 24-bit RGB and the 8-bit grayscale arrays. The commands

```
imshow(unconform1), figure, imshow(unconform2)
```

display the result. It is easy to see the difference between the two images in separate Figure Windows (Fig. 8.1 and 8.2). Let us now process the grayscale image. First, we compute a histogram of the distribution of intensity values.

```
imhist(unconform2)
```

A simple technique to enhance the contrast of such an image is to transform this histogram to obtain an equal distribution of grayscales.

```
unconform3 = histeq(unconform2);
```

We can view the difference again using

```
imshow(unconform2), figure, imshow(unconform3)
```

and save the results in a new file.

```
imwrite(unconform3,'unconform3.jpg')
```

We can read the header of the new file by typing

```
imfinfo('unconform3.jpg')
```

which yields

```
Filename: 'unconform3.jpg'
FileModDate: '18-Jun-2003 16:56:49'
FileSize: 138419
Format: 'jpg'
FormatVersion: ''
Width: 713
Height: 729
BitDepth: 8
ColorType: 'grayscale'
FormatSignature: ''
NumberOfSamples: 1
CodingMethod: 'Huffman'
CodingProcess: 'Sequential'
Comment: {}
```

Hence, the command `iminfo` can be used to obtain useful information (name, size, format and color type) about the newly-created image file.

There are many ways for transforming the original satellite image into a practical file format. For instance, the image data could be stored as *indexed color image*. Such an image consists of two parts, a colormap array and a data array. The colormap array is an *m*-by-3 array containing float-

Fig. 8.1 RGB true color image contained in the file *unconform.jpg*. After decompressing and reading the JPEG file into a 729×713×3 array, MATLAB interprets and displays the RGB composite using the function imshow. See detailed description of the image on the NASA TERRA-ASTER webpage http://asterweb.jpl.nasa.gov. Original image courtesy of NASA/GSFC/METI/ERSDAC/JAROS and U.S./Japan ASTER Science Team.

ing-point values between 0 and 1. Each column specifies the intensity of the colors red, green and blue. The data array is an x-by-y array containing integer elements corresponding to the lines m of the colormap array, i.e., the specific RGB representation of a certain color. Let us transfer the above RGB image into an indexed image. The colormap of the image should contain 16 different colors. The result of

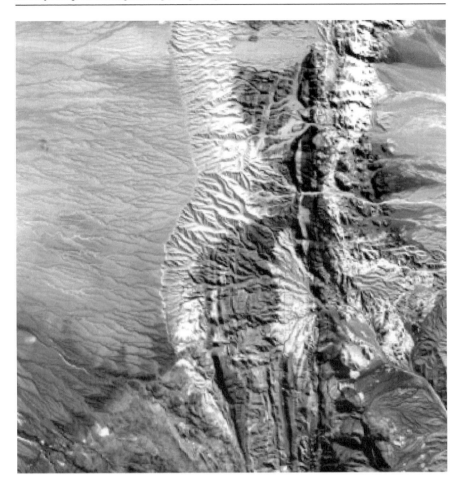

Fig. 8.2 Grayscale image. After converting the RGB image stored in a 729×713×3 array into a grayscale image stored in a 729×713 array, the result is displayed using `imshow`. Original image courtesy of NASA/GSFC/METI/ERSDAC/JAROS and U.S./Japan ASTER Science Team.

```
[x,map] = rgb2ind(unconform1,16);
imshow(unconform1), figure, imshow(x,map)
```

clearly shows the difference between the original 24-bit RGB image (256^3 or ca. 16.7 million different colors) and a color image of only 16 different colors (Fig. 8.1 and 8.3).

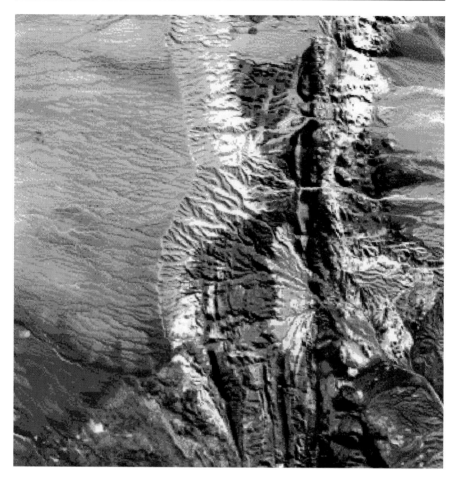

Fig. 8.3 Indexed color image using a colormap containing 16 different colors. The result is displayed using imshow. Original image courtesy of NASA/GSFC/METI/ERSDAC/ JAROS and U.S./Japan ASTER Science Team.

8.4 Importing, Processing and Exporting Satellite Images

In the previous chapter, we used a processed ASTER image that we have downloaded from the ASTER web page. The original ASTER raw data contain a lot more information and resolution than the free-of-charge image stored in *unconform.jpg*. The ASTER instrument produces two types of data, Level-1A and 1B. Whereas the L1A data are reconstructed, unprocessed instrument data, L1B data are radiometrically and geometrically corrected. Each ASTER data set contains 15 data arrays representing the intensity values from 15 spectral bands (see the ASTER-web page for more detailed information) and various additional information such as location, date and time. The raw satellite data can be purchased from the USGS online store:

```
http://edcimswww.cr.usgs.gov/pub/imswelcome/
```

Enter the data gateway as *guest*, pick a discipline/top (e.g., *Land: ASTER*), then choose from the list of data sets (e.g., *DEM, Level 1A* or *1B* data), define the search area and click *Start Search*. The system now needs a few minutes to list all relevant data sets. A list of data sets including various types of additional information (cloud coverage, exposure date, latitude and longitude) can be obtained by clicking on *List Data Granules*. Furthermore, a low resolution preview can be accessed by selecting *Image*. Having purchased a certain data set, the raw image can be downloaded using a temporary FTP-access. As an example, we process an image from an area in Kenya showing Lake Naivasha. The data are stored in two files

```
naivasha.hdf
naivasha.hdf.met
```

The first file (111 MB large) contains the actual raw data, whereas the second file (100 KB) contains the header with al types of information about the data. We save both files in our working directory. The image processing Toolbox contains various tools for importing and processing files stored in the hierarchical data format (HDF). The GUI-based import tool for importing certain parts of the raw data is

```
hdftool('naivasha.hdf')
```

This command opens a GUI that allows us to browse the content of the HDF-file *naivasha.hdf*, obtains all information the contents and imports certain frequency bands of the satellite image. Alternatively, the command hdf-read can be used as the quicker way of accessing image data. An image as the one used in the previous chapter is typically achieved by computing an RGB composite from the *vnir_Band3n, 2* and *1* in the data file. First, we read the data

```
I1 = hdfread('naivasha.hdf','VNIR_Band3N','Fields','ImageData');
I2 = hdfread('naivasha.hdf','VNIR_Band2','Fields','ImageData');
I3 = hdfread('naivasha.hdf','VNIR_Band1','Fields','ImageData');
```

These commands generate three 8-bit image arrays each representing the intensity within a certain infrared (IR) frequency band of a 4200×4100 pixel image. The *vnir_Band3n, 2* and *1* typically contain much information about lithology (including soils), vegetation and water on the Earth's surface.

Therefore, these bands are usually combined to 24-bit RGB images

```
naivasha_rgb = cat(3,I1,I2,I3);
```

Similar to the examples above, the 4200×4100×3 array can now be displayed using

```
imshow(naivasha_rgb);
```

MATLAB scales the images to fit the computer screen. Exporting the processed image from the Figure Window, we only save the image at the monitor's resolution. To obtain an image at a higher resolution (Fig. 8.4), we use

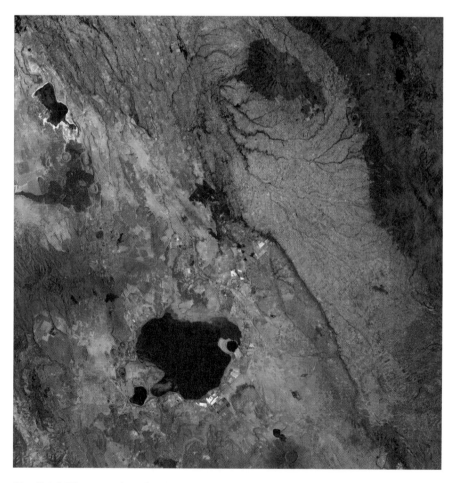

Fig. 8.4 RGB composite of a TERRA-ASTER image using the spectral infrared bands *vnir_Band3n*, *2* and *1*. The result is displayed using imshow. Original image courtesy of NASA/GSFC/METI/ERSDAC/JAROS and U.S./Japan ASTER Science Team.

the command

```
imwrite(naivasha_rgb,'naivasha.tif','tif')
```

This command saves the RGB composite as a TIFF-file *naivasha.tif* (ca. 50 MB large) in the working directory that can be processed with other software such as Adobe Photoshop.

8.5 Georeferencing Satellite Images

The processed ASTER image does not yet have a coordinate system. Hence, the image needs to be tied to a geographical reference frame (*georeferencing*). The raw data can be loaded and transformed into a RGB composite by typing

```
I1 = hdfread('naivasha.hdf','VNIR_Band3N','Fields','ImageData');
I2 = hdfread('naivasha.hdf','VNIR_Band2','Fields','ImageData');
I3 = hdfread('naivasha.hdf','VNIR_Band1','Fields','ImageData');

naivasha_rgb = cat(3,I1,I2,I3);
```

The HDF browser can be used

```
hdftool('naivasha.hdf')
```

to extract the geodetic coordinates of the four corners of the image. This information is contained in the header of the HDF file. Having launched the HDF tool, we activate *File* as *HDF* and select on the uppermost directory *naivasha.hdf*. This produces a long list of file attributes including *productmetadata.0*, which includes the attribute *scenefourcorners* that contains the following information:

```
upperleft   = [-0.319922,  36.214332];
upperright  = [-0.400443,  36.770406];
lowerleft   = [-0.878267,  36.096003];
lowerright  = [-0.958743,  36.652213];
```

These two-element vectors can be collected into one array `inputpoints`. Subsequently, the left and right columns can be flipped in order to have *x=longitudes* and *y=latitudes*.

```
inputpoints(1,:) = upperleft;
inputpoints(2,:) = lowerleft;
inputpoints(3,:) = upperright;
inputpoints(4,:) = lowerright;
inputpoints = fliplr(inputpoints);
```

The four corners of the image correspond to the pixels in the four corners of the image that we store in a variable named `basepoints`.

```
basepoints(1,:) = [1,4200];
basepoints(2,:) = [1,1];
basepoints(3,:) = [4100,4200];
basepoints(4,:) = [4100,1];
```

The function `cp2tform` now takes the pairs of control points `inputpoints` and `basepoints` and uses them to infer a spatial transformation matrix `tform`.

```
tform = cp2tform(inputpoints,basepoints,'affine');
```

This transformation can be applied to the original RGB composite `naivasha_rgb` in order to obtain a georeferenced version of the satellite image `newnaivasha_rgb`.

```
[newnaivasha_rgb,x,y] = imtransform(naivasha_rgb,tform);
```

Subsequently, an appropriate grid for the image may be computed. The grid is typically defined by the minimum and maximum values for the longitude and the latitude. The vector increments are then obtained by dividing the longitude and latitude range by the array dimension and by subtracting one from the result. Note the difference between the numbering convention of MATLAB and the common coding of maps used in the literature. The north/south suffix is generally replaced by a negative sign for south, whereas MATLAB coding conventions require negative signs for north.

```
X = 36.096003 : (36.770406-36.096003)/8569 : 36.770406;
Y =  0.319922 : ( 0.958743- 0.319922)/8400 :  0.958743;
```

Hence, both images can be displayed for comparison (Fig. 8.4 and 8.5).

```
iptsetpref('ImshowAxesVisible','On')
imshow(naivasha_rgb), title('Original ASTER Image')
figure
imshow(newnaivasha_rgb,'XData',X,'YData',Y);
xlabel('Longitude'), ylabel('Latitude')
title('Georeferenced ASTER Image')
grid on
```

The command `iptsetpref` makes the axis of the image visible. Exporting the results is possible in many ways, such as

```
print -djpeg70 -r600 naivasha_georef.jpg
```

as JPEG file *naivasha_georef.jpg* compressed at 70% and at a resolution of 600 dpi.

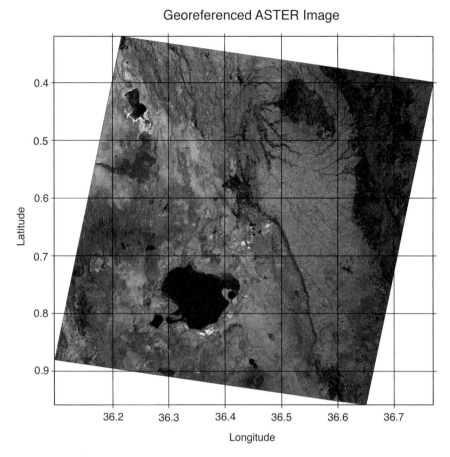

Fig. 8.5 Geoferenced RGB composite of an TERRA-ASTER image using the infrared bands *vnir_Band3n, 2* and *1*. The result is displayed using `imshow`. Original image courtesy of NASA/GSFC/METI/ERSDAC/JAROS and U.S./Japan ASTER Science Team.

8.6 Digitizing from the Screen

On-screen digitizing is a widely-used image processing technique. While practical digitizer tablets exist in all formats and sizes, most people prefer digitizing vector data from the screen. Examples for this application are digitizing of river networks and drainage areas on topographic maps, the outlines of lithologic units in maps, the distribution of landslides on satellite images or mineral grains in a microscope image. The digitizing procedure consists of the following steps. Firstly, the image is imported into the workspace. Subsequently, a coordinate system is defined. Finally, the objects of interest are entered by moving a cursor or cross hair and clicking the mouse button. The result is a two-dimensional array of *xy* data, such as longitudes and latitudes of the points of a polygon or the coordinates of the objects of interest in an area.

The function `ginput` included in the standard MATLAB toolbox provides graphical input using a mouse on the screen. It is generally used to select points such as specific data points from a figure created by an arbitrary graphics function such as `plot`. The function is often used for interactive plotting, i.e., the digitized points appear on the screen after they were selected. The disadvantage of the function is that it does not provide coordinate referencing on an image. Therefore, we use a modified version of the function that allows to reference an image to an arbitrary rectangular coordinate system. Save the following code in a text file *minput.m*.

```
function data = minput(imagefile)
% Specify the limits of the image
xmin = input('Specify xmin! ');
xmax = input('Specify xmax! ');
ymin = input('Specify ymin! ');
ymax = input('Specify ymax! ');

% Read image and display
B = imread(imagefile);
a = size(B,2); b = size(B,1);
imshow(B);

% Define lower left and upper right corner of image
disp('Click on lower left and upper right corner, then <return>')
[xcr,ycr] = ginput;
XMIN = xmin-((xmax-xmin)*xcr(1,1)/(xcr(2,1)-xcr(1,1)));
XMAX = xmax+((xmax-xmin)*(a-xcr(2,1))/(xcr(2,1)-xcr(1,1)));
YMIN = ymin-((ymax-ymin)*ycr(1,1)/(ycr(2,1)-ycr(1,1)));
YMAX = ymax+((ymax-ymin)*(b-ycr(2,1))/(ycr(2,1)-ycr(1,1)));

% Digitize data points
disp('Click on data points to digitize, then <return>')
[xdata,ydata] = ginput;
XDATA = XMIN + ((XMAX-XMIN)*xdata/size(B,2));
YDATA = YMIN + ((YMAX-YMIN)*ydata/size(B,1));
data(:,1) = XDATA; data(:,2) = YDATA;
```

The function `minput` has four parts. In the first part, the user enters the limits of the coordinate axis as the reference for the image. Next, the image is imported into the workspace and displayed on the screen. The third part uses `ginput` to define the upper left and lower right corners of the image. The relationship between the coordinates of the two corners on the figure window and the reference coordinate system is used to compute the transformation for all points digitized in the fourth part.

For instance, we use the image stored in the file *naivasha_georef.jpg* and digitize the outline of Lake Naivasha in the center of the image. We call the new function `minput` from the Command Window using the commands

```
data = minput('naivasha_georef.jpg')
```

The function first calls the coordinates for the limits of the *x*- and *y*-axis for the reference frame. We enter the corresponding numbers and press return after each input.

```
Specify xmin! 36.1
Specify xmax! 36.7
Specify ymin! -1
Specify ymax! -0.3
```

Next the function reads the file *naivasha_georef.jpg* and displays the image. We ignore the warning

```
Warning: Image is too big to fit on screen; displaying at 33%
```

and wait for the next response

```
Click on lower left and upper right corner, then <return>
```

The image window can be scaled according to user preference. Clicking on the lower left and upper right corner defines the dimension of the image. These changes are registered by pressing return. The routine then references the image to the coordinate system and waits for the input of the points we wish to digitize from the image.

```
Click on data points to digitize, then <return>
```

We finish the input again by pressing *return*. The *xy* coordinates of our digitized points are now stored in the variable `data`. We can now use these vector data for other applications.

Recommended Reading

Abrams M, Hook S (2002) ASTER User Handbook - Version 2. Jet Propulsion Laboratory and EROS Data Center, Sioux Falls

Campbell JB (2002) Introduction to Remote Sensing. Taylor & Francis, London

Francus P (2005) Image Analysis, Sediments and Paleoenvironments – Developments in Paleoenvironmental Research. Springer, Berlin Heidelberg New York

Gonzales RC, Eddins SL, Woods RE (2003) Digital Image Processing Using MATLAB. Prentice Hall, New Jersey

The Mathworks (2006) Image Processing Toolbox User's Guide - For the Use with MATLAB®. The MathWorks, Natick, MA

9 Multivariate Statistics

9.1 Introduction

Multivariate analysis aims to understand and describe the relationship between an arbitrary number of variables. Earth scientists often deal with multivariate data sets, such as microfossil assemblages, geochemical fingerprints of volcanic ashes or clay mineral contents of sedimentary sequences. If there are complex relationships between the different parameters, univariate statistics ignores the information content of the data. There is a number of methods, however, for investigating the scaling properties of multivariate data.

A multivariate data set consists of measurements of p variables on n objects. Such data sets are usually stored in n-by-p arrays:

$$X = \begin{pmatrix} x_{11} & x_{12} & \cdots & x_{1p} \\ x_{21} & x_{22} & \cdots & x_{2p} \\ \vdots & \vdots & \cdots & \vdots \\ x_{n1} & x_{n2} & \cdots & x_{np} \end{pmatrix}$$

The columns of the array represent the p variables, the rows represent the n objects. The characteristics of the 2nd object in the suite of samples is described by the vector in the second row of the data array:

$$X_2 = (x_{21} \quad x_{22} \quad \cdots \quad x_{2p})$$

As an example, assume the microprobe analysis on glass shards from volcanic ashes in a tephrochronology project. Then, the variables represent the p chemical elements, the objects are the n ash samples. The aim of the study is to correlate ashes by means of their geochemical fingerprints.

Most of the multi-parameter methods simply try to overcome the main difficulty associated with multivariate data sets. This problem relates to the data visualization. Whereas the character of an univariate or bivariate data set can easily be explored by visual inspection of a 2D histogram or an *xy* plot (Chapter 3), the graphical display of a three variable data set requires a projection of the 3D distribution of data points into 2D. It is impossible to imagine or display a higher number of variables. One solution to the problem of visualization of high-dimensional data sets is the reduction of dimensionality. A number of methods group highly-correlated variables contained in the data set and then explore a smaller number of groups.

The classic methods to reduce dimensionality are the *principal component analysis* (PCA) and the *factor analysis* (FA). These methods seek the directions of maximum variance in the data set and use these as new coordinate axes. The advantage of replacing the variables by new groups of variables is that the groups are uncorrelated. Moreover, these groups often help to interpret the multivariate data set since they often contain valuable information on process itself that generated the distribution of data points. In a geochemical analysis of magmatic rocks, the groups defined by the method usually contain chemical elements with similar ion size that are observed in similar locations in the lattice of certain minerals. Examples for such behavior are Si^{4+} and Al^{3+}, and Fe^{2+} and Mg^{2+} in silicates, respectively.

The second important suite of multivariate methods aims to group objects by their similarity. As an example, *cluster analysis* (CA) is often applied to correlate volcanic ashes as described in the above example. Tephrochronology tries to correlate tephra by means of their geochemical fingerprint. In combination with a few radiometric age determinations of the key ashes, this method allows to correlate sedimentary sequences that contain these ashes (e.g., Westgate 1998, Hermanns et al. 2000). More examples for the application of cluster analysis come from the field of micropaleontology. In this context, multivariate methods are employed to compare microfossil assemblages such as pollen, foraminifera or diatoms (e.g., Birks and Gordon 1985).

The following text introduces the most important techniques of multivariate statistics, principal component analysis and cluster analysis (Chapter 9.2 and 9.4). A nonlinear extension of the PCA is the *independent component analysis* (ICA) (Chapter 9.3). First, the chapters provide an introduction to the theory behind the techniques. Subsequently, the use of these methods in analyzing earth sciences data is illustrated with MATLAB functions.

9.2 Principal Component Analysis

The principal component analysis (PCA) detects linear dependencies between variables and replaces groups of correlated variables by new uncorrelated variables, the *principal components* (PC). The performance of the PCA is better illustrated with help of a bivariate data set than a multivariate one. Figure 9.1 shows a bivariate data set that exhibits a strong linear correlation between the two variables x and y in an orthogonal xy coordinate system. The two variables have their univariate means and variances (Chapter 3). The bivariate data set can be described by the bivariate sample mean and the covariance (Chapter 4). The xy coordinate system can be replaced by a new orthogonal coordinate system, where the first axis passes through the long axis of the data scatter and the new origin is the bivariate mean. This new reference frame has the advantage that the first axis can be used to describe most of the variance, while the second axis contributes only a little. Originally, two axes were needed to describe the data set prior to the transformation. Therefore, it is possible to reduce the data dimension by dropping the second axis without losing much information as shown in Figure 9.1.

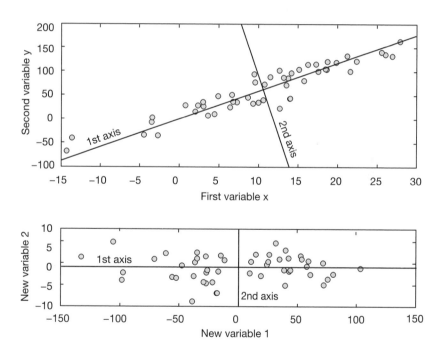

Fig. 9.1 Principal component analysis (PCA) illustrated on a bivariate scatter. The original xy coordinate system is replaced by a new orthogonal system, where the first axis passes through the long axis of the data scatter and the new origin is the bivariate mean. We can now reduce dimensionality by dropping the second axis without losing much information.

This is now expanded to an arbitrary number of variables and samples. Suppose a data set of measurements of p parameters on n samples stored in an n-by-p array.

$$X = \begin{pmatrix} x_{11} & x_{12} & \cdots & x_{1p} \\ x_{21} & x_{22} & \cdots & x_{2p} \\ \vdots & \vdots & \cdots & \vdots \\ x_{n1} & x_{n2} & \cdots & x_{np} \end{pmatrix}$$

The columns of the array represent the p variables, the rows represent the n samples. After rotating the axis and moving the origin, the new coordinates Y_j can be computed by

$$Y_1 = a_{11}X_1 + a_{12}X_2 + \ldots + a_{1p}X_p$$
$$Y_2 = a_{21}X_1 + a_{22}X_2 + \ldots + a_{2p}X_p$$
$$\vdots$$
$$Y_n = a_{n1}X_1 + a_{n2}X_2 + \ldots + a_{np}X_p$$

The first principle component PC_1 denoted by Y_1 contains the greatest variance, PC_2 the second highest variance and so forth. All PCs together contain the full variance of the data set. The variance is concentrated in the first few PCs, which explain most of the information content of the data set. The last PCs are generally ignored to reduce the data dimension. The factors a_{ij} in the above equations are the *principal component loads*. The values of these factors represent the relative contribution of the original variables to the new PCs. If the load a_{ij} of a variable X_j in PC_1 is close to zero, the influence of this variable is low. A high positive or negative a_{ij} suggests a strong contribution of the variable X_j. The new values Y_j of the variables computed from the linear combinations of the original variables X_j weighted by the loads are called the *principal component scores*.

In the following, a synthetic data set is used to illustrate the use of the function `princomp` included in the Statistics Toolbox. Our data set contains the percentage of various minerals contained in sediment samples. The sediments are sourced from three rock types: a magmatic rock contains amphibole (*amp*), pyroxene (*pyr*) and plagioclase (*pla*), a hydrothermal vein characterized by the occurrence of fluorite (*flu*), sphalerite (*sph*) and galenite (*gal*), as well as some feldspars (plagioclase and potassium feldspar, *ksp*) and quartz (*qtz*), and a sandstone unit containing feldspars, quartz and clay minerals (*cla*).

Ten samples were taken from various levels of this sedimentary sequence containing varying amounts of these minerals. The PCA is used to verify the influence of the three different source rocks and to estimate their relative contribution. First, the data are loaded by typing

```
data = load('sediments.txt');
```

Next, we define labels for the various graphs created by the PCA. We number the samples 1 to 10, whereas the minerals are characterized by three-character abbreviations.

```
for i = 1:10
    sample(i,:) = ['sample',sprintf('%02.0f',i)];
end
clear i

minerals = ['amp';'pyr';'pla';'ksp';'qtz';'cla';'flu';'sph';'gal']
```

A successful PCA requires linear correlations between variables. The *correlation matrix* provides a technique for exploring such dependencies in the data set (Chapter 4). The elements of the correlation matrix are Pearson's correlation coefficients for each pair of variables as shown in Figure 9.2. Here, the variables are minerals.

```
corrmatrix = corrcoef(data);
corrmatrix = flipud(corrmatrix);

imagesc(corrmatrix), colormap(hot)
title('Correlation Matrix')
axis square, colorbar, hold
set(gca,'XTickLabel',minerals,'YTickLabel',flipud(minerals))
```

This pseudocolor plot of the correlation coefficients shows strong positive correlations between the minerals *amp*, *pyr* and *pla*, the minerals *ksp*, *qtz* and *cla*, and the minerals *flu*, *sph* and *gal*, respectively. Moreover, some of the minerals show negative correlations. We also observe no dependency between some of the variables, for instance between the potassium feldspar and the vein minerals. From the observed dependencies, we expect interesting results from the application of the PCA.

Various methods exist for scaling the original data before applying the PCA, such as *mean centering* (zero means) or *autoscaling* (mean zero and standard deviation equals one). However, we use the original data for computing the PCA. The output of the function `princomp` includes the principal component loads `pcs`, the scores `newdata` and the variances `variances`.

```
[pcs,newdata,variances] = princomp(data);
```

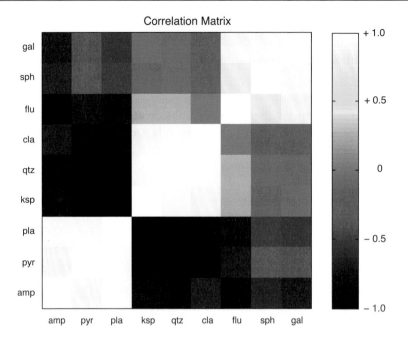

Fig. 9.2 Correlation matrix containing Pearson's correlation coefficients for each pair of variables, such as minerals in a sediment sample. Light colors represent strong positive linear correlations, whereas dark colors document negative correlations. Orange suggests no correlation.

The loads of the first five principal components PC_1 to PC_5 can be shown by typing

```
pcs(:,1:5)

ans =
    -0.3303     0.2963    -0.4100    -0.5971     0.1380
    -0.3557     0.0377     0.6225     0.2131     0.5251
    -0.5311     0.1865    -0.2591     0.4665    -0.3010
     0.1410     0.1033    -0.0175     0.0689    -0.3367
     0.6334     0.4666    -0.0351     0.1629     0.1794
     0.1608     0.2097     0.2386    -0.0513    -0.2503
     0.1673    -0.4879    -0.4978     0.2287     0.4756
     0.0375    -0.2722     0.2392    -0.5403    -0.0068
     0.0771    -0.5399     0.1173     0.0480    -0.4246
```

We observe that PC_1 (first column) has high negative loads in the first three variables *amp*, *pyr* and *pla* (first to third row), and a high positive load in the fifth variable *qtz* (fifth row). PC_2 (second column) has high negative loads in the vein minerals *flu*, *sph* and *gal*, and again a positive load in *qtz*. We create a number of plots of the PCs.

```
subplot(2,2,1), plot(1:9,pcs(:,1),'o'), axis([1 9 -1 1])
text((1:9)+0.2,pcs(:,1),minerals,'FontSize',8), hold
plot(1:9,zeros(9,1),'r'), title('PC 1')

subplot(2,2,2), plot(1:9,pcs(:,2),'o'), axis([1 9 -1 1])
text((1:9)+0.2,pcs(:,2),minerals,'FontSize',8), hold
plot(1:9,zeros(9,1),'r'), title('PC 2')

subplot(2,2,3), plot(1:9,pcs(:,3),'o'), axis([1 9 -1 1])
text((1:9)+0.2,pcs(:,3),minerals,'FontSize',8), hold
plot(1:9,zeros(9,1),'r'), title('PC 3')

subplot(2,2,4), plot(1:9,pcs(:,4),'o'), axis([1 9 -1 1])
text((1:9)+0.2,pcs(:,4),minerals,'FontSize',8), hold
plot(1:9,zeros(9,1),'r'), title('PC 4')
```

The loads of the index minerals and their relationship to the PCs can be used to interpret the relative influence of the source rocks. PC_1 characterized by strong contributions of *amp*, *pyr* and *pla*, and a contribution with an opposite sign of *qtz* probably describes the amount of magmatic rock clasts in the sediment. The second principal component PC_2 is clearly dominated by hydrothermal minerals hence suggesting the detrital input from the vein. PC_3 and PC_4 show a mixed and contradictory pattern of loads and are therefore not easy to interpret. We will later see that this observation is in line with a rather weak and mixed signal from the sandstone source on the sediments.

An alternative way to plot of the loads is a bivariate plot of two principal components. We ignore PC_3 and PC_4 at this point and concentrate on PC_1 and PC_2.

```
plot(pcs(:,1),pcs(:,2),'o')
text(pcs(:,1)+0.02,pcs(:,2),minerals,'FontSize',14), hold
x = get(gca,'XLim'); y = get(gca,'YLim');
plot(x,zeros(size(x)),'r')
plot(zeros(size(y)),y,'r')
xlabel('First Principal Component Loads')
ylabel('Second Principal Component Loads')
```

Here, we observe the same relationships on a single plot that were previously shown on several graphs (Fig. 9.3). It is also possible to plot the data set as functions of the new variables. This needs the second output of `princomp` containing the principal component scores.

```
plot(newdata(:,1),newdata(:,2),'+')
text(newdata(:,1)+0.01,newdata(:,2),sample), hold
x = get(gca,'XLim'); y = get(gca,'YLim');
plot(x,zeros(size(x)),'r')
plot(zeros(size(y)),y,'r')
xlabel('First Principal Component Scores')
ylabel('Second Principal Component Scores')
```

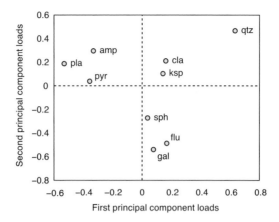

Fig. 9.3 Principal components loads suggesting that the PCs are influenced by different minerals. See text for detailed interpretation of the PCs.

This plot clearly defines groups of samples with similar influences. The samples 1, 2, 8 to 10 dominated by magmatic influences cluster in the left half of the diagram, the samples 3 to 5 dominated by the hydrothermal vein group in the lower part of the right half, whereas the two sandstone domi-nated samples 6 and 7 fall in the upper right corner.

Next, we use the third output of the function `princomp` to compute the variances of the corresponding PCs.

```
percent_explained = 100*variances/sum(variances)

percent_explained =
    80.9623
    17.1584
     0.8805
     0.4100
     0.2875
     0.1868
     0.1049
     0.0096
     0.0000
```

We see that more than 80% of the total variance is contained in PC_1, around 17% is described by PC_2, whereas all other PCs do not play any role. This means that most of the variability in the data set can be described by two new variables only.

9.3 Independent Component Analysis (by N. Marwan)

The principal component analysis (PCA) is the standard method for separating mixed signals. Such analysis provides signals that are linearly uncorrelated. This method is also called *whitening* since this property is characteristic for white noise. Although the separated signals are uncorrelated, they could still can be dependent, i.e., nonlinear correlation remains. The *independent component analysis* (ICA) was developed to investigate such data. It separates mixed signals into independent signals, which are then nonlinearly uncorrelated. Fast ICA algorithms use a criterion which estimates how gaussian distributed the joint distribution of the independent components is. The less gaussian this distribution is, the more independent the individual components are.

According to the model, n independent signals $x(t)$ are linearly mixed in m measurements.

$$x(t) = As(t)$$

and we are interested in the source signals s_i and in the mixing matrix A. For example, we can imagine that we are on a party and a lot of people talk independently with others. We hear a mixing of these talks and perhaps cannot distinguish the single talks. Now we could install some microphones and use these measurements to separate the single conversations. Hence, this dilemma is also called the *cocktail party problem*. Its correct term is *blind source separation* that is given by

$$s(t) = W^T x(t)$$

where W^T is the separation matrix in order to reverse the mixing and get the original signals. Let us consider a mixing of three signals s_1, s_2 and s_3 and their separation using PCA and ICA. First, we create three periodic signals

```
clear
i = (1:0.01:10 * pi)';
[dummy index] = sort(sin(i));

s1(index,1) = i/31; s1 = s1 - mean(s1);
s2 = abs(cos(1.89*i)); s2 = s2 - mean(s2);
s3 = sin(3.43*i);
```

```
subplot(3,2,1), plot(s1), ylabel('s_1'), title('Raw signals')
subplot(3,2,3), plot(s2), ylabel('s_2')
subplot(3,2,5), plot(s3), ylabel('s_3')
```

Now we mix these signals and add some observational noise. We get a three-column vector x which corresponds to our measurement (Fig. 9.4).

```
randn('state',1);

x = [.1*s1 + .8*s2 + .01*randn(length(i),1),...
     .4*s1 + .3*s2 + .01*randn(length(i),1),...
     .1*s1 +   s3  + .02*randn(length(i),1)];

subplot(3,2,2), plot(x(:,1)), ylabel('x_1'), title('Mixed signals')
subplot(3,2,4), plot(x(:,2)), ylabel('x_2')
subplot(3,2,6), plot(x(:,3)), ylabel('x_3')
```

We begin with the separation of the signals using the PCA. We calculate the

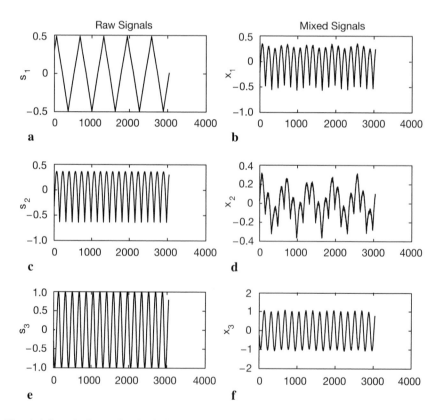

Fig. 9.4 Sample input for the independent component analysis. We first generate three period signals (**a**, **c**, **e**), mix the signals and add some gaussian noise (**b**, **d**, **f**).

principal components and the whitening matrix `W_PCA` with

```
sPCA = sPCA./repmat(std(sPCA),length(sPCA),1);
```

The PC scores `sPCA` are the linearly separated components of the mixed signals x (Fig. 9.5).

```
subplot(3,2,1), plot(sPCA(:,1))
ylabel('s_{PCA1}'), title('Separated signals - PCA')
subplot(3,2,3), plot(sPCA(:,2)), ylabel('s_{PCA2}')
subplot(3,2,5), plot(sPCA(:,3)), ylabel('s_{PCA3}')
```

The mixing matrix A can be found with

```
A_PCA = E * sqrt (D);
W_PCA = inv(sqrt(diag(D))) * E';
```

Next, we separate the signals into independent components. We will do

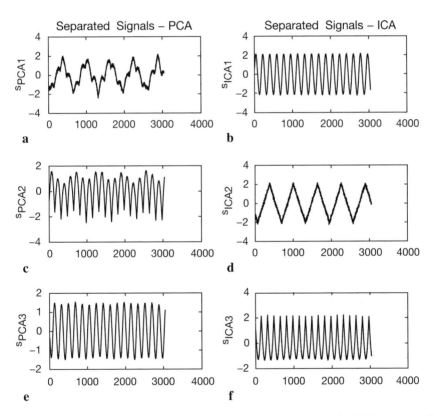

Fig. 9.5 Output of the principal component analysis (**a, c, e**) compared with the output of the independent component analysis (**b, d, f**). The PCA has not reliably separated the mixed signals, whereas the ICA found the source signals almost perfectly.

this by using a FastICA algorithm which is based on a fixed-point iteration scheme to find the maximum of the non-gaussianity of the independent
components $W^T x$. As the nonlinearity function we use a power of three
function for instance.

```
rand('state',1);

div = 0;
B = orth(rand(3, 3) - .5);
BOld = zeros(size(B));

while (1 - div) > eps
    B = B * real(inv(B' * B)^(1/2));
    div = min(abs(diag(B' * BOld)));
    BOld  = B;
    B = (sPCA' * ( sPCA * B) .^ 3) / length(sPCA) - 3 * B;
    sICA = sPCA * B;
end
```

We plot the separated components with (Fig. 9.5)

```
subplot(3,2,2), plot(sICA(:,1)), ylabel('s_{ICA1}'),
    title('Separated signals - ICA')
subplot(3,2,4), plot(sICA(:,2)), ylabel('s_{ICA2}')
subplot(3,2,6), plot(sICA(:,3)), ylabel('s_{ICA3}')
```

The PCA algorithm has not reliably separated the mixed signals. Especially
the saw-tooth signal was not correctly found. In contrast, the ICA has found
the source signals almost perfectly. The only remarkable differences are the
noise, which came through the observation, the wrong sign and the wrong
order of the signals. However, the sign and the order of the signals are not
really important, because we have generally not the knowledge about the
real sources nor their order. With

```
A_ICA = A_PCA * B;
W_ICA = B' * W_PCA;
```

we compute the mixing matrix A and the separation matrix W. The mixing matrix A can be used in order to estimate the portion of the separated
signals on our measurements The components a_{ij} of the mixing matrix A
correspond to the principal components loads as introduced in Chapter 9.2.
A FastICA package is available for MATLAB and can be found at

```
http://www.cis.hut.fi/projects/ica/fastica/
```

9.4 Cluster Analysis

Cluster analysis creates groups of objects that are very similar compared to other objects or groups. It first computes the similarity between all pairs of objects, then it ranks the groups by their similarity, and finally creates a hierarchical tree visualized as a dendrogram. Examples for grouping objects in earth sciences are the correlations within volcanic ashes (Hermanns et al. 2000) and the comparison of microfossil assemblages (Birks and Gordon 1985).

There are numerous methods for calculating the similarity between two data vectors. Let us define two data sets consisting of multiple measurements on the same object. These data can be described as the vectors:

$$X_1 = (x_{11} \quad x_{12} \quad \dots \quad x_{1p})$$
$$X_2 = (x_{21} \quad x_{22} \quad \dots \quad x_{2p})$$

The most popular measures of similarity of the two sample vectors are the

- *Euclidian distance* – This is simply the shortest distance between the two points in the multivariate space:

$$\Delta_{12} = \sqrt{\left(x_{11} - x_{21}\right)^2 + \left(x_{12} - x_{22}\right)^2 + \dots + \left(x_{1p} - x_{2p}\right)^2}$$

The Euclidian distance is certainly the most intuitive measure for similarity. However, in heterogenic data sets consisting of a number of different types of variables, it should be replaced by the following measure.

- *Manhattan distance* – In the city of Manhattan, one must walk on perpendicular avenues instead of diagonal crossing blocks. The Manhattan distance is therefore the sum of all differences:

$$\Delta_{12} = \left[\left(x_{11} - x_{21}\right) + \left(x_{12} - x_{22}\right) + \dots + \left(x_{1p} - x_{2p}\right)\right]$$

- *Correlation similarity coefficient* – Here, we use Pearson's linear product-moment correlation coefficient to compute the similarity of two objects:

$$r_{x1x2} = \frac{\sum_{i=1}^{n}(x_{1i} - \bar{x}_1)(x_{2i} - \bar{x}_2)}{(n-1)s_{x1}s_{x2}}$$

This measure is used if one is interested in ratios between the variables measured on the objects. However, Pearson's correlation coefficient is highly sensitive to outliers and should be used with care (see also Chapter 4).

- *Inner-product similarity index* – Normalizing the data vectors to one and computing the inner product of these yield another important similarity index. This is often used in transfer function applications. In this example, a set of modern flora or fauna assemblages with known environmental preferences is compared with a fossil sample to reconstruct the environmental conditions in the past.

$$s_{12} = \frac{1}{|X_1|}\frac{1}{|X_2|}\left(x_{11}\ x_{12}...x_{1p}\right)\begin{pmatrix} x_{21} \\ x_{22} \\ \vdots \\ x_{2p} \end{pmatrix}$$

The inner-product similarity varies between 0 and 1. A zero value suggests no similarity and a value of one represents maximum similarity.

The second step in performing a cluster analysis is to rank the groups by their similarity and build a hierarchical tree visualized as a dendrogram. Defining groups of objects with significant similarity and separating clusters depends on the internal similarity and the difference between the groups. Most clustering algorithms simply link the two objects with highest similarity. In the following steps, the most similar pairs of objects or clusters are linked iteratively. The difference between groups of objects forming a cluster is described in different ways depending on the type of data and application.

- *K-means clustering* – Here, the Euclidean distance between the multivariate means of the K clusters is used as a measure for the difference between the groups of objects. This distance is used if the data suggest that there is a true mean value surrounded by random noise.

- *K-nearest-neighbors clustering* – Alternatively, the Euclidean distance of the nearest neighbors is used as measure for this difference. This is used if there is a natural heterogeneity in the data set that is not attributed to random noise.

It is important to evaluate the data properties prior to the application of a clustering algorithm. First, one should consider the absolute values of the variables. For example, a geochemical sample of volcanic ash might show SiO_2 contents of around 77% and Na_2O contents of 3.5%, although the Na_2O content is believed to be of great importance. Here, the data need to be transformed to zero means (*mean centering*). Differences in the variances *and* in the means are corrected by *autoscaling*, i.e., the data are standardized to zero means and variances that equal one. Artifacts arising from closed data, such as artificial negative correlations, are avoided by using *Aitchison's log-ratio transformation* (Aitchison 1984, 1986). This ensures data independence and avoids the constant sum normalization constraints. The log-ratio transformation is

$$x_{tr} = \log(x_i / x_d)$$

where x_{tr} denotes the transformed score ($i=1, 2, 3, \dots, d-1$) of some raw data x_i. The procedure is invariant under the group of permutations of the variables, and any variable can be used as divisor x_d.

As an example for performing a cluster analysis, the sediment data stored in *sediment.txt* are loaded and the plotting labels are defined.

```
data = load('sediments.txt');

for i = 1:10
  sample(i,:) = ['sample',sprintf('%02.0f',i)];
end
clear i

minerals= ['amp';'pyr';'pla';'ksp';'qtz';'cla';'flu';'sph';'gal'];
```

Subsequently, the distances between pairs of samples can be computed. The function pdist provides many ways for computing this distance, such as the Euclidian or Manhattan *city block* distance. We use the default setting which is the Euclidian distance.

```
Y = pdist(data);
```

The function pdist returns a vector Y containing the distances between each pair of observations in the original data matrix. We can visualize the distances on another pseudocolor plot.

```
squareform(Y);
imagesc(squareform(Y)), colormap(hot)
title('Euclidean distance between pairs of samples')
xlabel('First Sample No.')
ylabel('Second Sample No.')
colorbar
```

The function `squareform` converts Y into a symmetric, square format, so that the elements `(i,j)` of the matrix denote the distance between the `i` and `j` objects in the original data. Next, we rank and link the samples with respect to their inverse distance using the function `linkage`.

```
Z = linkage(Y);
```

In this 3-column array `z`, each row identifies a link. The first two columns identify the objects (or samples) that have been linked, the third column contains the individual distance between these two objects. The first row (link) between objects (or samples) 1 and 2 has the smallest distance corresponding to the highest similarity. Finally, we visualize the hierarchical clusters as a dendrogram which is shown in Figure 9.6.

```
dendrogram(Z);
xlabel('Sample No.')
ylabel('Distance')
box on
```

Clustering finds the same groups as the principal component analysis. We observe clear groups consisting of samples 1, 2, 8 to 10 (the magmatic source rocks), samples 3 to 5 (the hydrothermal vein) and samples 6 and 7 (the sandstone). One way to test the validity of our clustering result is the *cophenet correlation coefficient*. The value of

```
cophenet(Z,Y)

ans =
    0.7579
```

looks convincing, since the closer this coefficient is to one, the better is the cluster solution.

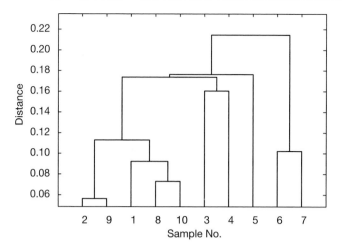

Fig. 9.6 Output of the cluster analysis. The dendrogram shows clear groups consisting of samples 1, 2, 8 to 10 (the magmatic source rocks), samples 3 to 5 (the magmatic dyke containing ore minerals) and samples 6 and 7 (the sandstone unit).

Recommended Reading

Aitchison J (1984) The Statistical Analysis of Geochemical Composition. Mathematical Geology 16(6):531–564

Aitchison J (1999) Logratios and Natural Laws in Compositional Data Analysis. Mathematical Geology 31(5):563–580

Birks HJB, Gordon AD (1985) Numerical Methods in Quaternary Pollen Analysis. Academic Press, London

Brown CE (1998) Applied Multivariate Statistics in Geohydrology and Related Sciences. Springer, Berlin Heidelberg New York

Hermanns R, Trauth MH, McWilliams M, Strecker M (2000) Tephrochronologic Constraints on Temporal Distribution of Large Landslides in NW-Argentina. Journal of Geology 108:35–52

Pawlowsky-Glahn V (2004) Geostatistical Analysis of Compositional Data – Studies in Mathematical Geology. Oxford University Press, Oxford

Reyment RA, Savazzi E (1999) Aspects of Multivariate Statistical Analysis in Geology. Elsevier Science, Amsterdam

Westgate JA, Shane PAR, Pearce NJG, Perkins WT, Korisettar R, Chesner CA, Williams MAJ, Acharyya SK (1998) All Toba Tephra Occurrences Across Peninsular India Belong to the 75,000 yr BP Eruption. Quaternary Research 50:107–112

10 Statistics on Directional Data

10.1 Introduction

Methods to analyze circular and spherical data are widely used in earth sciences. For instance, structural geologists measure and analyze the orientation of slickenlines (or striae) on fault planes. Circular statistics is also common in paleomagnetic applications. Microstructural investigations include the analysis of the grain shape and quartz c-axis orientation in thin sections. Paleoenvironmentalists reconstruct paleocurrent directions from fossil alignments (Fig. 10.1). In principle, two types of directional data exist in earth sciences: *directional data sensu stricto* and *oriented data*. Directional data have a true polarity, such as the paleocurrent direction of a river as documented by flute marks or the flow direction of a glacier as indicated by glacial striae. Oriented data describe axial data and lines without sense of direction, such as the orientation of joints.

MATLAB is not the first choice to analyze directional data since it does not provide the relevant functions such as an algorithm to compute the probability distribution function of a *von Mises distribution* or to run a Rayleigh's test for the significance of a mean direction. Therefore, earth scientists have developed numerous standalone programs to analyze such data, e.g., the excellent software developed by Rick Allmendinger available for Mac OS 9 and X as well as for Microsoft Windows:

```
http://www.geo.cornell.edu/geology/faculty/RWA/programs.html
```

The following tutorial on the analysis of directional data is independent of these tools. It provides simple MATLAB codes to display directional data, to compute the von Mises distribution and to run simple statistical tests. The first subchapter introduces rose diagrams as the most widely used method to display directional data (Chapter 10.2). Similar to the concept of Chapter 3 on univariate statistics, the next chapters are on empirical and theoretical distributions to describe directional data (Chapters 10.3 and 10.4). The last three chapters describe the three most important tests for directional data:

Fig. 10.1 Orthoceras fossils from an outcrop Neptuni Acrar near Byxelkrok on Öland, Sweden. Orthoceras is a cephalopod with a straight shell and lived in the Ordovician era about 450 million years ago. Such elongated, asymmetric objects tend to orient themselves in the hydrodynamically most stable position. Therefore, the fossils can indicate paleocurrent directions. The statistical analysis of the cephalopod orientation at Neptuni Acrar reveals a significant southward paleocurrent direction, which is an agreement with the paleogeographic reconstructions for Ordovician times.

The test for randomness of directional data (Chapter 10.5), the significance of a mean direction (Chapter 10.6) and the difference of two sets of directional data (Chapter 10.7).

10.2 Graphical Representation

The classic way to display directional data is the *rose diagram*. A rose diagram is a histogram for measurements of angles. In contrast to a bar histogram with the height of the bars proportional to frequency, the rose diagram comprises segments of a circle with the radius of each sector being proportional to the frequency. We use synthetic data to illustrate two types of rose diagrams to display directional data. We load a set of directional data from the file *directional_1.txt*.

```
data_degrees_1 = load('directional_1.txt');
```

The data set contains forty measurements of angles in degrees. We use the function `rose(az,nb)` to display the data. The function plots an angle histogram for the angles `az` in radians, where `nb` is the number of classes. Since the original data are in degrees, we have to convert all measurements to radians before we plot the data.

```
data_radians_1 = pi*data_degrees_1/180;
rose(data_radians_1,12)
```

The function `rose` counts in a counterclockwise direction in which zero degrees lies along the *x*-axis of the coordinate graph. In geosciences, however, 0° points due North, 90° points due East and the angles increase clockwise. The command `view` rotates the plot by +90° (the azimuth) and mirrors the plot by −90° (the elevation) (Fig. 10.2).

```
rose(data_radians_1,12)
```

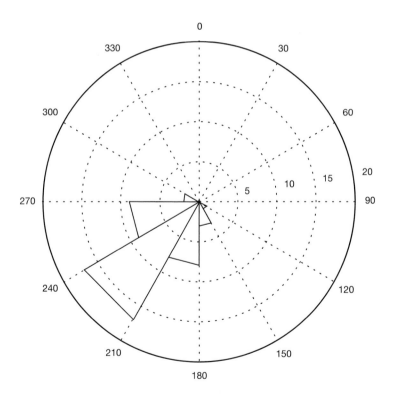

Fig. 10.2 Rose diagram to display directional data using function `rose`. The radii of the area segments are proportional to the frequencies for each class.

```
view(90,-90)
```

The area of the arc segments increases with frequency. Therefore, the rose diagram is scaled to the square root of the class frequency in a final modification. The function `rose` does not allow to plot the square root of the frequencies by default. However, the corresponding file *rose.m* can be easily modified. After the histogram of the angles is computed in line 58 by using the function `histc`, add a line with the command `nn = sqrt(nn);` which computes the square root of the frequencies `nn`. Save the modified function as file *rose_sqrt.m* and apply the new function to the data set.

```
rose_sqrt(data_radians_1,12)
view(90,-90)
```

This plot satisfies all conventions in geosciences (Fig. 10.3).

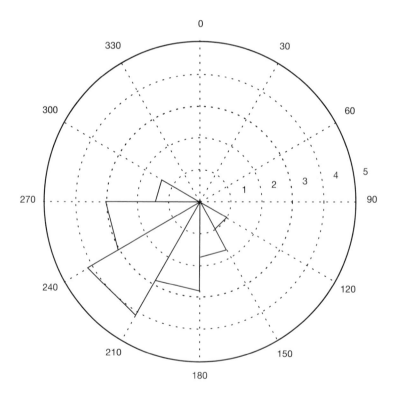

Fig. 10.3 Modified rose diagram to display directional data using function `rose`. In this version of `rose`, 0° points due North, 90° points due East and the angles increase clockwise. The plot scales the rose diagram to the square root of the class frequency. Now the area of the arc segments increases with frequency.

10.3 Empirical Distributions

This chapter introduces the statistical measures to describe empirical distributions of directional data. The characteristics of directional data are described by measures of central tendency and dispersion, similar to the statistical characterization of univariate data sets (Chapter 3). Assume that we have collected a number of angular measurements such as fossil alignments. The collection of data can be written as

$$\theta_1, \theta_2, \theta_3, \ldots, \theta_N$$

containing N observations θ_i. Sine and cosine values are computed for each direction θ_i to compute the resultant for the set of angular data.

$$x_r = \sum \sin \theta_i$$
$$y_r = \sum \cos \theta_i$$

The resultant or mean direction of the data set is

$$\bar{\theta} = \tan^{-1}(x_r / y_y)$$

The length of the resultant is

$$R = \sqrt{(x_r^2 + y_r^2)}$$

The resultant length clearly depends on the dispersion of the data. Normalizing the resulting length to the number of observations yields the *mean resultant length*.

$$\bar{R} = R / N$$

The value of the mean resultant length decreases with increasing dispersion. Therefore, the difference between one and the mean resultant length is often used as a measure of dispersion for directional data,

$$\sigma_0 = 1 - \bar{R}$$

which is the *circular variance*.

The following example illustrates the use of these parameters by means of synthetic directional data. We first load the data from the file *directional_1.txt* and convert all measurement to radians.

```
clear
data_degrees_1 = load('directional_1.txt');
data_radians_1 = pi*data_degrees_1/180;
```

Now we calculate the resultant vector *R*. Firstly, we compute the *x* and *y* component of the resultant vector.

```
x_1 = sum(sin(data_radians_1))
y_1 = sum(cos(data_radians_1))

x_1 =
  -24.3507

y_1 =
  -25.9552
```

The mean direction is the inverse tangent of the ratio of *x* and *y*.

```
mean_radians_1 = atan(x_1/y_1)
mean_degrees_1 = 180*mean_radians_1/pi

mean_radians_1 =
    0.7535

mean_degrees_1 =
    43.1731
```

This result suggests that the resultant vector *R* is around 0.75 radians or 43°. However, since both *x* and *y* are negative, the true value of mean_degrees is located in the third quadrant and we add 180°.

```
mean_degrees_1 = mean_degrees_1 + 180

mean_degrees_1 =
   223.1731
```

Therefore, the mean direction is around 223°. The length of this vector is the absolute of the vector, which is

```
R_1 = sqrt(x_1^2 + y_1^2)

R_1 =
   35.5897
```

The resultant length depends on the dispersion of the directional data.

Normalizing the resultant length to the sample size yields the mean resultant length of

```
Rm_1 = R_1 / (length(data_radians_1))

Rm_1 =
    0.8897
```

Higher `Rm` suggests less variance. Therefore, we compute the circular variance `sigma` which is

```
sigma_1 = 1 - Rm_1

sigma_1 =
    0.1103
```

10.4 Theoretical Distributions

As in Chapter 3, the next step in a statistical analysis is to find a suitable theoretical distribution that fits the empirical distribution visualized and described in the previous chapter. The classic theoretical distribution to describe directional data is the *von Mises distribution*, named after the Austrian mathematician Richard Edler von Mises (1883–1953). The probability density function of a von Mises distribution is

$$ f(\theta) = \frac{1}{2\pi I_0(\kappa)} e^{\kappa \cos(\theta - \mu)} $$

where μ is the mean direction and κ is the concentration parameter (Fig. 10.4). $I_0(\kappa)$ is the modified *Bessel function* of the first kind and order zero of κ. The Bessel functions are solutions of a second-order differential equation, the Bessel's differential equation, and are important in many problems of wave propagation in a cylindrical waveguide and heat conduction in a cylindrical object. The von Mises distribution is also known as *circular normal distribution* since it has similar characteristics as the normal distribution (Chapter 3.4). The von Mises distribution is used when the mean direction is the most frequent and most likely direction. The probability of deviations is equal towards both directions and decreases with increasing distance from the mean direction.

As an example, let us assume a mean direction of `mu=0` and five different values for the concentration parameter `kappa`.

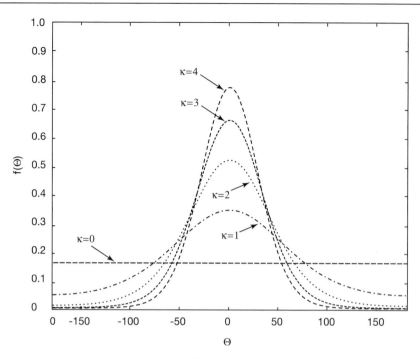

Fig. 10.4 Probability density function $f(\Theta)$ of a von Mises distribution with $\mu=0$ and five different values for κ.

```
mu = 0; kappa = [0 1 2 3 4]';
```

In a first step, an angle scale for a plot that runs from −180 to 180 degrees is defined in intervals of one degree.

```
theta = -180:1:180;
```

All angles are converted from degrees to radians.

```
mu_radians = pi*mu/180;
theta_radians = pi*theta/180;
```

In a second step, we compute the von Mises distribution for these values. The formula uses the modified Bessel function of the first kind and order zero that can be calculated by using the function `besseli`. We compute the probability density function for the five values of `kappa`.

```
for i = 1:5
   mises(i,:) = (1/(2*pi*besseli(0,kappa(i))))* ...
   exp(kappa(i)*cos(theta_radians-mu_radians));
   theta(i,:) = theta(1,:);
end
```

The results are plotted by

```
for i = 1:5
    plot(theta(i,:),mises(i,:))
    axis([-180 180 0 max(mises(i,:))])
    hold on
end
```

The mean direction and concentration parameter of such theoretical distributions are easily modified to compare them with empirical distributions.

10.5 Test for Randomness of Directional Data

The first test for directional data compares the data set with a uniform distribution. Directional data following a uniform distribution are purely random,
i.e., there is no preference for any direction. We use the χ^2-test (Chapter 3.8)
to compare the empirical frequency distribution with the theoretical uniform distribution. We load our sample data.

```
clear
data_degrees_1 = load('directional_1.txt');
```

We use the function `hist` to count the number of observations within
12 classes. The width of the classes is 30 degrees.

```
counts = hist(data_degrees_1,15:30:345);
```

The expected number of observations is 40/12, where 40 is the total number
of observations and 12 is the number of classes.

```
expect = 40/12 * ones(1,12);
```

The χ^2-test explores the squared differences between the observed and expected frequencies. The quantity χ^2 is defined as the sum of these squared
differences divided by the expected frequencies.

```
chi2 = sum((counts - expect).^2 ./expect)

chi2 =
    94.4000
```

The critical χ^2 can be calculated by using `chi2inv`. The χ^2-test requires the
degrees of freedom Φ. In our example, we test the hypothesis that the data are
uniformly distributed, i.e., we estimate one parameter, which is the number
of possible values N. The number of classes is 12. Therefore, the degrees of

freedom are $\Phi=12-(1+1)=10$. We test our hypothesis on a $p=95\%$ significance level. The function chi2inv computes the inverse of the χ^2 CDF with
parameters specified by Φ for the corresponding probabilities in p.

```
chi2inv(0.95,12-1-1)

ans =
    18.3070
```

The critical χ^2 of 18.3070 is well below the measured χ^2 of 94.4000.
Therefore, we reject the null hypothesis and conclude that our data do not
follow a uniform distribution, i.e., they are not randomly distributed.

10.6 Test for the Significance of a Mean Direction

Having measured a set of directional data in the field, we wish to know
whether there is a prevailing direction documented in the data. We use the
Rayleigh's test for the significance of a mean direction. This test uses the
mean resultant length introduced in Chapter 10.3, which increases with a
more significant preferred direction.

$$\bar{R} = \frac{1}{n}\sqrt{\left(\sum \sin\theta_i\right)^2 + \left(\sum \cos\theta_i\right)^2}$$

The data show a preferred direction if the calculated mean resultant length
is below the critical value (Mardia 1972). As an example, we load the data
contained in file *directional_1.txt* again.

```
clear
data_degrees_1 = load('directional_1.txt');
data_radians_1 = pi*data_degrees_1/180;
```

We calculate the mean resultant vector Rm.

```
x_1 = sum(sin(data_radians_1));
y_1 = sum(cos(data_radians_1));

mean_radians_1 = atan(x_1/y_1);
mean_degrees_1 = 180*mean_radians_1/pi;
mean_degrees_1 = mean_degrees_1 + 180;

Rm_1 = 1/length(data_degrees_1) .*(x_1.^2+y_1.^2).^0.5

Rm_1 =
    0.8897
```

The mean resultant length in our example is 0.8897. The critical Rm ($\alpha = 0.05$, $n = 40$) is 0.27 (Table 10.1 from Mardia 1972). Since this value is lower than the Rm from the data, we reject the null hypothesis and conclude that there is a preferred single direction, which is

```
theta_1 = 180 * atan(x_1/y_1) / pi

theta_1 =
    43.1731
```

The negative signs of the sine and cosine, however, suggest that the true result is in the third sector ($180-270°$) and, therefore, the correct result is $180 + 43.1731 = 223.1731$.

10.7 Test for the Difference of Two Sets of Directions

Let us consider two sets of measurements in two files *directional_1.txt* and *directional_2.txt*. We wish to compare the two sets of directions and test the hypothesis that these are significantly different. The test statistic for testing equality of two mean directions is the F-statistic (Chapter 3.7)

$$F = \left(1 + \frac{3}{8\kappa}\right)\frac{(n-2)(R_A + R_B - R_T)}{n - R_A - R_B}$$

where κ is the concentration parameter, R_A and R_B are the resultant of samples A and B, respectively, and R_T is the resultant of the combined samples. The concentration parameter can be obtained from tables using R_T (Batschelet 1965, Gumbel et al. 1953, Table 10.2). The calculated F is compared with critical values from the standard F tables. The two mean directions are not significantly different if the measured F-value is lower than the critical F-value, which depends on the degrees of freedom $\Phi_a = 1$ and $\Phi_b = N-1$, and the significance level α. Both samples must follow a von Mises distribution (Chapter 10.4).

We use two synthetic data sets of directional data to illustrate the application of this test. We load the data and convert these to radians.

```
clear
data_degrees_1 = load('directional_1.txt');
data_degrees_2 = load('directional_2.txt');
```

Table 10.1 Critical values of mean resultant length for Rayleigh's test for the significance of a mean direction of N samples (Mardia 1972).

N	Level of Significance, α				
	0.100	0.050	0.025	0.010	0.001
5	0.677	0.754	0.816	0.879	0.991
6	0.618	0.690	0.753	0.825	0.940
7	0.572	0.642	0.702	0.771	0.891
8	0.535	0.602	0.660	0.725	0.847
9	0.504	0.569	0.624	0.687	0.808
10	0.478	0.540	0.594	0.655	0.775
11	0.456	0.516	0.567	0.627	0.743
12	0.437	0.494	0.544	0.602	0.716
13	0.420	0.475	0.524	0.580	0.692
14	0.405	0.458	0.505	0.560	0.669
15	0.391	0.443	0.489	0.542	0.649
16	0.379	0.429	0.474	0.525	0.630
17	0.367	0.417	0.460	0.510	0.613
18	0.357	0.405	0.447	0.496	0.597
19	0.348	0.394	0.436	0.484	0.583
20	0.339	0.385	0.425	0.472	0.569
21	0.331	0.375	0.415	0.461	0.556
22	0.323	0.367	0.405	0.451	0.544
23	0.316	0.359	0.397	0.441	0.533
24	0.309	0.351	0.389	0.432	0.522
25	0.303	0.344	0.381	0.423	0.512
30	0.277	0.315	0.348	0.387	0.470
35	0.256	0.292	0.323	0.359	0.436
40	0.240	0.273	0.302	0.336	0.409
45	0.226	0.257	0.285	0.318	0.386
50	0.214	0.244	0.270	0.301	0.367
100	0.150	0.170	0.190	0.210	0.260

```
data_radians_1 = pi*data_degrees_1/180;
data_radians_2 = pi*data_degrees_2/180;
```

We compute the length of resultant vectors.

```
x_1 = sum(sin(data_radians_1));
```

```
y_1 = sum(cos(data_radians_1));
x_2 = sum(sin(data_radians_2));
y_2 = sum(cos(data_radians_2));

mean_radians_1 = atan(x_1/y_1);
mean_degrees_1 = 180*mean_radians_1/pi;
mean_radians_2 = atan(x_2/y_2);
mean_degrees_2 = 180*mean_radians_2/pi;

mean_degrees_1 = mean_degrees_1 + 180
mean_degrees_2 = mean_degrees_2 + 180

mean_degrees_1 =
   223.1731

mean_degrees_2 =
   200.8098

R_1 = sqrt(x_1^2 + y_1^2);
R_2 = sqrt(x_2^2 + y_2^2);
```

The orientation of resultant vectors is ca. 223° and 201°. Now, we also need
the resultant length of both samples, so we combine both data sets and compute the resultant length again.

```
data_radians_T = [data_radians_1;data_radians_2];

x_T = sum(sin(data_radians_T));
y_T = sum(cos(data_radians_T));

mean_radians_T = atan(x_T/y_T);
mean_degrees_T = 180*mean_radians_T/pi;

mean_degrees_T = mean_degrees_T + 180;

R_T = sqrt(x_T^2 + y_T^2)
Rm_T = R_T / (length(data_radians_T))

R_T =
    69.4941

Rm_T =
    0.8687
```

We apply the test statistic to the data for `kappa`=3.91072 for `Rm_T`=0.8687
(Table 10.2). The computed value for `F` is

```
n = length(data_radians_T);

F = (1+3/(8*2.07685)) * (((n-2)*(R_1+R_2-R_T))/(n-R_1-R_2))

F =
   13.5160
```

Table 10.2 Maximum likelihood estimates of concentration parameter κ for calculated mean resultant length (adapted from Batschelet, 1965 and Gumbel et al., 1953).

R	κ	R	κ	R	κ	R	κ
0.000	0.000	0.260	0.539	0.520	1.224	0.780	2.646
0.010	0.020	0.270	0.561	0.530	1.257	0.790	2.754
0.020	0.040	0.280	0.584	0.540	1.291	0.800	2.871
0.030	0.060	0.290	0.606	0.550	1.326	0.810	3.000
0.040	0.080	0.300	0.629	0.560	1.362	0.820	3.143
0.050	0.100	0.310	0.652	0.570	1.398	0.830	3.301
0.060	0.120	0.320	0.676	0.580	1.436	0.840	3.479
0.070	0.140	0.330	0.700	0.590	1.475	0.850	3.680
0.080	0.161	0.340	0.724	0.600	1.516	0.860	3.911
0.090	0.181	0.350	0.748	0.610	1.557	0.870	4.177
0.100	0.201	0.360	0.772	0.620	1.600	0.880	4.489
0.110	0.221	0.370	0.797	0.630	1.645	0.890	4.859
0.120	0.242	0.380	0.823	0.640	1.691	0.900	5.305
0.130	0.262	0.390	0.848	0.650	1.740	0.910	5.852
0.140	0.283	0.400	0.874	0.660	1.790	0.920	6.539
0.150	0.303	0.410	0.900	0.670	1.842	0.930	7.426
0.160	0.324	0.420	0.927	0.680	1.896	0.940	8.610
0.170	0.345	0.430	0.954	0.690	1.954	0.950	10.272
0.180	0.366	0.440	0.982	0.700	2.014	0.960	12.766
0.190	0.387	0.450	1.010	0.710	2.077	0.970	16.927
0.200	0.408	0.460	1.039	0.720	2.144	0.980	25.252
0.210	0.430	0.470	1.068	0.730	2.214	0.990	50.242
0.220	0.451	0.480	1.098	0.740	2.289	0.995	100.000
0.230	0.473	0.490	1.128	0.750	2.369	0.999	500.000
0.240	0.495	0.500	1.159	0.760	2.455	1.000	
0.250	0.516	0.510	1.191	0.770	2.547		

Using the F statistic, we find that for 1, $80-2$ degrees of freedom and $\alpha = 0.05$, the critical value is

```
finv(0.95,1,78)

ans =
    3.9635
```

which is well below the observed value of $F = 13.5160$. Therefore, we reject the null hypothesis and conclude that the two samples could have not been drawn from populations with the same mean direction.

Recommended Reading

Batschelet E (1965) Statistical Methods for the Analysis of Problems in Animal Orientation and Certain Biological Rhythms. American Institute of Biological Sciences Monograph, Washington, D.C.

Borradaile G (2003) Statistics of Earth Science Data – Their Distribution in Time, Space and Orientation. Springer, Berlin Heidelberg New York

Davis JC (2002) Statistics and Data Analysis in Geology, Third Edition. John Wiley and Sons, New York

Gumbel EJ, Greenwood JA, Durand D (1953) The Circular Normal Distribution: Tables and Theory. Journal of the American Statistical Association 48:131–152

Mardia KV (1972) Statistics of Directional Data. Academic Press, London

Middleton GV (1999) Data Analysis in the Earth Sciences Using MATLAB. Prentice Hall, New Jersey

Swan ARH, Sandilands M (1995) Introduction to geological data analysis. Blackwell Sciences, Oxford

General Index

D

Daubechies 115
degrees of freedom 33, 48
Delauney triangulation 177
DEM 171
demcmap 196
dendrogram 260
dependent variable 61, 68
descriptive statistics 29
difference equation 143
digital elevation model 171, 195
digital filter 133
digitizing 165, 241
dilation 115
dimension 16
directional data 6, 263
directional data sensu stricto 263
directional variograms 218
dispersion 30, 34
display 25
disttool 51
divergent flow 201
dots per inch 229
dpi 229
drift 206
DTEM 171

E

edge effect 185
edit 13
Edit Mode 27
Editor 12, 13, 20
Edit Plot 26
element-by-element 18
elevation 265
ellipsis 71

embedding dimension 123
empirical distribution 29, 41
Encapsulated PostScript 230
end 21, 22
EPS 230
error bounds 71
ETOPO2 168
Euclidian distance 257
Evolutionary Blackman-Tukey
        powerspectrum 104
expected frequencies 58
experimental variogram 209
export data 19
exposure 195

F

F-statistic 273
F-test 53
factor analysis 246
Fast Fourier Transformation 90
F distribution 48
field 71
Figure 25
Figure Window 25, 26
File 14
File menu 26, 28
filter 133, 139, 141, 154
filter2 196
filter design 153
filter weights 139, 157
filtfilt 139, 154
find 38, 174
finite differences 196
finv 55
flow accumulation 199
for 21
Fourier transform 145
frequency 85, 89